COMMUNICATION AND IDENTITY ACROSS CULTURES

INTERNATIONAL AND INTERCULTURAL COMMUNICATION ANNUAL

Volume XXI   **1998**

INTERNATIONAL AND INTERCULTURAL COMMUNICATION ANNUAL
VOLUME XXI   1998

COMMUNICATION AND IDENTITY ACROSS CULTURES

edited by

Dolores V. TANNO
Alberto GONZÁLEZ

Published in cooperation with
National Communication Association
International and Intercultural Division

SAGE Publications
International Educational and Professional Publisher
Thousand Oaks London New Delhi

For information:

 SAGE Publications, Inc.
2455 Teller Road
Thousand Oaks, California 91320
E-mail: order@sagepub.com

SAGE Publications Ltd.
6 Bonhill Street
London EC2A 4PU
United Kingdom

SAGE Publications India Pvt. Ltd.
M-32 Market
Greater Kailash I
New Delhi 110 048 India

Printed in the United States of America

Library of Congress Cataloging-in-Publication Data

ISBN 0-7619-1302-5
ISBN 0-7619-1303-3 (pbk.)
ISSN 0270-6075

This book is printed on acid-free paper.

98 99 00 01 02 03 10 9 8 7 6 5 4 3 2 1

Acquiring Editor:	Margaret H. Seawell
Editorial Assistant:	Renée Piernot
Production Editor:	Sherrise M. Purdum
Production Assistant:	Karen Wiley
Typesetter/Designer:	Yang-hee Syn Maresca
Indexer:	Juniee Oneida
Print Buyer:	Anna Chin

Contents

Preface   vii

PART I: INTRODUCTION

1. Sites of Identity in Communication and Culture   3
   Dolores V. Tanno
   Alberto González

PART II: SITES OF IDENTITY

2. Patriotic Breeders or Colonized Converts: A
   Postcolonial Feminist Approach to Antifootbinding
   Discourse in China   11
   Wen Shu Lee

3. Swinging the Trapeze: The Negotiation of Identity
   Among Asian Indian Immigrant Women in the
   United States   34
   Radha S. Hegde

4. Razzing: Ritualized Uses of Humor as a Form of
   Identification Among American Indians   56
   Steven B. Pratt

5. The Cultural Deprivation of an Oklahoma Cherokee
   Family   80
   Lynda Dixon Shaver

6. Linguistic Agons: The Self and Society Opposition
   and American Quakers   100
   Nancy Wick

7. Researching Cultural Identity: Reconciling
   Interpretive and Postcolonial Perspectives   122
   Mary Jane Collier

8. "Diversity" Versus "National Unity": The Struggle
   Between Moderns, Premoderns, and Postmoderns in
   Contemporary South Africa   148
   Eric Louw

**PART III: FORUM: IDENTIFYING NATION-STATES
THROUGH CHANGE**

9. Distinguishing Cultural Systems: Change as a
   Variable Explaining and Predicting Cross-Cultural
   Communication   177
   James W. Chesebro

10. Problematizing "Nation" in Intercultural
    Communication Research   193
    Kent A. Ono

11. Response to Chesebro's Change Variable to Explain
    Cross-Cultural Communication   203
    Carley Dodd

12. Change, Nation-States, and the Centrality of a
    Communication Perspective   215
    James W. Chesebro

Index   226

About the Contributors   238

Preface

In this, the 21st volume of the **International and Intercultural Communication Annual,** we bring together chapters that address issues of communication and identity in multicultural contexts. The authors represented in this book provide insight into how cultural identity is constructed, maintained, represented, and/or negotiated between and within cultures. In so doing, they also provide us with examples of a broad scope of approaches to, and theories about, the process of inquiry into communication, identity, and culture.

The book is divided into three sections, the first of which is the introductory chapter that provides a brief overview of identity and previews the essays that make up the book. The second section, "Sites of Identity," presents seven perspectives of identity in different cultural contexts. The third and final section, the "Forum," continues a feature introduced in Volume 20 of the Annual. Three scholars engage in a dialogue about cultural issues surrounding research and identity.

The completion of this volume was the result of the efforts of many people to whom we express gratitude. We want to acknowledge the creative and scholarly efforts of the authors whose work appears herein. We want to express our appreciation to the consulting editors whose thoughtful insights made our work easier. We want to extend our gratitude to those who worked with us on a daily basis, specifically Caroline Krejci and Jennifer Willis. We say a grateful thank you to Bei Cai for her assistance. Finally, we want to acknowledge the support and encouragement we received from our respective institutions.

I

INTRODUCTION

1

Sites of Identity in Communication and Culture

DOLORES V. TANNO • *California State University,*
San Bernardino
ALBERTO GONZÁLEZ • *Bowling Green State University*

> Between inner, outer and peripheral "I"s . . . between the personal "I"s and the collective "we"
>
> —Gloria Anzaldúa (1990, p. xxv)

Identity is about the "I" and the "we." It is about the rituals and rules, the idioms and ideologies, and the languages and experiences of the multiple "I's" and "we's." Such is the complexity and the richness of identity.

The study of identity is not new. In *Mind, Self, and Society,* George Herbert Mead (1962) described the concept of "self" in terms of its relationship to society. Within that relationship, Mead stressed the role of communication, or symbolic interaction, as central to the development of "self"-consciousness. But because Mead stressed the relationship of self-shaped-by-society-shaped-by-self, self-consciousness was only half of the equation of identity. Also necessary was self-objectification, the ability to turn an objective eye on self and on society, in an effort to effect change. This was the mind at work, a pragmatic mind at that, because Mead's approach was fundamentally functional and behaviorist. It is important to note that, despite Mead's recognition of the interdependence of self-identity and society, his was a conception of universal self. That is, he did not assume the existence of, for example, multiple ideologies and/or experiences within a given culture.

In contrast to Mead was Martin Heidegger's (1962) conception of self as *Dasein,* based on an ontological rather than a pragmatic approach to the study of identity. Heidegger's skepticism about the scientific method led to his ontological perspective of the development of self (Malhotra, 1987). Rather than existing as a singular self (Mead's unitary view), dasein existed as a multiplicity of selves. This multiplicity resulted in layers of meaning, the understanding of which is gained through Hermeneutic phenomonology. Heidegger, like Mead, believed that symbolic interaction played a key role in the development and maintenance of identity. Also like Mead, Heidegger did not assume multiple ideologies and/or experiences within a given culture; his conception of multiplicity was based on the doing, expressing, being behaviors of a universal self.

Following Mead's (1962) functional approach and his self-society-self-interaction, Gumperz and Cook-Gumperz (1982) emphasized *social* identity and the role of language in the development and maintenance of it. But they deviated from Mead's (and also Heidegger's) conception of self when they recognized the influence of gender, ethnicity, and class in the formation of identity.

In *The Saturated Self: Dilemmas of Identity in Contemporary Life,* Kenneth Gergen (1991) offers a more recent conception of self. Like Mead and Heidegger, Gergen places language at the center of self-identity, arguing that the vocabulary to describe the romantic and modern selves no longer exists. Rather, what we have is the postmodern (saturated) self that has no "new vocabulary for understanding ourselves" and, as a result, selves are "dismantled" (p. 7). Gergen offers possibilities for reassembling the self by recognizing and honoring the "heteroglossia of being, a living out of the multiplicity of voices within the sphere of human possibility" (p. 247).

Within our discipline, multiple voices are speaking out (Banks & Banks, 1995; Chen, 1992; Giles, Williams, Mackie, & Rosselli, 1995; Morris, 1997; Shome, 1996). The authors within the pages of this volume add their voices to the choir. It is not only the question of "What is multicultural identity?" that captures their imagination and curiosity. It is also the questions, "Where is multicultural identity to be found? How is it formed and maintained?" As scholars, we have imagined identity being caught between countries, finding it "at the edge" of borders (Anzaldúa, 1987). We have found it at the "interstices" of cultures (Saldivar, 1990). We can imagine the dimensions of identity: the psychology, the sociology, and the spirituality of it. We wonder about the sites of identity, a kind of "geography" of the physical, intellectual, social, and political locations where identity develops its dimensions.

OVERVIEW OF CHAPTERS

The studies in this volume illustrate different sites of identity. Within their respective chapters, the authors mark particular rules, rituals, and/or experiences within a particular culture that provide insight into individual and collective identity.

Wen Shu Lee begins her chapter with a brief history of footbinding in China that includes also a brief personal account of the impact of footbinding on her family. In this way, she not only foreshadows her argument about the importance of authorial self-reflexivity with which she ends her chapter, she also sets a historical and personal context for her postcolonial feminist approach to identity. In Lee's chapter, women's feet were the "site of constant identity battles" for Chinese women, Chinese men, and alien colonizers.

Radha S. Hegde addresses identity as emergence, the result of multiple discursive frames and contradictory ways of being. In her chapter, the site of identity is the interface of the "past" self and the "present" self when individuals have a desire to preserve history as they establish a presence in a new environment. But Hegde argues that identity is also an evolution, a process in the gendered experiences of Asian Indian women as they "walk in and out of cultural frames."

Steven B. Pratt examines self-identity as *choice*. He distinguishes between "contact Indians," who have contact with other tribal groups and other cultures, and "grass roots Indians," who have limited or no contact with other tribal groups or other cultures. Focusing on "contact Indians," he addresses the problematic nature of identity by describing the structure and function of razzing as one type of identity ritual that requires participation by other cultural members. "Indianness," Pratt concludes, "is not something that one can simply be, but is something one becomes, is, or both" with the help of others in the community. Thus, cultural identity is a function of both self-identification and the recognition and acceptance of that self-identification by "culturally competent members" of the culture.

Lynda Dixon Shaver offers a different perspective of identity within the American Indian culture. Her focus is on a single family within the Cherokee culture and their process of cultural rediscovery. Shaver provides a historical context within which this rediscovery can be understood. This is a story of movement from "enforced" identity (the social pressures "not to be Indian") to identity by choice; "they have chosen to be an Oklahoma Cherokee family."

Nancy Wick explains the process by which identity is developed and maintained in a group of Quakers. By isolating meanings behind symbols and connecting them with views of personhood and sociality, Wick concludes that within this particular group, identity is located in the interstices of two conflicting symbol systems with contrasting meanings. Between the secular and the spiritual, members of this particular

Quaker group give priority to their Quaker or spiritual identity, favoring the self in relation to God over the self in relation to society.

Mary Jane Collier begins her chapter by contrasting the ontological and epistemological claims of postcolonial and interpretive approaches of cultural and intercultural communication as they influence understanding of cultural identity theory. Going beyond the study of cultural identity, Collier begins the process of recognizing herself as an "intimately engaged participant" in the research process; it is a move toward a new "identity" as researcher.

Eric Louw's focus is on South Africa. When discussing the struggle among modern, premodern, and postmodern discourses and cultures, Louw attempts to discover "what it is going to 'mean' to be South African." He places his examination of these discourses in the context of South Africa's modes of production (rural subsistence, industry, information). Louw makes clear that neither the discourses nor the modes of production can be easily separated but, rather, that they are overlapping and interdependent. The result is the immense complexity of South African identity.

In the Forum section of this book, James Chesebro, Kent A. Ono, and Carley Dodd engage in dialogue about the identities of nation-state cultural systems and their influence on cross-cultural communication. Chesebro argues that, despite the complexity of culture, it is possible to propose four cultural dimensions by which cultures may be identified: individualism or collectivism, context, power or distance, and masculinity or femininity. Chesebro then proposes a fifth—change or, more accurately, the positive or negative response to change by a given culture. His continuum of change ranges from revolution to evolution to stability to involution.

Kent A. Ono's response underscores the benefits of including a culture's response to change as a variable. Ono, however, argues that "nation-state" is a problematic conception because it may often lead to "broad generalizations about massive numbers of diverse peoples." He attributes this partly to the fact that the concept of nation-centered research is insufficiently theorized and also undertheorized.

Like Ono, Carley Dodd finds value in the idea of cultural responses to change as a variable in the study of cross-cultural communication. Unlike Ono, he finds meaningful the use of "nation-state" as a unit of analysis. Noting that Chesebro's approach addresses only macro issues, Dodd elaborates on Chesebro's dimensions of culture to include the interpersonal and relational roles that also influence change.

In his rejoinder, Chesebro responds to these and other issues raised by Ono and Dodd.

The concept of cultural identity is bound to get more, rather than less, complex as we move into the 21st century. We will have to continuously assess not only the assumptions we bring to the research process but also the research process itself as we seek understanding. Dialogues such as the ones included here allow for that assessment to occur.

REFERENCES

Anzaldúa, G. (1990). Haciendo caras, una entrada. In G. Anzaldúa (Ed.), *Making face, making soul: Haciendo caras* (pp. xv-xxvii). San Francisco: Aunt Lute Books.

Banks, A., & Banks, S. P. (1995). Cultural identity, resistance, and "good theory": Implications for intercultural communication theory from Gypsy culture. *Howard Journal of Communications, 6,* 146-163.

Chen, V. (1992). The construction of Chinese American women's identity. In L. F. Rakow (Ed.), *Women making meaning* (pp. 225-243). New York: Routledge.

Gergen, K. J. (1991). *The saturated self: Dilemmas of identity in contemporary life.* New York: Basic Books.

Giles, H., Williams, A., Mackie, D. M., & Rosselli, F. (1995). Reactions to Anglo- and Hispanic-American-accented speakers: Affect, identity, persuasion and English-only controversy. *Language and Communication, 15,* 107-120.

Gumperz, J. J., & Cook-Gumperz, J. (1982). Introduction: Language and the communication of social identity. In J. J. Gumperz (Ed.), *Language and social identity* (pp. 1-21). New York: Cambridge University Press.

Heidegger, M. (1962). *Being and time* (J. Macquarrie & E. Robinson, Trans.). New York: Harper.

Malhotra, V. A. (1987). From "self" to "Dasein": A Heideggerian critique of Mead's social psychology. *Studies in Symbolic Interaction, 8,* 23-42.

Mead, G. H. (1962). *Mind, self, and society.* Chicago: University of Chicago Press.

Morris, R. (1997). Educating savages. *Quarterly Journal of Speech, 83,* 152-171.

Saldivar, R. (1990). *Chicano narrative: The dialectics of difference.* Madison: University of Wisconsin Press.

Shome, R. (1996). Postcolonial interventions in the rhetorical canon: An "other" view. *Communication Theory, 6,* 40-59.

II

SITES OF IDENTITY

2

Patriotic Breeders
or Colonized Converts

A Postcolonial Feminist Approach
to Antifootbinding Discourse in China

WEN SHU LEE • San Jose State University

Footbinding lasted for roughly 800 years in China. It was a gendered practice that physically mutilated the feet of Chinese women of the Han ethnicity from middle- and upper-class families. In the late 19th century, silence surrounding this atrocity was strategically broken in public. Nevertheless, antifootbinding discourse advanced by different hegemonies presented a paradox for Chinese women with bound feet. To unbind one's feet meant to embrace two newer, nonetheless oppressive, identities: a "patriotic breeder" to bolster China's superior nationhood, or a "colonized convert" to bathe in foreign colonizers and missionaries' benevolence. To understand this paradoxical situation—emancipatory oppression—this chapter argues for (a) a processual epistemology that treats differentiation and identification as a simultaneous process and (b) a content orientation to study multiple dimensions of predicates, such as race, class, gender, and nationality. On the basis of these two theoretical tenets, this chapter advances a postcolonial feminist approach. It sensitizes our analysis to women's different genders and gender differences among the colonized. This chapter concludes with a note on authorial self-reflexivity and the use of a provisional postcolonial feminism to rethink teaching and scholarship in the field of speech communication.

I was told that a girl had to suffer twice, through ear-piercing and footbinding.

—A Chinese woman with bound feet (Levy, 1966, p. 26)

The rhetoric of power all too easily produces an illusion of benevolence when deployed in an imperial setting.

—Edward Said (1993, p. xvii)

AUTHOR'S NOTE: A previous version of this chapter was presented at the Wake Forest Argumentation Conference, Venice, Italy, 1996. This chapter was supported by her sabbatical leave of San Jose State University. The author wishes to thank Bob Newman, Richard Morris, Janet Metzger, and Phillip Wonder for their helpful comments on the chapter.

11

Finally, any case made in behalf of a heterogeneous group of women will be stronger the clearer it is the product of an exploration of the complexity of the situations of women. It must make visible that we make a common struggle, if at all, in and through our differences from one another, not around them.

—Elizabeth Spelman (1988, pp. 176-177)

A BRIEF HISTORY OF FOOTBINDING IN CHINA

Footbinding is a relatively recent custom in Chinese history, given that this history spans 3,500 years. According to Chen (1927), footbinding began during the Five Dynasties period (A.D. 907-960) among female courtesans and dancers in the imperial court. As the imperial court and the male elite class imposed an increasingly stringent moral-sexual code[1] on Chinese women during the Southern Sung dynasty (A.D. 1127-1279), footbinding became a reputably correct fashion,[2] consistent with feminine chastity, domesticity, and masculine possessiveness. Beginning as an innovative fashion in the imperial court, footbinding was transmitted from the imperial to the gentry class, and to the merchant and labor classes, from metropolis to rural areas, and from northern China to central and then southern China. During the Ming dynasty (A.D. 1368-1644), footbinding became more popular than it had been during previous dynasties. Footbinding lasted for roughly 800 years.[3] It was neither a permanent nor a natural trait of Chinese culture. Rather, footbinding coincided with the rise of officially endorsed efforts to control women's domestic and sexual conduct, and it was specific to social class (middle and upper), region (northern China), and ethnicity (Han).[4]

As a woman born in the early 1960s in Taiwan, I often recoil from the thought that, had I been born four or five decades earlier, I might have been subjected to the same atrocity. My mother, as a little girl of grade-school age, witnessed her grandmother's "tiny feet." During my childhood, an often told family story was about my paternal grandmother, a widow with bound feet, raising her only son in a wealthy household in the Shandeng Province in the 1930s. Outraged by the physical punishment of my father, because of his failure to recite a text, my grandmother walked on her 3-inch feet to the grade school to ask for justification from the male schoolmaster. Her suffering from footbinding, though, was never part of my father's narrative.

A relative of ours, now in her mid-80s, whose feet were bound at the age of 3, described her pain and suffering. She said that the binding

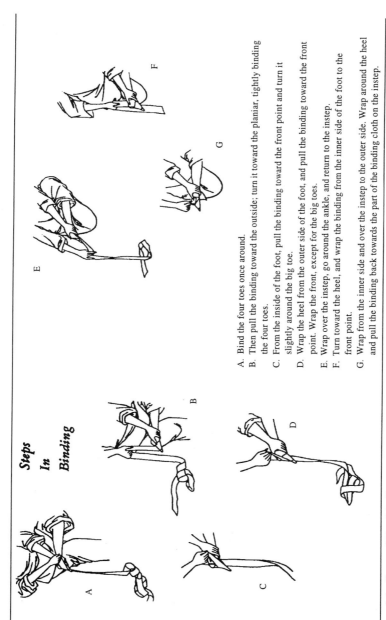

Steps
In
Binding

A. Bind the four toes once around.

B. Then pull the binding toward the outside; turn it toward the planiar, tightly binding the four toes.

C. From the inside of the foot, pull the binding toward the front point and turn it slightly around the big toe.

D. Wrap the heel from the outer side of the foot, and pull the binding toward the front point. Wrap the front, except for the big toes.

E. Wrap over the instep, go around the ankle, and return to the instep.

F. Turn toward the heel, and wrap the binding from the inner side of the foot to the front point.

G. Wrap from the inner side and over the instep to the outer side. Wrap around the heel and pull the binding back towards the part of the binding cloth on the instep.

gure 2.1. Steps of Footbinding
URCE: Reprinted from Levy (1966, pp. 24-25).

process began between the ages of 3 and 8. It was *hellish,* obliging at least 2 years of pain, pus, bleeding, begging, tears, and fear on the part of little girls. Binding was done by mothers or other matrons in the family, following specific steps (see Figure 2.1). There was usually a ceremony on the day of binding. Incense was burned so that female deities would assure perfect binding results. To coax little girls into conformity, the matron or binder would urge them to think about a good marriage prospect in the future. Then curses and beatings would follow if little girls unbound their feet during the night to relieve themselves of intense pain. A Chinese woman with bound feet described her suffering:

> She [Mother] shut the bedroom door, boiled water, and from a box withdrew binding, shoes, knife, needle and thread. I begged for a one-day postponement, but mother refused: "Today is a lucky day," she said. "If bound today, your feet will never hurt; if bound tomorrow, they will". . . . Beatings and curses were my lot for covertly loosening the wrappings. . . . Mother would remove the bindings and wipe the blood and pus which dripped from my feet. She told me that only with removal of the flesh could my feet become slender. . . . It took two years to achieve the three-inch model. My toenails pressed against the flesh like thin paper. The heavily-creased plantar couldn't be scratched when it itched or soothed when it ached. My shanks were thin, my feet became humped, ugly, and odoriferous; how I envied the natural-footed. (Levy, 1966, pp. 27-28)

It was a bone-crushing experience in a *literal* sense (see Figure 2.2). As illustrated in the reported testimony, children's resistance and their views on pain and suffering were actively suppressed.

Spivak (1990) is quite right in her analysis of oppression. The problem was not that the oppressed did not speak up in the past and now need to learn to voice their opinions. Rather, it is the unwillingness, for political and ideological reasons, *to grant them a hearing* that constitutes the core of oppression. Mitsuye Yamada (1983), a Japanese American poet, comments on this in her chapter, "Invisibility is an Unnatural Disaster":

> Not only the young, but those who feel powerless over their own lives know what it is like not to make a difference on anyone or anything. . . . The most insidious part of this conditioning process, I realize now, was that we have been trained not to expect a response in ways that mattered. (p. 39)

For centuries, these little girls' pleas went unheard in private and public situations (Chang, 1953/1981). Their mutilation remained unrecorded; their pleas drowned out by official endorsement and the rise of

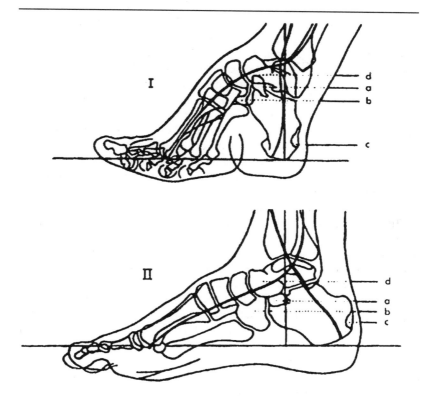

a. Small protuberance of the heel bone
b. Cuboid
c. Insertion of the Achilles tendon
d. Top of the anklebone

Figure 2.2. An X-Ray Comparison of Bound and Normal Foot (Provided by a Chinese and an Annamese Woman of the Same Weight)
SOURCE: Reprinted from Levy (1966, p. 29).

celebratory (rather than critical) literary works. But hundreds of years of silence surrounding footbinding was *strategically broken* in the late 19th century. This collective speaking-up movement resulted in Chinese girls' and women's exemption from a dire form of physical mutilation.

So great a boon was it for millions of Chinese females that at first glance antifootbinding appears to be an emancipatory movement. It argued and legislated for a better condition and identity for Chinese females with mutilated feet. As we enter into contact with the arguments formulated by different discursive hegemonies, however, other identities, closed to discursive scrutiny, begin to reveal themselves, identities that used Chinese females to preserve their privileges. Put differently, the case against footbinding, at this specific historical juncture, was almost never publicly made *by* Chinese women for their inalienable rights.[5] Instead, the arguments against footbinding formed a site of *identity struggle* involving imperial but well-meaning males and females, whose identities were bound up in privileges associated with their race, class, and nationality.

The fate of Chinese women's feet, bound or unbound, lay not in their own hands but in the hands of Chinese matrons and patrons (i.e., mothers, fathers, husbands) who endorsed or complied with patriarchal and imperial ideologies, their foreign-devil[6] missionaries, and their imperial colonizers. This chapter argues that the new identities prescribed by various antifootbinding agents for Chinese females advance oppression in newer and subtler forms. Yet how is it possible to foster oppression in the midst of an emancipatory movement? To answer this paradoxical question, I will use a theoretical notion advanced by Wander (1996), *rhetorical contextualization,* and couple it with Elizabeth Spelman's point (1988) that gender cannot be understood without uncovering issues related to race, class, *and* nationality.

RHETORICAL CONTEXTUALIZATION IN RACE, CLASS, GENDER, AND NATIONALITY

Pondering the critical links between Marxism and postcolonialism, Wander (1996) argues that in studying human communication we must not lose sight of a rhetorical triad—speaker, text, and audience. This notion takes us beyond textual analysis that often leaves unspoken (therefore unaccountable) the ideological positions of the speaker and her or his audience. To bring alive the speaker and audience is a contextualization move. To push this move further, we can identify the excluded speakers, the excluded texts, and the excluded audiences. These excluded rhetorical triads Wander calls *rhetorical voids.* In sum, contextualization involves two moves: (a) verbalizing the speaker and audience of a given text and (b) verbalizing the rhetorical voids (i.e., the excluded speaker, text, and audience).

Elizabeth Spelman (1988) offers insights into ways we may practice the above contextualizing moves. She argues that gender cannot be studied apart from race, class, and nationality, urging the following reforms in feminist scholarship: "When referring to women or to relations between men and women, note the class and race of the men and women in question. The situations in which those are relevant considerations far outweigh those in which they aren't" (p. 177). If gender cannot be fully understood apart from race, class, and nationality, we then are confronted with differences among women, or what Spelman calls "women of different genders" (p. 175). Difference or *plethora* presents opportunities for growth and mutual understanding, because we cannot assume that people of the same biological sex are open books to each other. *Plethoraphobia,* or treating differences as a problem, on the other hand, grows out of one's inability to challenge privileges due to one's race, class, and nationality. Put differently, to contextualize a given text (e.g., antifootbinding discourse) by verbalizing the race, class, gender, and nationality of the speaker and audience, and the race, class, gender, and nationality that form the rhetorical voids, is a project of challenging multiple forms of privilege. It is to this that I will turn.

RHETORICAL PRESENTS AND VOIDS
OF THE ANTIFOOTBINDING DISCOURSE

Benevolence as a virtue draws our liberal attention to a righteous cause: let us help change the dire condition of the victimized and grant them a better identity. Attention, as a result, falls on the yet-to-be-saved victims. The identities of the speaker—the "benevolent savior"—not surprisingly, remain unexamined and uninterpellated in the background. To move beyond this narrow focus on the "victims," we must uncover the *rhetorical presents and voids* even in benevolent discourse: Who speaks to whom and for whose interest? Who is not a speaker, who is not an audience, and whose interest is left out? Such questions lead to a rhetorically contextualized study of the benevolent and the victims along the lines of race, class, gender, and nationality. In relation to footbinding, I will deconstruct the discursive identities of (a) the Manchu conquerors and their Han subjects during the last dynasty (Qing) in China, (b) Japanese colonizers and their Han subjects in Taiwan between 1895 and 1945, (c) Western imperial powers (people at home and missionaries in China) and their Chinese colonized, and (d) Han males' heterogeneous voices regarding footbinding in the late 19th century.

Manchu Conquerors and Their Han Subjects

In 1644, the Manchus, as an ethnic minority, consolidated political power in China over their Han subjects, establishing the Qing dynasty (A.D. 1644-1912). As conquerors, the Manchus forced Han males to change their hairstyle into pigtails. Those who disobeyed this imperial edict were executed (by the tens of thousands). They also regarded footbinding as a sign of "cultural backwardness" and issued an edict banning this practice. The argument against footbinding was launched at the *ethnicity* level without considering *gender* as a critical marker of power imbalance. Instead of accusing Han males of mutilating Han females, the Manchus dismissed the Han as a "backward" people.

In the end, the pigtail edict was effectively enforced, whereas the antifootbinding one was rescinded. Both pigtails and footbinding[7] were Han-centric customs, a site of identity struggle between Han subjects and their Manchu conquerors. The selective enforcement of laws affecting Han males and females suggests that, whereas the Manchus demanded submission from Han males, they could relent when it came to Han females (Levy, 1966), in part because bound feet rendered females physically nonthreatening and difficult to relocate in the course of an armed struggle. In any case, footbinding was at first banned but then was tolerated when Manchu rule was consolidated. Han females from middle- and upper-class families still suffered mutilation. In such a context, it becomes obvious that the antifootbinding discourse, advanced in the early Qing dynasty by the Manchu ruling class, legitimated an ethnically different conqueror's domination of the Han subjects in China.

Japanese Imperialists and Their Han Subjects in Colonial Taiwan

Japan colonized Taiwan from 1895 to 1945. Long before the Japanese occupation, Taiwanese males of the Han ethnicity adopted Qing's pigtails. This symbolized the loss of Han identity and its subordination to the Manchu's imperial domination. The majority of Taiwanese women of Han ethnicity and from middle- and upper-class families, on the other hand, still practiced footbinding (Zhuo, 1993, pp. 69-71). Japanese imperialists looked down on pigtails and footbinding as ugly and unsanitary "Chinese" customs (Levy, 1966, p. 95). A policy of noninterference was adopted because it was not expedient to force the removal of ingrained customs when Japanese colonizers were still busy consolidating their military control in Taiwan, putting down armed rebellions by Taiwanese and aborigines.

In 1915, after 20 years of occupation, Japanese colonizers ordered the end of pigtails among Taiwanese men (of Han ethnicity) and the end of footbinding among Taiwanese women (of Han ethnicity). Most Taiwanese people complied. The imperialistic rationale behind this ban revealed itself in a poignant case during 1911, 4 years before the end of pigtails and footbinding in Taiwan. At issue was whether Taiwanese should be given Japanese citizenship. The Japanese Governor-General remarked, "such recipients [of Japanese nationality] would be ridiculed if they went to Europe and America wearing pigtails and dressed like old-style Chinese. This was considered detrimental to the national face of Japan and, as such, was officially deplored" (Levy, 1966, p. 102). Again, antifootbinding was not argued by Japanese colonizers to end oppression on behalf of Taiwanese women. Rather, it was advanced by a foreign colonizer, Japanese imperialists in this case, to bolster their superior national identity and legitimate their right to colonize Taiwan.

Western Imperial Powers and Their Chinese Colonized

Opposition to footbinding by Western imperial powers began at the time of the two Opium Wars in 1842 and 1858. It started in missionary circles in China and in Western public opinion at home. This change in attitude from early toleration to vague disapproval and finally to outright disgust and opposition (Drucker, 1981) coincided with the decline of the Qing empire and the rise of foreign colonization. These nations expanded their military sphere of influence by opening up Chinese ports, legalizing the export of opium to China, seizing lands, obtaining the right to disseminate gospels, and mediating disputes between Westerners and Chinese natives. Just like the Japanese imperialists discussed earlier, Western antifootbinding discourse was more strategically expedient than morally righteous. As these hegemonies became more established in China, their opposition to footbinding became more vehement. Footbinding, from the perspective of Western missionaries, was a *sin.* It violated the doctrine that men and women share a common fatherhood in God and should be treated equally. Footbinding distinguished the sinner from the pious. This argument was formulated at the level of *faith* rather than *gender.* It was a matter of theology, not a matter of women's rights (Drucker, 1981; Ono, 1978/1989).

In Western public opinion at home, footbinding was a *barbaric practice* (Yung, 1988). For example, the *Englishwoman's Review* (A.D. 1866-1910), the first periodical devoted to women's issues in England, treated footbinding as an example of barbarism to women, from which their superior culture ought to distinguish itself (Murray & Clark, 1985, p. xiii). Such arguments, though offered by early British feminists, were imperial in nature. They bolstered the identity of the colonizer as the bearer of a superior civilization and distorted the identity of the colonized as culturally backward savages.[8] These arguments stayed at the level of *national civilization* with *gender* left out as a critical marker.

Neither Western people at home nor missionaries in China denounced "Chinese patriarchal ideologies," nor did they sing the praises of the rights of women. Instead, they denounced a nation and its people as sinful and barbaric. Westerners plundered China, killed tens of thousands of its people, drugged millions of Chinese via opium, all the while posing as "civilized saviors." Again, antifootbinding was not advocated to end gendered and other forms of oppression against Chinese women. Rather, it justified colonizing China and subordinating the entire Chinese population, men and women, along with millions of peasant and gentry women whose feet remained bound.

Chinese Males' Heterogeneous Voices Regarding Footbinding

There were Chinese men who fetishized bound feet. They were called "lotus lovers" because the most beautifully bound feet of 3 inches in length were euphemized as "golden lotus." As discussed earlier, "golden lotus" had been adored as the identity of the Chinese gentry class (Veblen, 1934, p. 149) since the Sung dynasty, and it served as a symbol for the Han-centric resistance to the Manchus during the Qing dynasty. There were a few Chinese male scholars who criticized footbinding during the Sung, Ming, and Qing dynasties (Li, 1981; Lin, 1935/1981; Ropp, 1976), but antifootbinding discourse did not register in public opinions until the end of the 19th century (Chen, 1927; Ono, 1978/1989).

This was when reform-minded Chinese male elites (mainly of the Han ethnicity) criticized China's antiquated educational system and its backward scientific knowledge, technologies, and military weapons. Their focus was on the bruised identity of the Celestial Kingdom after the two Opium Wars. The rhetoric of "supporting Qing and destroying the foreign" [*fu qing mie yan*] was dominant. Antifootbinding speakers argued that unbound feet would improve the health of Chinese mothers, enabling them to bear and nurture stronger Chinese offspring, to perform their domestic duties as wives and daughters-in-law, and to visit their parents on a regular basis fulfilling their filial duties (Ono, 1978/1989). A popular slogan during the period was "strengthening the nation must first come from strengthening the breed" [*qiang guo bi xian qiang zhueng*]. Once again, antifootbinding rhetoric was less a women's and more a patriotic and filial movement. The focus was on bolstering China's national identity in the face of foreign invasions.

During the same period, male lotus lovers made their case for foot-binding (Levy, 1966). First, they argued that golden lotus, because it required pain to achieve something grander, was a measure of civilization. From this, they concluded that golden lotus symbolized the highest achievement in Chinese culture. Second, golden lotus marked the difference between men and women, putting each in their proper place. Third, golden lotus confined women to their private chambers all day. This made them more easily impressed by their husbands' strength and attention and less likely to seek favors elsewhere. Fourth, golden lotus made women shift their body weight to thighs and buttocks, tightening up their vagina. This made men feel especially excited and heavenly during intercourse. Fifth, golden lotus increased women's beauty and sexual desire. This was what "they wanted" because females would "naturally do" whatever they could to keep their men. Finally, an inability to appreciate golden lotus (antifootbinding rhetoric) was an alien, Western thing, evidence of inferior sensibilities and cultural backwardness. Only traitors to China would advance this movement. In the name of civilization and pleasure, lotus lovers ignored the pain, aspirations, and improved identity of Chinese women.

Chinese males differed in their opinions about footbinding. Antifootbinders denounced the lotus lovers' arguments as devilish and immoral; lotus lovers accused antifootbinders of their complicity with Western barbarism. But both sides did not criticize each other for being patriarchal or chauvinistic. Lotus lovers were, in general, not taken seriously, and reform-minded male elites tried to persuade "all Chinese"—both men and women—to abolish footbinding to strengthen China.

CHINESE WOMEN'S NEW IDENTITIES: PATRIOTIC BREEDER OR COLONIZED CONVERT?

In the process of radical international and domestic power redistribution, Chinese women's feet became a fetish, a site of constant identity battles. The Manchus, Japanese, and Western imperial powers denounced bound feet to legitimate different forms of colonization. Chinese elitist men denounced golden lotus as a barrier to China's "superior nationhood."

Han females from middle- and upper-class families escaped physical mutilation. This was good. But sadly enough, they left their *old identity,* as people with dainty feet, only to assume a new but still constricting identity of "patriotic" or "filial breeders" for their country, or "colonized converts" for their alien colonizers—the Manchus, Japanese, or the "Westerners."

Who benefited from the antifootbinding crusade? Footbinding was a "woman's question," *not for* Chinese women but as a means serving other ends. Within China, it was an argument serving chauvinistic-nationalistic ends; outside of China, it was a civilized and righteous argument, promoting imperialistic-religious domination. In this larger, historical context, the rhetoric of "antifootbinding" was used by different discursive hegemonies to forge a benevolent identity to mask different forms of domination.

Who benefited from this rhetoric? Chinese elitist males of the Han ethnicity gained a new identity. They became, in part because of their views on footbinding, reform-minded, progressive patriots. Colonizing powers became "civilized saviors." Out of their benevolence, they moved against the heathen to divide "his" wealth. Chinese women who unbound their feet and little girls of the new generation who did not have to go through such an atrocity had their oppressive countrymen and their plundering colonizers to thank.

What these benefactors gained in identity as patriots or saviors in relation to Han Chinese women left their gendered double standards intact. Chinese male elites could see the "weakness" of footbinding but neither the evils of polygamy[9] nor the denial of education and property rights to Chinese women. Alien imperial powers could see the "barbaric pathology" of footbinding but not their *own* gendered oppression. They remained silent about the miscarriages and deaths by corsets, the denial of women's suffrage, and the threat of poverty and prostitution facing unmarried women who had to leave their families (McClintock, 1995). Western missionaries placed the "sin" of footbinding against the backdrop of their religious doctrine. They failed to question their own gendered double standard of women as chaste mothers, husbands as the head of the family, and priesthood itself as bastion of male supremacy.

Antifootbinding was a paradoxical movement—it advanced emancipatory oppression. It saved Han Chinese women from physical mutilation but subjected all Chinese women and men to imperialistic colonization, religious dogma, and chauvinistic-nationalistic domination.

TOWARD A POSTCOLONIAL FEMINIST APPROACH TO IDENTITY AND ANTIFOOTBINDING DISCOURSE

"Identity" often remains *dormant* for those who are content with their living arrangements, social network, and ideological milieu. Identity, however, becomes an awakened, conscious issue when agency questions surface: Who am I? Why am I here? What am I doing? Who do I want to be? That is, identity becomes problematic when we enter into a discursive contest, when our "naturalized" privilege is challenged, when existing ideologies cannot contain imagination, and when it can no longer police alternatives (Trinh, 1991).

There is a link between identity and argumentation. Arguments about identity distinguish "is" from "is not," and "what to be" from "what not to be." Put differently, identification and differentiation constitute each other.[10] Understanding how people argue for an identity obliges us to consider how they differentiate identities, that is to say, distinguish themselves from others, making arguments *for* one and *against* another.

This theoretical point leads us back to Phil Wander's discussion of rhetorical presents and voids. A specific rhetorical triad takes on meaning only when layers of its rhetorical voids are uncovered. The juxtaposition of presents and voids recalls a processual definition of knowledge appearing in Lao Tsu in the *Book of Changes* and in Gregory Bateson's interdisciplinary works.

Processual epistemology involves a process of double-description (Bateson & Bateson, 1987; Lee, 1994; Lee, Chung, Wang, & Hertel, 1995). We cannot know "brightness" if we fail to experience the process that differentiates brightness and "darkness." "Self" becomes a significant symbol only in relation to the "other." It takes a process of "doubling" or a "pairing" to signify meaning. By ignoring this doubling in human discourse, we cannot interrogate (or deconstruct) political performances. To view bound feet as a sign of barbarism automatically commends another component in the doubling—advanced civilization. Making this doubling process explicit helps us sort out alternatives that one party or another tries to play down.

This principle of double description or doubling when rigidified and essentialized, however, has been labeled as the problem of *binary opposition*,[11] and attacked as an epistemological violence legitimating domination. This is an error and a serious one because the double-binary epistemology is a constitutive process of human communication. It is not binary naming that is oppressive. Rather, it is the conscious or unconscious "insistence" on a monolithic double or a monolithic binary-naming system, leaving no room for revision, provisionality, and alternatives that fuel oppression and domination. In the face of this, Butler (1993) argues for strategic provisionality.[12] Edward Said (1993) reminds us that imperialism, an extreme form of domination, thrives on its power to narrate and "to block other narratives from forming and emerging" (p. xiii).

The simultaneous processes of identification and differentiation as discussed by Bateson and Bateson (1987), Butler (1993), Lee et al. (1995), Spivak (1988), and Wander (1996) offer a *processual* epistemological guideline for conducting a systematic criticism of a discourse. What they do not offer is a guide to content. For this we must turn to Elizabeth Spelman.

Spelman (1988) addresses *content* issues—the ideological necessity to examine gender, race, class, and nationality. Among the various critical and content-related perspectives challenging domination and oppression, Marxism reminds us of the role played by social class, feminism the importance of gender, antiracism the hierarchy of race, gay and lesbian studies the issue of sexual orientation, and postcolonialism the influence of international imperialism. By way of contrast, postmodernism and poststructuralism lay out critical metaperspectives that are relatively content free. Each of the above viewpoints has been subjected to criticism due to its omission of certain "predicates" (Butler, 1990, p. 143), which is consistent with the position advocated by Spelman. But her work also poses a serious difficulty if one wants to theorize and mobilize political actions. The list of critical predicates is simply infinite! To deal with this dilemma, Judith Butler's (1990) notion of "excess" is instructive:

> The theories of feminist identity that elaborate predicates of color, sexuality, class, and ablebodiness invariably close with an embarrassed "etc." at the end of the list. Through this horizontal trajectory of adjectives, these positions strive to encompass a situated subject but invariably fail to be complete. This failure, however, is instructive: What political impetus is to be derived from the exasperated "etc." that so often occurs at the end of such lines? This is a sign of exhaustion as well as of the illimitable process of signification itself. It is the *supplement* [original italics], *the excess* [italics added] that necessarily accompanies any effort to posit identity once and for all. (p. 143)

As illustrated in my analyses above, the signification of footbinding changed as certain identities were affirmed and others rejected. Footbinding evolved from the Han-centric and gentry-class pride into (a) a barrier to a superior nationhood by elitist Han males (and some females), (b) a symbol of the Han-centric backwardness by the Manchu ruling class, and (c) a symbol of Chinese barbaric or heathen or inferior national status in the eyes of China's colonizers, be they Japanese or "Western" governments and missionaries. The critical predicates used were related to elitist nationalism in the case of Han males, ethnicity in the case of the Manchu rulers, and international imperialism in the case of foreign colonizers. They were unified in their omission of gender as a critical marker.

By now, it has become obvious that to do justice to "Chinese" "females" who suffered from the dual oppressions of Chinese nationalist chauvinism and foreign international imperialism, we need to couple a feminist perspective with a postcolonial perspective.[13] I urge a *postcolonial feminist perspective* while heeding Butler's (1990) instructive notion, "the excess of etc.," to avoid "posit[ing] identity once and for all" (p. 143). Let me spell out briefly why a feminist perspective or a postcolonial perspective cannot stand on its own without considering other critical predicates.

Feminisms and Women's Different Genders

Antifootbinding discourse argued by different hegemonies systematically left out the critical predicate of gender. A contemporary feminist, Mary Daly (1978), highlights this omission in her objection to footbinding,[14] to illustrate patterns of Sado-Ritual Syndrome and unmask "the universal sameness of phallocratic morality" (p. 112). Her exclusive emphasis on gender channels her arguments into a unitary debunking of the global patriarchy.

Mary Daly (1978) argues that because binding was done by matrons to little girls, Chinese females were pitted against each other. Their inability to challenge the co-opted superiority[15] set up by the Chinese elitist patriarchy, using mutilated feet as a way of climbing the social ladder, led to the "use of women as token torturers" (p. 139). In all this, the invisible hand of male domination remained unchallenged.

Arthur Waley ignores this invisible hand in his foreword to Levy's book on footbinding. Waley saw footbinding as "the most striking example of the strange things that women do or have done to them, in almost all cultures, to make themselves more attractive to men" (cited in Daly, 1978, p. 140). A woman's perspective challenging male domination, according to Daly, can sensitize the absurdity in treating footbinding as self-mutilations or self-modifications.

But what are the rhetorical voids in Mary Daly's (1978) antifootbinding arguments? It is ethical to argue against footbinding, against a gendered identity that equates mutilated feet with pride or privilege associated with specific ethnicity and social classes. But what were the new identities for these Chinese women after they unbound their feet? The road did not lead straight to equal rights. Quite to the contrary, the role of either a patriotic breeder or a colonized convert awaited Chinese females of unbound feet, and these are the invisible hands Mary Daly does not see nor feel.

She recognizes and defends her omissions of Chinese nationalism and foreign imperialism:

> Those who claim to see racism and/or imperialism in my indictment of these atrocities can do so only by blinding themselves to the fact that the oppression of women knows no ethnic, national, or religious bounds. These are variations on the theme of oppression, but the phenomenon is planetary. (p. 111)

Daly is after a bigger game—globalized patriarchy. Clearly, recalling Spelman's (1988) argument of "women of different genders," Daly's gender is different from the gender of a Chinese woman with bound feet. A white radical lesbian scholar who is economically independent and lives in a neocolonial empire, the United States, Daly has privileges not easily matched by a Han Chinese woman with bound feet, who had little chance to receive formal education, to be gainfully employed, and to have the right to vote and inherit property and, on top of all these, had to suffer international imperialism. Not that gender-specific critique should be replaced by a critique of nationalism or colonialism. They should be conducted *together,* because the female gender for one woman may differ from the female gender of another woman. Insisting that "the oppression of women knows no ethnic, national, or religious bounds" (p. 111), Daly cannot fathom, and therefore fails to urge a change from "patriotic breeders and colonized converts," the new but still oppressive identities associated with Chinese women with unbound feet.

A white bourgeois view of feminism has been contested by women of color[16] and Third World women[17] since the late 1970s and 1980s (Canning, 1994, p. 371; Martin, 1994, p. 631). Congenial to the tenets of a postcolonial feminism, bell hooks (1983) advances a view that is more consistently emancipatory than the feminism upheld by Mary Daly. For hooks, feminism means

> A struggle to end sexist oppression . . . to eradicate the ideology of domination that permeates Western culture on various levels as well as a commitment to reorganizing society so that the self-development of people can take precedence over imperialism, economic expansion, and material desires. (p. 24)

Such a feminism involves efforts to "end all forms of violence" (p. 130), without which a feminist intervention, like the one argued by Mary Daly, becomes paradoxical in its reluctance to challenge the privileges of white, middle-class women, the privileges associated with international imperialism, and the privileges of nationalism enjoyed by Chinese elites.

Postcolonialism and Different Genders of the Colonized

As more intellectuals, growing up during or after colonizing nations' spheres of influence, create increasingly influential narratives, alternative to the ones authorized by different empires (Achebe, 1959; Ngugi, 1981; Said, 1993; Shome, 1996), matters related to ethnicity, race, class, gender, and sexual orientation have to be reevaluated in conjunction with the influence of international imperialism. Western female missionaries, for example, occupied a quite paradoxical power position during the colonial era. They were colonized by their gender, but they were also implicated in their religion's domination of indigenous cultures (Flemming, 1992; Hunter, 1984; Jacobs, 1992). Like other imperial women of different positions and professions in the colonies (Chaudhuri & Strobel, 1992), they functioned "as both subordinates in colonial hierarchies and as active agents of imperial culture in their own right" (Stoler, 1991, p. 51).

Even though postcolonial analysis presents itself as a new and powerful method, it has its own pitfalls (McClintock, 1995, pp. 9-17). The prefix "post," for example, endorses a linearity of progress, which is the very spirit of empire that "postcolonialism" strives to fight against. Rey Chow (1995) also cautions us not to study "coloniality" in terms of "foreignness" or differences in race, land, and language; because it "can blind us to political exploitation as easily as it can alert us to it" (p. 62). When alien colonizers relinquished their sovereignty, most new governments formed by native elites were not quite immune from being dogmatic and oppressive of their own people (Said, 1993). Rey Chow puts it eloquently:

> The apparent absence of the "enemy" as such does not make the Chinese case any less "third world" (in the sense of being colonized) in terms of the exploitation suffered by the people, whose most important colonizer remains their own government. (p. 62)

The Chinese male elites' arguments against footbinding embodied a postcolonial critique of foreign imperialism. Nevertheless, with the omission of gender as a critical predicate, their crusade, in the eyes of Han Chinese women with bound feet, was both emancipatory and oppressive. "Patriotic breeders," a new nationalistic-patriarchal identity, urged Han women to become "healthy mothers." But this "becoming" made them depend on male figures for food and lodging. Their crusade entirely left out Chinese women who lived below the poverty line, whose feet were not bound to begin with and whose prospect was either lifelong labor, starvation, or prostitution. These serious omissions become clear from a postcolonial feminist perspective, which finds it important to identify that among the colonized, there were different genders—not only between Chinese males and females but also between females of different class privileges.

A NOTE ON AUTHORIAL SELF-REFLEXIVITY

This chapter advances three theoretical tenets. First, it argues for a postcolonial feminist approach rather than a unidimensional feminist perspective or a unidimensional postcolonial perspective. Put differently, this chapter is a postcolonial feminist "talking back" project in that it has critiqued (a) "alien empires" *outside* of China and Taiwan and (b) power operations *within China* in terms of gender, class, ethnicity, and nationality. Second, this chapter embraces a processual principle of doubling. In the case of antifootbinding discourse, this means a simultaneous discussion of identification and differentiation associated with Han women's feet. This doubling uncovers the paradox of emancipation and oppression faced by Chinese women. Third, this chapter acknowledges the "excess," the incompleteness of any discursive effort. Taken together, these three tenets lead to a critical issue in theorizing— authorial self-reflexivity.

Self-reflexivity[18] obliges an author to reflect on "who he or she is." Author identities, thus, become a critical issue in academic writing and speaking process.[19] Applying our three tenets, we have challenged the privileges of antifootbinding "authors" who argued for certain new identities for Han women. Advancing this critical process to the meta level, I can apply the same principles to my own identities as the "author of this chapter." My chapter is situated in my identities as a female coming from Taiwan and writing in the United States. As discussed earlier, my "femaleness" is related to the fact that I am only two generations away from footbinding. I view my "Taiwaneseness" via Taiwan's international status: a postcolonial country in relation to her Japanese colonizers; a tyrannical country due to Chiang Kai-Shek and his son's monolithic control for four decades (Lee et al., 1995); and a neocolonial country due to cultural imperialism from contemporary

Japan and the United States. My "scholarliness," as a consequence, is inherently diasporic or postcolonial in that I am speaking to a group of readers, lacking substantial knowledge of Chinese languages and histories, residing in the United States (the heart of a neocolonial country), and trained in a knowledge legitimation process preserving the privileges of the status quo.

The omissions of my chapter, another component in the doubling process, have to do with my family social status, sexual orientation, and academic position in the United States. Growing up in a middle-class family and having completed an elitist education in Taiwan, my arguments are not subaltern and, thus, lack a situated understanding of Chinese males and females who suffer from poverty and economic exploitation. My femaleness does not address the voices of lesbians living during the footbinding eras. Finally, my own privileges derived from teaching in higher education in a neocolonial empire are yet to be interrogated (Said, 1993). For these reasons (and others that may be added), my chapter is provisional and I by no means posit, once and for all, the identities (patriotic breeders and colonized converts) about Han women's unbound feet and my own identities associated with this chapter. I invite scholars who are interested in the discourse in the late imperial China and in other nations to interrogate my provisional stance and argue for alternative analyses. I also urge scholars in the discipline of communication to "unlearn our privilege" (Shome, 1996, p. 46). Forced ear piercing and footbinding are long gone in China. But unchallenged privileges still lurk in the rhetoric of benevolence. To make concrete changes in different women's lives, we need to challenge privileges and work *through* women's differences, not *around* them. With authorial self-reflexivity in mind, a postcolonial feminist perspective can serve as a useful starting point for rethinking our teaching and scholarship in the field of speech communication.

NOTES

1. Widows were discouraged from remarrying; chastity and virginity were primary; learning might make women promiscuous (Chen, 1927).

2. For a detailed discussion of material conditions and women's femininity (the use of corsets and footbinding), see Veblen (1934, pp. 145-149). He contrasts two values—reputably correct versus aesthetically true.

She is useless and expensive, and she is consequently valuable as evidence of pecuniary strength. . . . It results that at this cultural stage women take thought to alter their persons, so as to conform more nearly to the requirements of the instructed taste of the time; and under the guidance of the canon of pecuniary decency, the men find that resulting artificially induced pathological features attractive. So for instance, the constricted waist which has had so wide and persistent a vogue in the communities of the Western culture and so also the deformed foot of the Chinese. Both of these are mutilations of unquestioned repulsiveness to the untrained sense. It requires habituation to become reconciled to them. Yet there is no room to question their attractiveness to men into whose scheme of life they fit as honorific items sanctioned by the requirements of pecuniary reputability. They are items of pecuniary and cultural beauty which have come to do duty as elements of the ideal of womanliness. (p. 149)

3. In 1902, the Empress Dowager, Ci Xi, of the Qing dynasty issued the Anti-footbinding Edict (Levy, 1966, p. 79). This was an official call to end footbinding in China. Nevertheless, footbinding was still practiced in some areas (e.g., Shandeng Province, Da Tueng in the Shanxi Province) into the early 1940s (pp. 89-94).

4. China has always been multiracial and multilingual. Most Chinese dynasties were established by Han people, with two exceptions: the Yuan dynasty (A.D. 1279-1368) was established by the Mongols and the Qing dynasty (A.D. 1644-1912) by the Manchus. Footbinding was basically a Han-centric practice.

5. An exception was discussed by Beahan (1975). Between 1902 and 1911, with the rise of Chinese women's press, arguments against footbinding were made by Chinese female authors in the public sphere. Nevertheless, due to these women's middle- and upper-class background, the rise of revolutionary ideology against the Manchu rulers, and the harm done by foreign colonizers, women's rights "were henceforth a cause which was indissolubly linked with, yet subordinate to and defined by, the interests of the nation" (p. 414).

6. Beginning in the 19th century in China, Western imperial colonizers were called yang-gwei-zi, meaning "foreign devils" in Mandarin.

7. A subordinate style of communication comes in various forms. Han subordinate identity was performed via males' pigtails. Amongst multiple forms of subordination, however, we may find subtle strategies of subversion or insubordination. In this chapter, Han insubordination was effected via Han females' continued practice of footbinding. This suggests a fertile area of research—that is, different forms of communication present critical links between subordination and subversion regarding race, class, gender, sexual orientation, nationalism, and imperialism.

8. For a discussion of British imperial suffragism in relation to Indian women, see Burton (1991). She historicizes British feminists' imperial identity, "woman-as-savior," from 1900 to 1915 (p. 69).

9. Take as an example Kang Youwei (A.D. 1858-1927), one of the most prominent male reformists during the late Qing dynasty and the early Republic (founded by Sun Yesen). He argued for abolishing footbinding, encouraging women's education, and love-based, rather than arranged, marriage. But throughout his progressive life, a serious chauvinistic elision remained—his failure to come to terms with his polygamous practice. Kang had a wife and six concubines (Wang, 1994).

10. This point is supported by Judith Butler and Gayatri Spivak. Butler (1993) holds that the search for a new identity operates hand in hand with a process of "othering." Spivak (1990), an Indian diasporic intellectual and deconstructionist feminist, notes that in exploring reification, fetishisms, and brutality in imperial narratives, we should not forget to ask how "the other" (e.g., women of color from the Third World) functions in grand imperial narratives (p. 73).

11. For a critique of binary opposition, see Spivak (1990, p. 8) and Trinh (1991, p. 158).

12. "Strategic provisionality" (Butler, 1993, p. 312) argues that the meaning of a sign should not be foreclosed. "Provisionality" emphasizes that meaning (e.g., identity) is a constant "site of contest and revision." She advocates this notion as different from Spivak's (1988) "strategic essentialism" (p. 205).

13. This call for a postcolonial feminist perspective in our field is also made by Raka Shome (1996) when she urges a postcolonial turn in feminist rhetorical studies:

> Thus, feminist rhetorical scholarship, even though it is pushing the paradigms of the discipline in a laudable manner, still needs culturally localized perspectives, critical or theoretical, that address how *race and gender work together* [italics added] to influence and often inhibit women's communicative experiences. (p. 53)

14. Mary Daly also examines four other righteous rites that massacre women—namely, Indian suttee (widow burning), African genital mutilation, European witchburnings, and American gynecology.

15. Critiquing the Chinese imperial hierarchy and patriarchal hierarchy, Lee et al. (1995) coined the term *co-opted superiority:*

> Many, perhaps most, Chinese who do not or cannot afford to challenge the powerful, fight among themselves for superiority that is framed and encouraged by the dominant group. We label it *co-opted superiority* because the more the powerless fight for it, the less they pose a danger to the status quo, and the more co-opted they become. (p. 282)

16. For a discussion on the thesis that gendered oppression may be shared but is rarely identical among women of different race, class and sexual orientation, see Flores (1996), bell hooks (1981, pp. 119-196), Houston (1994), Lam (1994), and Moraga and Anzaldúa (1981).

17. For ways in which Western women who were colonized by their gender but acted to support the cause of their colonizing countries, see Chaudhuri and Strobel (1992), and Mohanty, Russo, and Torres (1991).

18. Critical reflexivity is supported by Judith Butler (1990): "Feminist critique ought to explore the totalizing claims of a masculinized signifying economy, but also remain self-critical with respect to the totalizing gestures of feminism" (p. 13). Raka Shome (1996), in her groundbreaking article, also argues for the practice of academic self-reflexivity to "examine our academic discourse against a larger backdrop of Western hegemony, neocolonialism and racial politics" (p. 45).

19. Dwight Conquergood (1991) advances a similar notion, rhetorical self-reflexivity, in the field of speech communication to examine "the rhetorical construction of its own disciplinary authority" (p. 193). Authors should examine explicitly what counts as "normative knowledge" and whose interests are served by such a knowledge-legitimation process.

REFERENCES

Achebe, C. (1959). *Things fall apart.* New York: McDowell, Obolensky.

Bateson, G., & Bateson, M. C. (1987). *Angels fear.* New York: Macmillan.

Beahan, C. L. (1975). Feminism and nationalism in the Chinese women's press, 1902-1911. *Modern China, 1,* 379-416.

Burton, A. (1991). The feminist quest for identity: British imperial suffragism and "global sisterhood," 1900-1915. *Journal of Women's History, 3,* 46-81.

Butler, J. (1990). *Gender trouble: Feminism and the subversion of identity.* New York: Routledge.

Butler, J. (1993). Imitation and gender insubordination. In H. Abelove, M. Barale, & D. Halperin (Eds.), *The lesbian and gay studies reader* (pp. 307-320). New York: Routledge.

Canning, K. (1994). Feminist history after the linguistic turn: Historicizing discourse and experience. *Signs: Journal of Women in Culture and Society, 19,* 368-404.

Chang M. (1981). Opposition to footbinding. In Y. Li (Ed.), *Chinese women through Chinese eyes* (pp. 125-128). New York: M. E. Sharpe. (Original work published 1953)

Chaudhuri, N., & Strobel, M. (Eds.). (1992). *Western women and imperialism: Complicity and resistance.* Bloomington: Indiana University Press.

Chen, D. (1927). *Zhongguo funu shenghuo shi* [A history of the lives of Chinese women]. Shanghai: Shangwu yinshuguan.

Chow, R. (1995). *Primitive passions: Visuality, sexuality, ethnography, and contemporary Chinese cinema.* New York: Columbia University Press.

Daly, M. (1978). *Gyn/ecology: The metaethics of radical feminism.* Boston: Beacon.

Drucker, A. R. (1981). The influence of Western women on the anti-footbinding movement, 1840-1911. In R. W. Guisso & S. Johannesen (Eds.), *Women in China: Current directions in historical scholarship* (pp. 179-199). New York: Philo.

Flemming, L. S. (1992). A new humanity: American missionaries' ideals for women in North India, 1870-1930. In N. Chaudhuri & M. Strobel (Eds.), *Western women and imperialism: Complicity and resistance* (pp. 191-206). Bloomington: Indiana University Press.

Flores, L. (1996). Creating discursive space through a rhetoric of difference: Chicana feminists craft a homeland. *Quarterly Journal of Speech, 82,* 142-156.

hooks, b. (1981). *Ain't I a woman?* Boston: South End.

hooks, b. (1983). *Feminist theory: From margin to center.* Boston: South End.

Houston, M. (1994). When black women talk with white women: Why dialogues are difficult. In A. González, M. Houston, & V. Chen (Eds.), *Our voices: Essays in culture, ethnicity, and communication* (pp. 133-139). Los Angeles, CA: Roxbury.

Hunter, J. (1984). *The gospel of gentility: American women missionaries in turn-of-century China.* New Haven, CT: Yale University Press.

Jacobs, S. M. (1992). Give a thought to Africa: Black women missionaries in Southern Africa. In N. Chaudhuri & M. Strobel (Eds.), *Western women and imperialism: Complicity and resistance* (pp. 207-230). Bloomington: Indiana University Press.

Lam, M. C. (1994). Feeling foreign in feminism. *Signs: Journal of Women in Culture and Society, 19,* 865-893.

Lee, W. (1994). On not missing the boat: A processual method for inter/cultural understanding of idioms and lifeworld. *Journal of Applied Communication Research, 22,* 141-161.

Lee, W., Chung, J., Wang, J., & Hertel, E. (1995). A sociohistorical approach to inter/ cultural communication. *Howard Journal of Communications, 6,* 262-291.

Levy, H. (1966). *Chinese footbinding: The history of a curious erotic custom.* New York: Walton Rawls.

Li, Y. (1981). Historical roots of changes in women's status in modern China. In Y. Li (Ed.), *Chinese women through Chinese eyes* (pp. 102-122). New York: M. E. Sharpe.

Lin, Y. (1981). Feminist thought in ancient China. In Li Yu-ning (Ed.), *Chinese women through Chinese eyes* (pp. 34-58). New York: M. E. Sharpe. (Original work published 1935)

Martin, J. R. (1994). Methodological essentialism, false difference, and other dangerous traps. *Signs: Journal of Women in Culture and Society, 19*, 630-657.

McClintock, A. (1995). *Imperial leather: Race, gender and sexuality in the colonial contest.* New York: Routledge.

Mohanty, C. T., Russo, A., & Torres, L. (Eds). (1991). *Third World women and the politics of feminism.* Bloomington: Indiana University Press.

Moraga, C., & Anzaldúa, G. (Eds.). (1981). *This bridge called my back.* New York: Kitchen Table, Women of Color Press.

Murray, J. H., & Clark, A. K. (1985). *The "Englishwoman's Review" of social and industrial questions: An index.* New York: Garland.

Ngugi, T. (1981). *Writers in politics.* London: Heinemann.

Ono, K. (1989). *Chinese women in a century of revolution, 1850-1950.* (J. Fogel, Ed., K. Bernhardt et al., Trans.). Stanford, CA: Stanford University Press. (Original work published 1978 in Japanese)

Ropp, P. S. (1976). The seeds of change: Reflections on the condition of women in the early and mid Ch'ing [Qing]. *Signs: Journal of Women in Culture and Society, 2*, 5-23.

Said, E. (1993). *Culture and imperialism.* New York: Vintage.

Shome, R. (1996). Postcolonial interventions in the rhetorical canon: An "other" view. *Communication Theory, 6*, 40-59.

Spelman, E. (1988). *Inessential woman: Problems of exclusion in feminist thought.* Boston: Beacon.

Spivak, G. C. (1988). *In other words: Essays in cultural politics.* New York: Routledge.

Spivak, G. C. (1990). *The post-colonial critic: Interviews, strategies, dialogues.* New York: Routledge.

Stoler, A. L. (1991). Carnal knowledge and imperial power: Gender, race, and morality in colonial Asia. In M. Leonardo (Ed.), *Gender at the crossroads of knowledge* (pp. 51-101). Berkeley: University of California Press.

Trinh, T. M. (1991). *When the moon waxes red: Representation, gender and cultural politics.* New York: Routledge.

Veblen, T. (1934). *The theory of the leisure class.* New York: Modernity Library.

Wander, P. (1996). Marxism, post-colonialism, and rhetorical contextualization. *Quarterly Journal of Speech, 82*, 402-426.

Wang, S. (1994). Kang Youwei dui nu xiang ji hun yin de kan fa [Kang Youwei's views on women and marriage]. *Jin Dai Zhong Guo Fu Nu Shi Yan Jiou* [Research on Women in Modern Chinese History], *2*, 27-50.

Yamada, M. (1983). Invisibility is an unnatural disaster: Reflection of an Asian American woman. In C. Moraga & G. Anzaldúa (Eds.), *This bridge called my back: Writings by radical women of color* (2nd ed., pp. 35-40). New York: Kitchen Table, Women of Color Press.

Yung, J. (1988). The social awakening of Chinese American women as reported in *Chung Sai Yat Pao, 1900-1911.* In *Chinese America: History and perspectives* (pp. 80-102). San Francisco: Chinese Historical Society of America.

Zhuo, Y. (1993). *Qing dai Taiwan fu nu de sheng huo* [Taiwanese women's lives in Qing Dynasty]. Taipei: Zi Li Wan Bao Wen Hua Chu Ban She [The Independence Nightly Publishing Co.].

3

Swinging the Trapeze

The Negotiation of Identity
Among Asian Indian Immigrant
Women in the United States

RADHA S. HEGDE • *Rutgers University*

Shuttling between cultural frames, immigrant women struggle to deal with the contradictions they face outside and within themselves. This chapter concentrates on the simultaneous interplay of race and gender on the process of displacement and re(dis)location. Interviews with Asian Indian immigrant women in the United States show that ethnic identities are ongoing negotiations between subjective experience and external representations faced in the practices of their everyday lives. To immigrant women, this means balancing multiple, often contradictory, ways of being both in interethnic and intraethnic contexts. This exploration of interpersonal experiences shows that narratives of self are products of social interchange, and identities emerge as enactments in relational contexts rooted within multiple discursive frames.

Migrants, Rushdie (1991) writes, root themselves in memories and define themselves by their otherness. They are a people "in whose deepest selves strange fusions occur, unprecedented unions between what they were and where they find themselves" (p. 124). This merging of the past and present together with the reality of the cultural in-between has some very specific consequences for Asian Indian women living in the United States.[1] Their identities and interactions are constituted within the prescriptive parameters of the old and new environments.

Ethnicity is a discourse created to invite a common system of meaning for a group. Ideological symbols of the past are revived by immigrants with renewed commitment. These symbols become doubly significant in the process of nostalgic connection with a distant history and a receding cultural past. Immigrants from the Indian subcontinent, in the United States, actively reproduce the traditional culture in which they were socialized.[2] They reenact the familiar synchrony of behavior and values within ethnic boundaries, where the traditional role of women plays a pivotal role in recapturing the past.

The position of Asian Indian immigrant women is defined through the interface of multiple ideologies that frame the experience of relocation, preserving history, and establishing presence in a new environment. Expectations and social sanctions for women's roles occupy a central place in all of these cultural articulations. Hurtling back and forth between distinct cultural worlds constitutes the lived reality of the migrant experience.[3] Nevertheless, the politics of shuttling has complex gendered overtones and assumes very different meanings for ethnic women. Adaptation to the U.S. context, for Asian Indian women, is like surviving a trapeze act replete with precarious swinging from the demands of one world to another.

This chapter explores the ways in which the interpersonal experiences of Asian Indian women in the United States shape their sense of self. Questions of identity emerge very prominently in an immigrant's consciousness and communicative experiences. As they walk in and out of cultural frames that are often incompatible, migrants struggle to deal with the contradictions they see outside and within themselves. The ambiguity of the hybrid zone, or what Anzaldúa (1987) powerfully names the borderlands, characterizes the nomadic struggles of those who are displaced. This chapter concentrates on the gendered nature of this conflict and its enactment in the context of interaction, where identities are constructed and deconstructed in multiple ways.

CONSTRUCTION OF A GENDERED
ETHNIC SUBJECTIVITY

Cultural relocation and experiential ambivalence is a central theme in the contemporary context of globalization. This separation of people from their native culture is one of the most formative experiences of our times, according to Bammer (1994). Rushdie (1991) claims that the migrant sensibility is "one of the central themes of this century of displaced persons" (p. 124). The reality of re(dis)location surrounding diasporic movement and the ensuing consciousness of the borderlands have prompted extensive theoretical articulations from various disciplinary angles (e.g., Anzaldúa, 1987; Bhabha, 1992; Donald & Rattansi, 1992; Hall, 1992; Rutherford, 1990; Said, 1993).

Issues of ethnic communication and identity are addressed in the scholarship on cultural adaptation—an important research domain in intercultural communication (for a review, see Kim, 1988).[4] Most of this research rests on the belief that the individual is responsible for his or her participation in the new society. The research on adaptation assumes that an immigrant should learn the ropes of communication of the host society and that adaptation will be relative to the extent that the ethnic members can competently participate in the new context. Kim's recent work (1996) argues that, in the progressive sequence of adaptive change, there is a link between the inherently stressful intercultural communication and the transformation of identity. The process of reorganization of self takes place in the context of intercultural interface and "involves continual reinventing of an inner self beyond the boundaries of the original cultural identity" (p. 356). "As the old 'person' breaks up, new cultural knowledge, attitudes and behavioral elements are assimilated into an enactment of growth—an emergent 'new' person at a higher level of integration" (p. 357).

Whereas Kim does build a strong case for viewing identity as a dynamic and evolving process, the focus is on the individual and his or her predisposition and ability to deal with the environment. Both of the assumptions, of the sovereign individual who is able to act independently and the idea of linear patterns of identity exchange, do not address the politics of the in-between, which characterizes the migrant situation. Kim's view, that people can embrace an intercultural identity development if they are open-minded and resilient enough to endure stress, seems too optimistic in a world in which hegemonic structures systematically marginalize certain types of difference. Individual ethnic subjectivity is framed within a complex web of factors and within ideologies that construct what Hall (1992) calls "the impassable symbolic boundaries between racially constituted categories" (p. 255).

Another underlying assumption in the scholarship on ethnic identity is that the cultural adaptation process is a common experience shared by men and women. The reason for this is the continued importance given to the individualist approach to the study of immigrants that overlooks the gendered experience of ethnic reality (Toro-Morn, 1995). Women's roles, however, are not enacted on an empty stage or in the ideal room of one's own. They are contained within the embedded discourse of race, gender, and class (hooks, 1981, 1989; Moraga & Anzaldúa, 1981; Trinh, 1989). As Spelman (1988) notes, any attempt to treat identity in an additive manner is to engage in "pop bead" metaphysics, in which the assumption is not only that each part of one's identity is separable from other parts but that the significance of any part is unaffected by the other parts. The experiences of women of color in their specific material and discursive locations make it very obvious that one is not a woman in addition to being a racial other. Attempts to study race and gender as separate variables result in reductionism, or even erasure, and denial of the total experience of ethnic women.

For ethnic women, achieving a personal coherence of self is a struggle in the face of negotiating experiences of marginalization and displacement. Asserting identity becomes an act of negotiation between private and public, of fragmentation and coherence, of past and present, and of self and other. The dynamic of being an immigrant woman of color from the Third World in the United States is not one that can be described or analyzed in independent parts. The reality of their lives is constituted simultaneously at the intersections of multiple hierarchies of race, class, and gender (Crenshaw, 1992). It is this simultaneity that West and Fenstermaker (1995) claim has eluded theoretical treatment. Research studies in communication that emphasize gender and race issues have been few and recent (see Chen, 1992; Houston, 1989, 1992, 1994; Kramarae, 1989).

With respect to Asian Indian women in the United States, these intersecting discourses are played out in tandem with the patriarchal sounds of the old society and its traditional paradigms for gender relations. The resultant complexity of these structures constrains agency, silences voices, and profoundly affects the lives of immigrant women. These systemic erasures carry over to research in which difference is sidestepped to make room for the normalized and generalizable explanations of social processes. The experiences of ethnic women, until recently, have received minimal attention in the mainstream and feminist literature (see Bhavnani, 1993). Monolithic representations of Third World women have discursively colonized the historical heterogeneities in the lives of women (Mohanty, 1991). By placing women's ethnic culture at the center, we can overcome this totalizing tendency and portray the diversity within nondominant cultures (Houston, 1992).

DISPLACEMENT AND IDENTITY

There has been considerable scholarship from critical theorists challenging the Western notion of the bounded self and the reliance on such oppositional dichotomies as the individual and society as fundamental units of analysis. The view of the self as socially constructed reproblematizes practices of everyday life as sites to understand subjectivity as an ongoing process. In the field of communication, there is increasing attention paid to the fact that identities, such as cultures, no longer can be conceptualized as self-contained, fixed, and stable but are, rather, constituted and reproduced within the process of communication and everyday interaction (Gergen & Davis, 1985; Hecht, 1993; Hecht, Collier, & Ribeau, 1993; Mokros, 1996; Shotter & Gergen, 1989). The fluid nature of identity has a particular resonance for understanding the experience of migrants, whose identities are constantly in the process of being repositioned by the attempt to integrate multiple cultural narratives. The major theoretical consequence of border crossings is "a rethinking of identities as constructed and relational, instead of on-tologically given and essential" (Conquergood, 1991, p. 184).

For most migrants, the need to assert a personal identity is related to the articulation of a group, or collective, identity. In their overwhelming desire for the past, migrants tend to believe that there is a collective true self that ethnic members share due to their common origins. Cultural identities are treated as a common reference point that provides a mirage of stability and continuity. But Hall (1990, 1992, 1993), in his discus-sions of identity and the diaspora experience, argues very provocatively that cultural identity is not just about what we are but also about what we have become. So instead of being fixed in the memory of the past, identities are subject to the continual play of history, culture, and power. Ethnic identities are not merely about recovering the past. The backward-looking conception of diaspora, as scattered peoples defined through their relation to a lost homeland, is, according to Hall (1990), a hegemonizing form of ethnicity. "Diaspora identities are those which are constantly producing and reproducing themselves anew, through transformation and difference" (p. 235). Hence, the theoretical point of departure for my discussion follows Hall's stand that cultural identity is equally a matter of *becoming* and *being* (p. 225).

In his critique of cultural identity as being an accomplished fact, Hall (1990) proposes that we should think of identity "as a production which is never complete, always in process, and always constituted from within, not outside, representation" (p. 222). So not only is the ethnic individual constructed as the *other,* but representation has the power to make migrants experience themselves as the *other.* Therefore, accord-ing to Hall, cultural identity can be conceptualized as framed by two axes—the axis of similarity and continuity and the axis of difference and rupture. "Cultural identities are the points of identification, the unstable points of identification or suture, which are made, within the discourses of history and culture, not an essence but a positioning" (p. 226). Framed by this tension between continuity and rupture, ethnic identities are produced in the hybrid narratives of displacement.

The common tendency to define ethnic identity in terms of a fixed essence results in freezing difference and reducing the complexity of ethnic others to simple categories.[5] The current onslaught of multicul-tural rhetoric is deeply wedded to naturalizing differences and fixing them in terms of deviations from the dominant norm, not in terms of their individual locations and discontinuities (see Donald & Rattansi, 1992). Ethnic groups themselves, in their need to assert their collective strength, also resort to reiterating a different type of essence in the process of excavating the past. This can be problematic for women (Brah, 1992) when the values that the group reproduces, as essential and intrinsic to what they consider fundamental say *Indianness,* are those that subordinate women.

As women negotiate their lives between two worlds, they find themselves inscribed within various discursive configurations that make available and prioritize certain subject positions from which meaning is constructed (de Lauretis, 1986; Gregg, 1993; Hollway, 1984). These representations permeate the everyday lives of immigrants and situate them at the crossroads of contradictory discourses. Immigrant women actively negotiate their positions in the cultural and discursive context that they encounter in their quotidian practices. Their locations are marked by the ambivalence and dialectical tension of resisting and learning the performative scripts of assimilation. The "traveling" between worlds, according to Lugones (1990), arises for the mestiza, or those of the borders, as a matter of necessity and survival. "Inhabiting more than one 'world' at the same time and traveling between 'worlds' is part and parcel of our experience and our situation" (p. 396). Whereas movement between cultures is part of the construction of hyphenated identities, the boundaries blur and are resurrected simultaneously. The challenge of the hyphen constitutes the poetics of the migrant condition—"the realm in-between where predetermined rules cannot fully apply" (Trinh, 1991, p. 57).

THE STANDPOINT OF ASIAN INDIAN WOMEN

Asian Indian women in the United States come from diverse linguistic, economic, and occupational backgrounds, in terms of their current life and their backgrounds in India. In 1988, more than 48.5% of the Asian Indian women in the United States born in India had 4 years or more of college (U.S. Bureau of the Census, 1991). Most Asian Indian women follow their husbands to the United States; the decision to emigrate, by and large, is not made by women. The system of arranged marriage is an accepted institution and it is common for an immigrant man living in the United States to travel to India and find a wife through family networking. Indian men living in the West are considered superior alliances in the marriage market in India. Women who arrive in the

United States face intense isolation and the fact that with migration follows a reconfiguration of familiar patriarchal power (Mani, 1993). Reincarnating a form of mythologically informed Indian womanhood and femininity are part of the immigrant contract with continuity and tradition.

Immigrants from the Indian subcontinent are a recent and growing minority group with a total population of 815,447 of which 377,604 are women (U.S. Bureau of the Census, 1990). The major influx of immigrants from the subcontinent occurred after 1960 when changes in the immigration law phased out the national quota system. This initial wave of immigrants was characterized by high levels of education and professional attainment in scientific and technological fields (Saran, 1985). The community has grown far beyond the small homogeneous elite group and is concentrated on the west and east coasts of the United States.

Asian Indians tend to be very conscious of their ethnic heritage (Fisher, 1980; Nandi, 1980). Coming from a deeply religious traditional culture, these immigrants form very tightly organized ethnic networks. Various ethnic organizations are built around points of commonality: language, place of origin, religion, and music, to name a few. The ethnic group becomes the context within which to engage in known lines of interaction and to affirm one's past.

In the routines of border crossings, Asian Indian women find themselves facing competing versions of being an embodied cultural being. The various locations in which they enact and make sense of their lives serve as sites from which to understand the crisscrossing of ideological structures and the construction of gendered subjectivity. Alcoff's (1988) notion of positionality is useful here, not only to critically situate identity as performance but to cast social practices of immigrants as border negotiations. If we assume with Alcoff that identity is relative to a constantly shifting context, then locating women's position relative to a social and cultural network provides a vantage point from which to see meaning being constructed rather than the place where meaning can be discovered.[6] By examining how women locate themselves within their multiple communities, we begin to see identities emerge as enactments in relational contexts rooted within ideological structures.

The stories women tell of their lives show us how identities are constructed and the conflicts that are embedded in this process. Each woman's account, according to Gregg (1993), opens a window on the work done to reproduce the social relations and subject positions that make diverse identities both possible and sustainable (p. 197). Narratives have long been an important way of accessing women's lives in feminist research (e.g., Franz & Stewart, 1994; Personal Narratives Group, 1989; Torres, 1992). The focus of my research is to gain access to women's standpoints through unstructured in-depth interviews. The interviews were intended to understand how meanings emerge in the hybrid spaces of the migrant experience, as women talk about their everyday practices. How do Asian Indian women negotiate the categories woman, Indian, Asian Indian, immigrant, foreigner, and define boundaries between them? The choice of method was driven by the need to engage in a discussion of identity and communication that is grounded in the perspective and material realities of Asian Indian women. With the problematics generated from the perspective of women's experiences (Harding, 1987, p. 7), this chapter attempts to present the voices of a small group of immigrant women.

I spoke to Asian Indian women about their lives, their conflicts, their isolation, and the meaning and challenges of being an immigrant and female. I met them in their homes, their work environments, and in coffee shops. My identity as an Asian Indian immigrant woman was central to the relational dynamics of the interviews. I was conscious of my position as a "gendered, racial, social-classed voice interacting with other gendered, racial, social-classed voices" (Kauffman, 1992, p. 200). The women were not only eager but also anxious to talk about their experiences. There was a rapport and involvement that characterized our engagement, as the issues they raised were equally significant to my life world. I spoke to 20 women from the Indian subcontinent living in the eastern United States. Ten of them were born in India (eight were married) and ranged in age from 28 to 55. The other 10 were second-generation Asian Indian women between the ages of 20 and 25. This group of single women raised in this country included two who had come to the United States when they were very young. Whereas the two generational groups shared a common focus, their concerns and narrative emphases were strikingly different. According to Visweswaran (1993), second-generation immigrants who have been "interpolated from early childhood into the racialist structures of U.S. identity politics, are compelled to confront race in their narratives" (p. 308) and do so far more frequently than the generation of their mothers.

The women who were interviewed all spoke English. There were four professional career women, two part-time administrative or lab assistants, one housekeeper and factory worker, one fast-food business manager, and two homemakers. The 10 second-generation women were all students in a university in the eastern United States.[7]

The conversations were initiated with two primary questions: (a) What is your life in this country like, and (b) what does it mean to be an Indian woman in this country? We usually started talking about being

Indian in the United States, in general, and this led to various thematic areas. The major themes that arose in the interviews are discussed to show the multiple ways in which Asian Indian women's subjectivity is framed and constituted.

NEGOTIATION OF IDENTITY IN INTER- AND INTRAETHNIC CONTEXTS

To Asian Indian immigrants, the interpersonal experiences in inter- and intraethnic communication contexts are like moving in and out of two distinctly different relational contexts (Hegde, 1991). Immigrants are faced with the sudden slipping away of certainty and familiarity and find themselves on a new game board, facing new rules. Within these contexts, immigrant women see themselves represented in discernible patterns along the two axes defined by Hall (1990)—divergence or rupture and identification or continuity.[8] The experience of seeing oneself represented as "the other" makes immigrants highly speculative and anxious to develop oppositional narratives that explain and connect their relationship to *otherness*. Therefore, the politics of location is central to the understanding of identities as the active negotiation between external representations of self as other and the subjective experiences of displacement and alienation (Parmar, 1990).

Axes of Difference and Rupture

Over my mask
  is your mask
    of me

—Yamada (1990, p. 114)

As the Asian Indian women talked about their interpersonal experiences, it was clear that identity was the ongoing contestation or reproduction of various forms of representation. From their various locations as immigrant women, they articulated how their lives and identities were played out in a constantly shifting interpersonal terrain. The women I interviewed continuously referred to the us-and-them binary to distinguish the interethnic and intraethnic situations as two separate domains. When they talked about interethnic contexts of communication, they most often referred to the interactions at the workplace, interactions with colleagues or fellow students. Three prominent themes framed their subject positions: stereotypical representations, racist encounters, and isolation.

Stereotypical Representations

There was repeated emphasis on how Asian Indian women are represented stereotypically and how this affects them on a daily basis. "There is nothing one can do, they have made up their mind that we are submissive, too timid and well, too Indian," said a professional woman who works for a research and development organization. Once these meanings have already been attributed, they are reproduced and perpetuated; interactions get played out in predictable ways. The women effortlessly recalled the stereotypes that they perceived were held about them: submissive, docile, soft spoken, not aggressive enough, lacking leadership, overly traditional, unsociable.

The individual disappears behind such phrases as "you people," "you Indians," which Asian Indians hear regularly. The women I spoke to were painfully aware of the totalizing manner in which their culture was constructed, but at the same time there was a skepticism and resignation about these stereotypes. Stereotypes, writes hooks (1992), are a form of representation.

> Like fictions, they are created to serve as substitution, standing in for what is real. They are there not to tell it as it is but to invite and encourage pretense. They are a fantasy, a projection onto the other that makes them less threatening. (p. 170)

The difficulties of breaking through and dealing with the consequences of not fitting in with the stereotype were recalled, often with anguish. One illustrative remark came from a postdoctoral fellow who talked about how she had worked through a harrowing conflict situation with her university superiors. She felt she was being mistreated and wanted to make her position clear. On hearing this, her American peers were amazed at her response: "They told me, 'You are so aggressive, how come? You don't fit into the mold of the Indian woman.' " She was required to explain the shift away from the essentialist conception of Indian woman.

Other comments showed how South Asian women have internalized the assimilationist call, to protect themselves from these representations. Yamuna talked of a corporate leadership training program for Asian women she had attended, which helped her unlearn everything she had been socialized into:

> My mother used to tell me all the time "don't talk about yourself." Now when I work with white men I know I have to forget my mother and what she told

me. I have to learn to be a new person to survive, everything I was raised to be doesn't seem to fit in.

A secretary in a large organization spoke of a similar transformation. "I had to cut my long hair, change my style of dressing; Indian clothes are out—they don't take you seriously if you don't blend in." The superficial veneer of assimilation is the first thing that Indian women resort to in the process of *blending in*: "I love to wear my beautiful Indian saris, but no, I feel too conspicuous, too foreign."

There was a recognition that a stereotypical conception of the Asian Indian woman is systematically sustained. Whether one conforms or deviates from this expectancy, the stereotypes remained constant, curtailing options and erasing individual differences. "I try to do my own thing and ignore these comments but it is not possible," said Mohana, a computer programmer.

Mohana, whose colleagues decided to call her "Mo" because "Indian names are so hard to pronounce," has lived in the United States for more than 20 years. "Yet, even today, at work, when my colleagues talk about their social life, they still say, Do you get it, Mo? " Mohana has decided that her colleagues will never "get it" about her and has decided, "Who cares?" The *becoming* aspect of ethnic identity is denied in the process of fixing difference within an eternal past.

Racist Encounters

The subject of racism inevitably loomed large in these conversations. I include all interactions that interpellate the subject to assume the ideological space of the dominant group. For these women, recalling specific incidents, some of which were subtle and others overtly antagonistic, was painful and difficult. The women talked of such significant details as faces being forgotten: "It is amazing how soon they forget your face. My friend, an Indian, and I get constantly mistaken for each other—we look the same they say; I don't think so." Frequent reference was made to names being forgotten or conveniently changed. Many women mentioned Anglicizing their names intentionally, choosing names for their daughters that "are easy for the Americans to pronounce and won't embarrass the children," or both. Others resent this appropriation of their identity: "My name is Sudha, do not call me Sue." "My name is Paulomi, and no it does not sound like Paloma as in the perfume."

The embarrassment over an Indian accent was recounted in terms of how it was received and derided. Minauti, a second-generation student who remembers being teased "Naughty, Naughty, Minauti," recalled an instance from her sixth-grade class:

> I remember saying something in class, and when the class ended, we were leaving and somebody, you know, just chewed me out. He said, "Why don't you learn to talk right before you say anything." I remember I did not talk after that. I didn't say anything in class for 3 or 4 months. I would be scared to go to school.

The second-generation women recalled more fearful forms of racism they had encountered in middle and high school. "They called me names, made fun of my name, made fun of Indian food, called me a Dot-head[9] even though I have never wore a dot on my forehead." The masking of cultural origins was another way to deal with racism: "If they mistook me for some other nationality, that was a relief, a compliment." Minauti recalled that it was so chilling an experience for a teenager to handle that she tried to act as un-Indian as she possibly could: "I did not know who I was."

Others recalled being hooted in the malls, jeered at on the streets to such insults as "dot-head," "Bombay bitch," and other expletives, including, ironically, the terms *Hindu* and *Gandhi*! One of my respondents, who runs a fast-food store, said, "I don't know about this 'Gandhi' thing, they keep yelling 'Gandhi' when I cross the street. I mean I still hear it, but it was really bad when the movie 'Gandhi' came out."

A ride in a public transportation bus was recalled. "These boys brought pebbles and threw it at me saying _____ I can't repeat the words. I said nothing, I did nothing, no one on the bus did anything either." Others are unable to shrug off this racist name-calling: "I feel so helpless, I feel they are killing me. I don't know what we have got into."

The self-doubts and search for personal meaning were so interconnected with the obliteration of self that these women experienced through racism. The effect of these encounters with racism was always a sense of disempowerment and total lack of control over one's environment. A sense of inadequacy and being denied their selfhood was persistent in the tone and recall of these encounters. "Who am I? Why should I go through this? What am I doing here?"

Isolation of the Other

The existential ambivalence of living as the *other* is compounded by the notorious *home* question that immigrants hear, regardless of the number of years they have spent in the United States: "When are you going back home?" The concept of home plays a serious role in the migrant consciousness. As Mohanty (1993) wonders, "Is home a geographical space, a historical space, an emotional, sensory space?" (p. 352). However we approach it, the question, according to Mohanty (1993), is profoundly political. Home signifies belonging and continuity and as the Asian Indian women yearned for a sense of identification, the reality they faced was one of pervasive isolation. There was a feeling of not belonging anywhere, of not being accepted and a deep sense of alienation from their surroundings, a sense of not being *home*. Self-reflexiveness seemed intertwined with the migrant situation: "I sometimes don't know what we are doing here, but we are not a part of that world either."

The word *they,* which was used to refer to the American world outside, also reappeared to mean India, in its geographical and psychological distance. "They don't understand my life when I go back either," said Urmila when we talked of life in the borderlands, of biculturality and of the meaning of home.[10] The sense of loss, having cut connections and being marooned without roots, was a theme echoed frequently. "What will happen to our children in the future? Will they know who they are?"

Anchoring that anguish about the future to the present was Rema, a homemaker who has just come from India to join her husband after having waited in India for 2 years for her alien registration card.[11] "I arrived here after all that waiting and I feel like a prisoner jailed in a strange land. It is his environment, his house, his friends, I have nothing here."

Neena, a second-generation Asian Indian, is an undergraduate student. She recounted interactions that had made her stop and reflect: "Wait a minute, who do you think I am? What am I, anyway?" This was in reference to a white female friend who had told Neena, "It's really a pity there are no black men or Indian men around here for you to date." To Neena, the statement was meant to indicate that she belongs to another group that is denied access to the centers of white social networks. Socializing with her American friends at parties was "a nightmare" to Neena. She would join her friends to go to a fraternity party and

> They would just overlook me, shut me out. I was having the worst time and I know it's not me. I would get all dressed up and go and it's like I don't even exist. This is worse than being treated poorly.

The anguish and resistance came together repeatedly: "There is always this cultural barrier between them and us." "They view me as just another Indian, I am not me." Whether it was attending an exercise class, a meeting, or a party, they were extremely conscious of their invisibility. This stripping away of particularities about self was deeply felt and lamented by the women I met. As Mrs. Dalal, the factory worker, told me in anguish, "My family is all here, *nobody is there* in India; I am still unhappy; why?"

In negotiating their subject positions, issues of status surfaced as an identity marker. The emphasis on their class and social status in India prior to coming to the United States was an important reminder to counter the marginalization they felt here. "After all, we had status in India; they don't know anything about our background." The educated, professional women tended to be very conscious of selecting their networks. Seeta, the research scientist, relates,

> My neighbor is a redneck and won't talk to me and I won't either. The only Americans who are close to me are the 60s type you know, the liberal ones who were into meditation and yoga in the 60s.

The narratives echoed the same themes of alienation, isolation, and rejection. "It is like wearing a mask." "It is like playing charades." "It is a double life." "You can never forget who you are or your past; even if you do, there is always someone reminding you."

Axes of (Mis)identification and Continuity

In the process of recreating little Indias, Asian Indian immigrants have created an extensive organizational structure. There are religious institutions, temples, and cultural organizations all over the United States (Saran, 1985). These ethnic activities and organizations are very diverse and organized around caste, language, and religious differences, all of which make a noticeable reappearance in the diaspora. The traditional literature on adaptation has always maintained that ethnic networking creates insular communities that effectively slow down the acculturation process (Shibutani & Kwan, 1965). The Indian community establishes for immigrants a sense of continuity and familiarity to face the disruptions and lack of coherence they experience in their adopted worlds. "Even though the Indians I mix with are so different from me, in America, we are just Indians and I need them." So the differences of class and language seem to be overlooked for a common bond of cultural origins. The sense of relief was mentioned: "Once in an ethnic gathering, one can let down the mask and finally be oneself."

For these reasons, all the women interviewed said their closest friends were Asian Indian women. This need to bond among Asian Indian women arises not only out of the need to counter the isolation of the outside but also to provide support for the ideological curtailments of women within the ethnic group.

Representations of Authenticity and Modernity

In the production of "familiar essentials" (Bhattacharjee, 1992), women become emblematic of what constitutes authentic cultural tradition. The image of the Indian woman as inscribed in traditional patriarchal ideologies of Indian society is reinvented in the new world (p. 28). The model of pure Indian womanhood is an important signifier of Indianness in the new U.S. context and this translates into various forms of control and domination. According to Chatterjee (1989), the dichotomy of inner and outer, home and the world, is a powerful ideological device used in Indian nationalist rhetoric. The world outside is the domain of the male whereas the home, with its essence untouched by materiality, is represented by the women. "In the world, imitation and adaptation to Western norms was a necessity, at home, they were tantamount to annihilation of one's identity" (p. 625). The binary is very true in the context of Asian Indians in the United States, where critical questioning of tradition, particularly by women, is associated with a negation of Indianness (Mani, 1993).

The home is the unsullied Indian cultural space in the lives of immigrants. It is the women who run it, celebrate the Indian religious holidays, maintain the rituals and customs that re-create a version of *Indianness*. Commenting on the nationalist ideology, Chatterjee (1989) writes, "No matter what the changes in the external conditions of life for women, they must not lose their essentially spiritual (that is, feminine) virtues; they must not, in other words, become essentially Westernized" (p. 629). There is powerful resonance again to the lives of Asian Indians in the United States who actively engage in freezing the essence of India.

The theme was echoed in my interviews, in the recall of domestic conflicts, raising of daughters, dating, and sexuality. Mala, the lab technician, protested about having to make Indian food every night at home. "He wants Indian food, I can't be the *pativrata*[12] his mother used to be." The politics of housework is a common source of conflict be- cause the husband did not participate in household chores. "We cannot live like we did in India" was a frequent cry of resistance to the fact that the transplanted Indian home was the domain of the woman alone.

The stress and contradictions in trying to raise bicultural children and maintain an Indian home was repeatedly raised. The inner and outer binary makes its way into everyday life, providing a template to critique women's assertions of self and identity. It is a taboo, my respondents stated, within the Indian community to be too *American*. Facing the contradictions of growing up in an immigrant home, Mona brought up the issue of tradition versus modernity: "My parents use the term *modern*. They say we have to remember our traditions; kids from India are getting too modern."

The control of women's sexuality is an important part of maintaining authenticity of tradition. The second-generation women were vocal in resisting this silence around sexual topics and the control of their sexual lives, which is prodigiously maintained in Indian homes. "Anyone who has a brother, knows they can do so much more; they don't have to play this double thing as much as we have to," said Mona. Dating was an American practice that was regarded as cultural contamination of the worst sort, and Asian Indian parents particularly protected their daughters from the sexual world outside. To 22-year-old Nisha, this restriction bordered on the ridiculous: "I'm like, mom, you know the Kama Sutra does come from India, right?"

With the mothers, the dating problem took on different dimensions. "You see, whenever my husband sees my daughter going out, he says she is getting too Americanized and it is because of my poor mothering." To the first generation of Asian Indian women, socialized in India, talking to their daughters about sexuality was a difficult thing to do. Sexuality in middle-class families in India is never an issue that is addressed. From my conversations, I noticed that the responsibility of keeping daughters in check and controlling their sexual behavior was solely left to the mother. Women in their roles as daughters, wives, and mothers are implicated in every aspect of this immigrant project to preserve tradition.

The mandatory requirements for the right image of Indian womanhood were reiterated, often sarcastically: "Asian Indian men want a nice Indian girl, accomplished but not too Americanized." The level of some illusory assimilative end is also determined as a part of the prescriptions for women's identity. To second-generation Asian Indian women, the warnings about growing up to be a good Indian woman posed tremendous social pressure. The lack of total acceptance by their peers in college and the experience of being different, in addition to the cultural conflicts at home, contributed to their daily struggle with questions of identity and belonging.

OF INTERSECTIONS AND THE "OTHER"

As I talked to these Asian Indian immigrant women, it was clear that the processes of cultural relocation and the evolution of identity are complex negotiations of claiming a position in the present and reclaiming versions of the past. Running through the experiences of the everyday is a quest for self, a search for a narrative that can connect and make sense of the disjunctures and historical discontinuity of their lives. The experiences that were recounted to me were not discrete instances but the unfolding of a persistent theme of trying to reconcile subjectivity with the representations of self as *other*. As women, this meant trying to balance multiple, often contradictory, ways of being that framed interactions in the inter- and intraethnic worlds they frequented. From a theoretical perspective, this exploration of experiences reiterated the fact that narratives of self are products of social interchange and are constituted relationally.

The frequent immersion in self-doubt and questioning seemed to relate to the need to historically situate self in terms of a distant past and an uncertain present and establish some form of a future trajectory. Gergen (1994) maintains that narratives of self not only strive for coherence and continuity, but also work toward maintaining consistency between the nested macro- and microlevel narratives. In this context, the macronarratives are the ones that historically situate the immigrant context with a past, a history, and a genealogy. The micronarratives relate to the representations of self in quotidian practices that inscribe migrants in subject positions removed from their historical flow and context. The jarring between the two levels and the lack of narrative linkages create the tensions of migrant life. With women specifically, both levels of narrative are appropriated, thereby doubly displacing self. Each context fixes immigrant women, pitting various essences of appropriate and normative womanhood against each other. The dual realities of immigrant life are compounded for Asian Indian women by multiple illusions (or delusions!) about what a woman's identity should and should not be.

The simultaneity of race and gender are inextricably woven into the narratives of self. Considering the multiplicity of forces acting at any given time, it is counterproductive to lift immigrant women's identities and communication out of the context of racism and sexism. Consequently the question of which subject position is more valid at any given time is also irrelevant. Women of color often are asked what is more oppressive, being a woman or being the racial other? When I hear harassing slurs hurled at me (as I often do), is it due to the sari that I wear, the red dot on my head, the fact that I am brown skinned, or that I am a woman?[13] Prioritizing one discourse over another is merely setting up a false agenda. Clearly, cultural identities are not snapped on together, to again use Spelman's (1988) famous pop bead metaphor.

In this chapter I have attempted to provide a picture of how Asian Indian women's identities are constituted at the intersection of multiple forces. The community of Asian Indians has grown beyond the original elite professional group that came in the 1960s. There are many working-class immigrant women whose lives are circumscribed in even more complex ways than the particular group to which I spoke. Work that begins from the standpoint of marginalized lives will provide a way of including minority women in our scholarship. This is a domain that has too long been ignored, particularly in intercultural communication scholarship. This groundwork of descriptive data and details, regarding the complexities of women's lives, is necessary to understand the processes by which women generate meaning about their identities and interaction.

Migrant identities are enacted at the intersections, with the old and the new environments occurring simultaneously or, as Said (1990) describes it, "contrapuntally." The theme of being the *other* continually echoes in the lives of immigrants, displacing and deferring their sense of coherence about self. In an ironic twist, on their trips *home* to India, immigrant women from the United States become the westernized others who have lost touch with the native land. So my respondents and I swing between contexts and build "imaginary homelands" in the hybrid zone, even as we hear, "Hey Gandhi, when are you going home?"

NOTES

1. *Asian Indian* is the term created by the U.S. Bureau of the census in the 1980s to refer to Asian immigrants from South Asia,—that is, India, Pakistan, Sri Lanka, Bangla Desh, Nepal, and Bhutan. Whereas there are some thematic similarities between these countries, there are striking contextual differences. To assert a collective, political voice, the term *South Asian diaspora* is currently used. This study focuses exclusively on immigrants from India.

2. For some studies on the acculturation patterns of recent immigrants from India, see Helweg and Helweg (1990) and Saran and Eames (1985).

3. The use of the words migrant and immigrant are intentional. The word *migrant* is used to refer to the state of being nomadic, a consciousness described by Bhabha (1992), Rushdie (1991), and Said (1993), among others, to refer to the existential ambivalence and hybridity that is associated with living between cultures. The word *immigrant* refers to the material condition of being "a resident alien."

4. Y. Y. Kim's work has been very instrumental in directing attention of communication scholars to the study of cultural adaptation. In a series of studies (reviewed in Kim, 1988), she established the central role played by communication in the acculturation process of immigrants.

5. This essentialist fixing of difference is seen routinely in the media and particularly in the new rhetoric of diversity that prevails in institutional settings. By concentrating on the superficial differences and essences, an engagement with the more complex issues of hierarchies and margins are not addressed.

6. Alcoff (1988) remarks that her notion of positionality does not imply that a woman is a passive recipient of an externally determined identity and thereby without any agency. On the contrary, it helps provide a perspective "that being a woman is to take up a position within a moving historical context" (p. 435).

7. Most of the names of my respondents are pseudonyms that sound like the original names. Only first names are used.

8. These axes, suggested by Hall (1990), are used primarily as a model to frame the inter- and intraethnic contexts. Nevertheless, the terms themselves are by no means mutually exclusive, nor are they solely representative of each context.

9. *Dot-head* is a term of derision used against Indian women who wear a traditional cosmetic mark on their foreheads. In the mid-1980s, a group called "Dot Busters" in Jersey City, New Jersey, violently harassed Asian Indian immigrants in that area. The term is still heard by Indian women in the United States.

10. See Gayatri Spivak (1990). Speaking of her position as an Indian intellectual in the United states, she says, "I am bicultural, but my biculturality is that I'm not home in either of the places" (p. 83).

11. Women in India who get married to an immigrant usually have a very long waiting period for their alien registration card, which enables them to travel and live in the United States. With the system of arranged marriages, usually the husband files the papers after the marriage, and the wife typically waits with her family in India for the period of time. Waiting for the card is a common narrative among newly married immigrant couples.

12. *Pativrata* is a very traditional Indian term for a woman whose life is one of total dedication to her husband. In ancient social texts of India, a woman's identity was defined always in terms of a man—that is, her father, husband, and sons. There are numerous mythological tales that celebrate the virtues and selflessness of such a paragon.

13. This is a modification of an example used by K. Bhavnani (1993): "When I walk down a street in Europe or North America wearing jeans and am harassed or abused, I cannot say that my sex is privileged above my Blackness or vice versa" (p. 40).

REFERENCES

Alcoff, L. (1988). Cultural feminism versus post-structuralism: The identity crisis in feminist theory. *Signs, 13,* 405-436.

Anzaldúa, G. (1987). *Borderlands/la frontera: The new mestiza.* San Francisco: Aunt Lute Books.

Bammer, A. (1994). *Displacements: Cultural identities in question.* Bloomington: Indiana University Press.

Bhabha, H. (1992). *The location of culture.* New York: Routledge.

Bhattacharjee, A. (1992). The habit of ex-nomination: Nation, woman and the Indian immigrant bourgeoisie. *Public Culture, 5*(1), 19-44.

Bhavnani, K. (1993). Talking racism and the editing of women's studies. In D. Richardson & V. Robinson (Eds.), *Thinking feminism: Key concepts in women's studies* (pp. 27-48). New York: Guilford.

Brah, A. (1992). Difference, diversity and differentiation. In J. Donald & A. Rattansi (Eds.), *Race, culture, and difference* (pp. 126-145). Newbury Park, CA: Sage.

Chatterjee, P. (1989). Colonialism, nationalism, and colonialized women: The contest in India. *American Ethnologist, 16*(4), 622-633.

Chen, V. (1992). The construction of Chinese American women's identity. In L. Rakow (Ed.), *Women making meaning* (pp. 225-243). New York: Routledge.

Conquergood, D. (1991). Rethinking ethnography: Towards a critical cultural politics. *Communication Monographs, 58,* 179-194.

Crenshaw, K. (1992). Whose story is it anyway? Feminist and anti-racist appropriations of the Anita Hill story. In T. Morrison (Ed.), *Race-ing justice, en-gendering power* (pp. 402-440). New York: Pantheon.

de Lauretis, T. (1986). Feminist studies/critical studies: Issues, terms, and contexts. In T. de Lauretis (Ed.), *Feminist studies/critical studies* (pp. 1-19). Bloomington: Indiana University Press.

Donald, J., & Rattansi, A. (Eds.). (1992). *Race, culture, and difference.* Newbury Park, CA: Sage

Fisher, M. P. (1980). *The Indians of New York City: A study of immigrants from India.* New Delhi: Heritage.

Franz, C. E., & Stewart, A. J. (1994). *Women creating lives: Identities, resilience and resistance.* Boulder, CO: Westview.

Gergen, K. (1994). *Realities and relationships: Soundings in social construction.* Cambridge, MA: Harvard University Press.

Gergen, K. J., & Davis, K. E. (Eds.). (1985). *The social construction of the person.* New York/Berlin: Springer-Verlag.

Gregg, N. (1993). Trying to put things first: Negotiating subjectivities in a workplace organizing campaign. In S. Fisher & K. Davis (Eds.), *Negotiating at the margins: The gendered discourses of power and resistance* (pp. 172-204). New Brunswick, NJ: Rutgers University Press.

Hall, S. (1990). Cultural identity and diaspora. In J. Rutherford (Ed.), *Identity: Community, culture, difference* (pp. 222-237). London: Lawrence & Wishart.

Hall, S. (1992). New ethnicities. In J. Donald & A. Rattansi (Eds.), *Race, culture and difference* (pp. 252-259). Newbury Park, CA: Sage.

Hall, S. (1993). What is this "black" in black popular culture? In G. Dent (Ed.), *Black popular culture* (pp. 21-33). Seattle, WA: Bay.

Harding, S. (1987). *Feminism and methodology.* Bloomington: Indiana University Press.

Hecht, M. L. (1993). 2002—A research odyssey: Toward the development of a communication theory of identity. *Communication Monographs, 60,* 76-82.

Hecht, M. L., Collier, M. J., & Ribeau, S. (1993). *African American communication.* Newbury Park, CA: Sage.

Hegde, R. S. (1991). *Adaptation and the interpersonal experience: A study of Asian Indians in the United States.* Unpublished doctoral dissertation, Ohio State University, Columbus.

Helweg, A. W., & Helweg, U. M. (1990). *An immigrant success story: East Indians in America.* Philadelphia: University of Pennsylvania Press

Hollway, W. (1984). Gender difference and the production of subjectivity. In J. Henriques, W. Hollway, C. Urwin, C. Venn, & V. Walkerdine (Eds.), *Changing the subject* (pp. 227-263). New York: Methuen.

hooks, b. (1981). *Ain't I a woman: Black women and feminism*. Boston: South End.

hooks, b. (1989). *Talking back: Thinking feminist, talking black*. Boston: South End.

hooks, b. (1992). *Black looks: Race and representation*. Boston: South End.

Houston, M. (1989). What makes scholarship about black women and communication feminist scholarship? *Women's Studies in Communication, 11,* 28-31.

Houston, M. (1992). The politics of difference: Race, class and women's communication. In L. Rakow (Ed.), *Women making meaning* (pp. 45-59). New York: Routledge.

Houston, M. (1994). When black women talk with white women: Why dialogues are difficult? In A. González, M. Houston, & V. Chen (Eds.), *Our voices: Essays in culture, ethnicity and communication* (pp. 133-139). Los Angeles: Roxbury.

Kauffman, B. (1992). Feminist facts: Interview strategies and political subjects in ethnography. *Communication Theory, 2*(3), 187-206.

Kim, Y. Y. (1988). *Communication and cross cultural adaptation*. Philadelphia: Multilingual Matters.

Kim, Y. Y. (1996). Identity development: From culture to intercultural. In H. B. Mokros (Ed.), *Interaction and identity* (pp. 347-369). New Brunswick, NJ: Transaction Books.

Kramarae, C. (1989). Redefining gender, class and race. In C. Lont & S. Friedly (Eds.), *Beyond boundaries: Sex and gender diversity in communication* (pp. 317-327). Fairfax, VA: George Mason University Press.

Lugones, M. (1990). Playfulness, "world"-traveling and loving perception. In G. Anzaldúa (Ed.), *Making face, making soul: Creative and critical perspectives by feminists of color* (pp. 390-402). San Francisco: Aunt Lute Books.

Mani, L. (1993). Gender, class and culture conflict: Indu Krishnan's "Knowing her place." In Women of South Asian Descent Collective (Eds.), *Our feet walk the sky: Women of the South Asian diaspora* (pp. 32-36). San Francisco: Aunt Lute Books.

Mohanty, C. T. (1991). Under western eyes. In C. Mohanty, A. Russo, & L. Torres (Eds.), *Third World women and the politics of feminism* (pp. 51-80). Bloomington: Indiana University Press.

Mohanty, C. T. (1993). Defining genealogies: Feminist reflections on being South Asian in North America. In Women of South Asian Descent Collective (Eds.), *Our feet walk the sky: Women of the South Asian diaspora* (pp. 351-358). San Francisco: Aunt Lute Books.

Mokros, H. B. (1996). From information and behavior to interaction and identity. In H. B. Mokros (Ed.), *Interaction and identity* (pp. 1-22). New Brunswick, NJ: Transaction Books.

Moraga, C., & Anzaldúa, G. (1981). *This bridge called my back: Writings by radical women of color*. Latham, NY: Kitchen Table, Women of Color Press.

Nandi, P. (1980). *Quality of life of Asian Americans*. Chicago: Pacific/Asian American Mental Health Research Center.

Parmar, P. (1990). Black feminism: The politics of articulation. In J. Rutherford (Ed.), *Identity, community, culture, difference* (pp. 101-126). London: Lawrence & Wishart.

Personal Narratives Group. (1989). *Interpreting women's lives*. Bloomington: Indiana University Press.

Rushdie, S. (1991). *Imaginary homelands*. New York: Penguin.

Rutherford, J. (Ed.). (1990). *Identity, community, culture, difference*. London: Lawrence & Wishart.

Said, E. (1990). Reflections on exile. In R. Ferguson, M. Gever, T. Trinh, & C. West (Eds.), *Out there: Marginalization and contemporary cultures* (pp. 357-366). New York: The New Museum of Contemporary Art.

Said, E. (1993). *Culture and imperialism*. New York: Alfred Knopf.

Saran, P. (1985). *The Asian Indian experience.* Cambridge, MA: Schenkman.

Saran, P., & Eames, E. (Eds.). (1985). *The new ethnics: Asian Indians in United States.* New York: Praeger.

Shibutani, T., & Kwan, K. M. (1965). *Ethnic stratification: A comparative approach.* New York: Macmillan.

Shotter, J., & Gergen, K. J. (Eds.). (1989). *Texts of identity.* London: Sage.

Spelman, E. (1988). *Inessential woman.* Boston: Beacon.

Spivak, G. C. (1990). *The post-colonial critic: Interviews, strategies, dialogues.* New York: Routledge.

Toro-Morn, M. I. (1995). Gender, class, family and migration: Puerto Rican women in Chicago. *Gender & Society, 9*(6), 712-726.

Torres, L. (1992). Women's narratives in a New York Puerto Rican community. In L. Rakow (Ed.), *Women making meaning* (pp. 244-262). New York: Routledge.

Trinh, T. M. (1989). *Woman, native, other: Writing postcoloniality and feminism.* Bloomington: Indiana University Press.

Trinh, T. M. (1991). *When the moon waxes red.* New York: Routledge.

U.S. Bureau of the Census. (1990). *1990 census of the population: General population characteristics* (Series P-1-1). Washington, DC: Government Printing Office.

U.S. Bureau of the Census. (1991). Profiles of foreign-born population in the United States: June, 1988. *Current Population Reports* (Series P-23, No. 176). Washington, DC: Government Printing Office.

Visweswaran, K. (1993). Predicaments of the hyphen. In Women of South Asian Descent Collective (Eds.), *Our feet walk the sky: Women of the South Asian diaspora* (pp. 301-312). San Francisco: Aunt Lute Books.

West, C., & Fenstermaker, S. (1995). Doing difference. *Gender & Society, 9*(1), 8-37.

Yamada, M. (1990). Desert run. In G. Anzaldúa (Ed.), *Making face, making soul: Creative and critical perspectives by feminists of color* (pp. 114-116). San Francisco: Aunt Lute Books.

4

Razzing

Ritualized Uses of Humor as a Form of Identification Among American Indians

STEVEN B. PRATT • *University of Central Oklahoma, Edmond*

During the course of managing our day-to-day affairs, we often engage in social encounters in which one's ethnic identity is salient to one or both interactants. As such, the cultural identity of one or both of the interactants may be suspect. The standard communicative practices, which are appropriate to the occasion, may, in such cases, be emphasized to determine whether or not the interactants are truly cultural members. Such is the case for those who would make themselves known as American Indian and who make this assumption about others. The purpose of this study is to examine and explicate "razzing," a teasing ritual used by many contemporary American Indians that functions as a means of testing and establishing cultural identity. Specifically, this research will discuss the problematic nature of identifying as an Indian, explain the concept of Indianness, and provide an exemplar of razzing.

Whenever members of a particular group come together, the cultural identity (the competent membership) of one or more of the interactants may be suspect. Nonverbal cues often serve as a means of reducing ambiguity in initial interaction—that is, determining the identity of another. Nevertheless, nonverbal cues are often inadequate for making predictions of a person's cultural identity. The standard communicative practices, which are appropriate to the occasion, may, in such cases, be emphasized to determine whether or not the interactants are truly cultural members.

Let us suppose that a student, who has been educated in the traditional European American educational setting, enters a classroom for the first

AUTHOR'S NOTE: I would like to acknowledge the contributions of D. Lawrence Wieder and Hartmut B. Mokros. I wish to thank Larry for the many conversations we had concerning the notion of Indianness and helping me to see what constitutes Indianness. Hartmut provided much needed editorial advice and I am appreciative of the time he spent reading my first manuscript. An earlier version of this chapter appeared in 1996, in H. B. Mokros (Ed.), Inter-action and identity: Vol 5. Information and Behavior. *New Brunswick, NJ: Transaction Books.*

time and observes a person standing at the head of the room, positioned behind a podium. On the basis of context and previous experiences, this student could then appropriately recognize this person as the teacher of the class. The student would then know how to engage in the communicative behaviors that the roles—that is, teacher and student—elicit on the basis of this context. Yet if the person perceived as the teacher were to engage in communicative behaviors that were inappropriate to the situation, for example, shouting profanities at no one in particular, this person's identity as a teacher would obviously become suspect. The situation requires that we observe and test further communicative behaviors to determine just exactly who this person is, for example, raising one's hand and being called on.

Such is the case in the day-to-day affairs of those who would make their personal and social identity known as an American Indian.[1] For those who would make themselves known as an Indian and make this assumption about others, physical characteristics, self-identification, and tribal certification do not provide sufficient evidence. Rather, those who ascribe to being a "real" Indian, those who primarily live their lives according to Indian culture, tribal culture, or both,[2] rely on a set of presupposed and tacit communicative behaviors in making this interpretation.

For the culturally competent member, identity is established or reestablished by engaging in appropriate speech behaviors. Competency is displayed by appropriately engaging others in the culture's communication rituals or "when the behavior of one interactant confirms the enacted ethnic identity of the other interactant" (Hecht, Collier, & Thomas, 1988, p. 59). Wieder and Pratt (1990) identified seven prominent modes of communication behavior that are "critical" for the identification of an Indian. Among these seven prominent modes of communication behavior that are "critical" in the identification of Indianness, they identify ritualized uses of humor as a central mode.

The purpose of this chapter is to examine and explicate a communicative practice that functions in this way—that is, a means of testing and establishing cultural identity—as a means of answering the question "Is he or she really one of us?" A particular communicative behavior that American Indians use in testing and establishing whether or not someone is a culturally competent member is "razzing," a teasing ritual that is enjoyed as humor. Razzing is a collective form of storytelling in which participants take some episode, humorous or not, from a present or past experience and relate it "humorously" to the others in attendance. The story, which is often lengthy, is then characteristically embellished and altered by others who are present.

Specifically, this chapter will (a) discuss the problematic nature of identifying as an Indian and explain the concept of Indianness, (b) delineate the structure and functions of razzing, and (c) provide an exemplar of razzing in which cultural competence is displayed.

THE SCOPE OF THE INQUIRY: CONTACT INDIANS

The communicative behaviors identified here function as criteria for what I refer to as "contact Indians" (Pratt, 1985), or those Indians who have frequent contact with members of differing tribal groups and with members of other cultures, as opposed to "grassroots Indians," who reside in isolated reservation areas and who have limited, if any, contact with members of other tribes and other cultures.

Contact Indians make up a segment of the Indian population that, in many cases, live in urban settings and travel throughout their own geographical region, as well as other geographical regions. Travel and the attendant contact with members of other tribes and other cultures are frequently the result of work, attendance at such intertribal activities as powwows (social gatherings) and religious events (Native American Church, sweat lodge), or attendance at schools, colleges and universities, and so forth. On the other hand, grassroots Indians seldom venture from their reservation, and their primary contact with the outside world is through interactions with those contact Indians who have left the reservation and returned either for a visit or to resume residency.

Because of their prolonged residence in areas in which there are relatively few Indians with whom to interact, contact Indians have a problem maintaining social identity. The social identity and subsequent cultural competency of the contact Indian becomes suspect, by the grass roots and other contact Indians, as a result of their living in a primarily non-Indian environment. For example, many Indians who move away from the Indian community to attend college, or for employment opportunities, often find that they have to reaffirm their identity and competency with those whom they knew earlier. That is, whenever an Indian interacts with another Indian his or her identity and cultural competency is not readily taken for granted, nor is it immediately conferred. During the course of the interaction, a type of testing is done to reveal the true identity of the persons involved and to satisfy the question of whether or not "you are still one of us." The common question, when speaking of such persons, is, "Are they really Indians?"

To address the phenomena of Indianness, I have employed a qualitative-ethnographic methodology. This entails "research procedures which produce descriptive data: people's own written and spoken words and observable behavior" (Bogden & Taylor, 1975, p. 4). This also entails a heavy dependence on inductive procedures that contrast with an a priori specification of the categories of analysis. My study permitted the subjects to specify what constitutes Indianness, rather than rely on a preconceived conception of what Indianness is, based on the criteria established by the Bureau of Indian Affairs (BIA), physical characteristics, and so forth.

Method

The particular qualitative approach I used involved participant observation that McCall and Simmons (1969) define as "research characterized by a period of social interaction between the researcher and the subject in the milieu of the latter" (p. 3). Participant observation allows the researcher to enter a particular setting and unobtrusively observe the members in the course of managing their everyday affairs. In the course of observation, the researcher's life may actually become a part of the activities that he or she is observing. Because of my own life circumstance, I was already involved on a day-to-day basis with the very phenomena that are the focus of this study. In many important ways, I have been my own primary informant.

Initial Research Procedures and the Development of Other Techniques

During the initial stage of data gathering, I simply intensified my involvement in the American Indian community and functioned as a reflective observer and a participant. I sought out those who were regarded as true members known to other members of the cultural group and began observing them in the process of "doing Indianness" in the course of their daily affairs.

Some of the participants were told of my research and were asked to be a part of it. They were asked specific questions about a certain phenomenon. In other instances, I was simply regarded as a participant in a specific event and did not readily make my presence as a researcher known. For example, although I tried, I found it impossible to structure a razzing event, in that it is a spontaneous event. I did, however, covertly tape-record several instances of razzing and later informed the participants that I had done so. I then asked for their permission to use the tapes.

Data Collection

The observations in this chapter are based on my own intuitions as a participant in the speech community and discussions with more than 60 informants. I am an actively participating member of the Osage Nation and was able to unobtrusively observe and engage in this communication ritual. Informal interviews were conducted with Indians, which were recorded on field notes, with many of the instances tape-recorded. Some of the data come from my own cultural expertise and recounted experiences. Some of these materials were elicited by D. L. Wieder treating me as an informant. I have found it useful to use Del Hymes's (1972) categories of (a) topic, (b) purpose, (c) act sequence, (d) setting, and (e) participants, to describe the organization of the razzing ritual.

Participants

As I have already noted, I was a primary participant of my own research. The other participants for this study were primarily members of the various Southern Plains Indian tribes who reside in urban, rural, and reservation environments and are considered to be real Indians by other real Indians and those who consider themselves to be real Indians. Nevertheless, as should be clear in the characterizations that follow, the extent of their contact experience with members of other tribes, when their Indianness would have been potentially at issue, more than strongly suggests that their experiences as real Indians transcends tribe and region.

The participants from whom the primary data were gathered ranged in age from 19 to 87. Blood quantum ranged from one-eighth degree Indian blood to four fourths. The educational backgrounds of the informants, who were male and female, ranged from college students (graduates and undergraduates) to those who had not completed high school. The participants were employed in a variety of occupations. They were attorneys, physicians, counselors, business persons, laborers, governmental employees, those who work in Indian organizations and tribal offices, and the unemployed. The participants were "powwow goers" and "nonpowwow goers," traditionalists and non-traditionalists, and the young and tribal elders.

On the Generalizability of the Results of This Study

This study seeks to establish the existence of a folk concept, "the real Indian," to describe its constituent criterion razzing, and to show its participation in interactions between Indians (who may be identified in those interactions as "real Indians," "candidate real Indians," "interactionally clumsy," "inauthentic Indians," "nouveau Indians," or "apples," etc.) and, to a lesser extent, in interactions between Indians and whites.

A reader of this study who did not fully grasp the fact that my intent is to describe a concept and its "uses" might object to the generality of my findings by complaining in the following manner: "You seem to be talking about all Indians, but your data were gathered primarily in Oklahoma, from Oklahoma-based Indians."

Let me address my hypothetical interlocutor directly: "Your remarks rather miss the point in several ways. This study is *not* concerned with a population of persons and their characteristics. It would not serve the interests of this study to construct a 'real Indianness scale,' to administer that scale to a large random sample of all possible Indians (or, alternatively, to all U.S. residents), and to assess and describe, thereby, the distribution of 'real Indians' throughout the United States. Such a procedure fundamentally misconstrues the phenomenon and would lose sight of it. The phenomenon of interest here is a pure interactional communicative phenomenon. It occurs exclusively in communicative transactions, as they occur 'in real time,' as they are anticipated, and as they are recollected, talked about, and reconstructed."

My imaginary interlocutor might reply, "How do you make valid claims about phenomena like that? How can we be assured that you have not simply reported a set of 'anecdotes' (whatever those might be) and that your phenomenon, if it does indeed exist, has more generality than the particular episodes that you did observe or that were reported to you—that is, that what you have is not simply a collection of non-generalizable, historical particulars?"

"In my defense, please remember that I have already told you that this study was an ethnography of communication, much in the same sense that Hymes (1979) proposes it. Although I am not looking at linguistic phenomena in the same way that a linguist does, my procedures and claims to validity and generality have their foundation in the same chain of reason that underlies linguistics. I observed many actual episodes of 'doing real Indianness' (think of speaking real French). I also employed informants who 'did real Indianness' in my presence and at my request (think of a linguist who gets native speakers to speak in his or her presence and at his or her request). Unlike the typical linguist, I did get my informants to reflect on and speak about 'doing Indianness.' Nevertheless, like many linguists, especially those who follow Noam Chomsky, I also used my own sensibilities as a native 'doer of being a real Indian' (think of a native speaker of French) to grasp the structure of the phenomena. I report to you the patterns that I have seen and grasped along with exemplars that support and illuminate what I am talking about. Like the linguist, I haven't given you the particulars of the whole corpus of my data. I *could* show it to you if you asked."

My interlocutor might reply, "I think I get the general picture, but you still haven't mentioned anything that assures me that you can generalize beyond that corpus of data that you collected in Oklahoma."

"In response, my primary informants and I are 'contact Indians,' and our contacts with Indians from around the United States are widespread. We meet and interact with other Indians in their 'home territories.' We find that we are accepted as real Indians by them and that we can recognize them as real Indians. We *do* 'being real Indians' together with them. Furthermore, they (Indians from other parts of the country) come to visit us here in Oklahoma and, here too, we *do* 'being real Indians' together with them. As active contact Indians, we (from Oklahoma) also meet and interact with other 'real Indians' as 'real Indians' at national meetings, religious ceremonies, and so forth, where members of all tribes are present.

"I am talking about a phenomenon that is much like competence in the linguistic and the ethnomethodological sense of that term, and my claims concerning that phenomenon are grounded in much the same way as the claims of linguists and ethnomethodologists."

ON THE PROBLEMATIC AND
CONSEQUENTIAL NATURE OF "INDIANNESS"

The question of what constitutes "Indianness" is problematic and consequential to members of the Indian community. Determining who is an Indian is problematic in that "Indianness to many scholars represent a set of tacit presuppositions that members of the Indian community adhere to, rather than something that is readily defined" (Pratt, 1985, p. 29).

Indianness can be interpreted in a variety of ways. For the non-Indian, anyone who looks like an Indian may be considered an Indian who has been socialized in a traditional lifestyle and is knowledgeable of Indian culture. Nevertheless, Indianness to Indian people is a concept that espouses the eclectic lifestyles of indigenous people that serves to unify the various tribal groups under one rubric.

Indian identity is not the same as tribal identity, which is derived from adherence to and acceptance of a unique lifestyle, although belonging to an Indian tribe is a constituent of Indianness. All tribes have different languages and customs, but under the rubric of "Indian," it is a generalization of a combination of various tribal lifeways; thus, it is this generalizability that creates Indianness.

Most reviewers, and those who conduct scholarly research concerning American Indians (or Native Americans), have questioned the generalizability of the findings of studies that identify communicative behaviors of American Indians. The generalizabilty of the behaviors identified in scientific research is exactly what constitutes Indianness. For the purpose of this study I am concerned with communicative behaviors that are enacted "Indian-ly" as opposed to "tribal-ly," that is, a set of communicative behaviors that serves as a means for intertribal and "inter-Indian" interaction, rather than intratribal.

Let us consider the role of Indianness with regard to tribalism. For example, it is possible to be an Indian and an Osage—that is, a person who has been socialized in Osage culture and is accepted as an Osage by other Osages and also maintains an identity with members of other tribes. He or she performs appropriate communicative behaviors that enable acceptance by other Indians. Moreover, one can be an Indian but not be Osage. This person has been socialized in an urban or Indian environment and is accepted by other Indians but has not been socialized into the Osage tribe and is not accepted by other Osages. Finally, it is also possible to be an Osage but not be an Indian. This individual has been socialized into the Osage culture, has limited contact with members of other tribes, and primarily views his or her world from the cultural template created by Osage lifeways.

Motivations for Identifying as an Indian

One may choose to self-identify as an Indian because one derives the essence of his or her self-concept and subsequent self-esteem from Indian and tribal culture. This person views himself or herself and others as from a cultural template created by American Indian values, beliefs, world view, patterns of thought, and so forth. Others may opt to self-identify to be certified by federal or tribal officials primarily for the economic benefits associated with tribal identification, for example, tribal scholarships, health care, and hiring preferences. Typically, this person does not derive his or her primary identity from Indian culture but in most cases identifies with European American culture.

Problematic Matters of Identifying as an Indian

There is a variety of criteria by which a person may achieve the identity of Indianness. These criteria, as will be seen, vary according to the constituency that accords an individual identity as Indian.

For example, to be "legally" considered an Indian one must belong to a federally recognized tribe according to the Bureau of Indian Affairs. If a person belongs to a tribe that is not federally recognized, then he or she is not considered to be an Indian. Thus, it is possible that an Indian, recognized as Indian by other Indians, may indeed fail to hold such an identity (legally) if not certified as an Indian. Federal or tribal certification does not establish the social identity of Indianness; rather, Indianness is a personal and instrumental identity.

Another determinant is blood quantum, which is established by each tribal group. The degree of blood that one must possess to be considered a member varies among the recognized tribal groups. Some tribes maintain that a person must possess at least one-half degree of Indian blood, whereas others may require only one fourth, one eighth, or one sixteenth, or that a person must only provide evidence of lineage.

Along with degree of Indian blood and tribal membership, physical appearances also serves as a possible criterion for identifying someone as an Indian. For many non-Indians, the question of who is an Indian is resolved by the folk definition: anyone who physically possesses the physical characteristics of an Indian is an Indian. Any attempt to use physical characteristics as the criterion of Indianness would fail to take account of the fact that there are many who are physically identifiable as Indian but who have assimilated into European American culture. They do not self-identify to others as Indians, nor do they in any way consider themselves to be Indians. Conversely, many Indians are not easily identified as Indian and may be denied an identity of Indianness by non-Indians or Indians alike, because they lack the stereotypic physical characteristics, for example, having, instead, light skin, hair, and eye color. Yet they have been socialized in a traditional Indian environment and continue to reside on a reservation or in a rural Indian community.

Moreover, this question is problematic in that being an Indian "is not something one can simply be but is something one becomes and/or is, in and as the doing of being and becoming a real Indian" (Wieder & Pratt, 1990, p. 50). Wieder and Pratt found that "doing," being, and becoming a competent member requires the participation of other culturally competent members, for a person must know not only how to "do" being and becoming a culturally competent member, but one must continue to practice what one knows—that is, comport oneself as an Indian.

Consequentiality of the Question

The question of Indianness is consequential because members of the Indian community ask this about others who present themselves as

Indians, and the answers determine admissibility to parts of the community's life and to the receipt of particular benefits offered by the community and by tribal and governmental agencies.

This is the problem that Indians face daily in intercultural, intertribal, and intratribal settings—determining the cultural identity and subsequent competency of those who present themselves as Indians. When an Indian meets another Indian the question arises about how to appropriately interact. In European American culture, categorization is often used to reduce ambiguity in initial interactions. As a result of this categorization process a person is predicted to possess specific cultural traits associated with the category. Nevertheless, among Indians, those who look like Indians are not afforded immediate competency. Rather, confirmation is held until a span of interactive testing has been initiated and passed before bestowing cultural competency.

RAZZING AND SIMILAR FORMS

Razzing has a surface similarity to "sounding" (Kochman, 1981) or "playing the dozens" (Abrahams, 1976), which are verbal dueling games of black speakers in urban ghetto areas. Razzing and sounding (a) require the interactants to be skillful in the use of humor and verbal sparring, (b) are dependent on audience, (c) are contextual, and (d) require an awareness of the rules involved. Although both of these culturally based forms are types of ritualized insults, razzing differs significantly from sounding or playing the dozens in the sense that playing the dozens often requires the participants to direct insults, generally of a sexual nature, toward a specific family member, for example, someone's mother (Garner, 1983; Labov, 1972). Moreover, sounding and playing the dozens often occur in the form of standardized rhymed couplets, as opposed to razzing, which is not standardized and seldom occurs in rhymed couplets.

Basso (1979) observed a similar form of ritualized humor among the Western Apache. In his study, Basso identified the intratribal behavior of ridiculing the behaviors and attitudes of the "Whiteman." He found that, "By making of the 'Whiteman' an improbable buffoon, Apache jokers isolate and accentuate significant contrasts between their own cultural practices and those of Anglo-Americans" (p. 64).

The butt of the joking ritual is the Whiteman, who is portrayed "as a loud-talking, overbearing, self-righteous, unswervingly presumptuous bumbler" (p. 60).

Although there are similarities between this form of ritual humor and razzing, I describe a ritualized pattern that is conducted inter- and intratribally that is used as a mode of cultural acceptance, rather than as a vehicle that provides "substance to Apache conceptions of Anglo-Americans and the problems they face when they engage Anglo-Americans in social interaction" (p. 64).

Vine Deloria (1988), in his chapter on the "Indian Manifesto" also discussed the prevalence of humor among Indian people and described the functions that humor serves for the maintenance of Indian culture. In his chapter, he discussed how teasing is used as a method of controlling social situations, teaching, and how Indian people simply enjoy relating humorous episodes to each other. He further notes how humor is used in creating unity and as a method of increasing social and political awareness such that "Humor has come to occupy such a prominent place in national Indian affairs that any kind of movement is impossible without it" (p. 146). It should be noted that, in his discussion of humor, he speaks of this behavior as it is enacted by Indian people in inter-Indian settings and does not treat this behavior as being reflective of only one tribe.

Shutiva (1994), in a chapter exploring Indian humor, discussed its usefulness in interpersonal communication and noted that "contrary to popular belief, Native Americans are not a stoic, quiet people. . . . They are generally a joyful people . . . who appreciate and dote upon humor" (p. 117).

Razzing as a Ritual

As mentioned above, the approach used to conceptualize and analyze razzing is based on the ethnography of speaking, as articulated by Hymes (1972). The categories of (a) topic, (b) purpose, (c) act sequence, (d) setting, and (e) participants, as discussed by Hymes, are particularly useful for describing the organization of the razzing ritual.

Topics in Razzing Rituals

Within the Indian community, razzing is performed inter- and intratribally and is directed toward the divergent behavior of an individual, group, or tribe. Unlike sounding and playing the dozens, razzing does not include such topical areas as family members, physical disabilities, or socioeconomic status. In fact, one informant with whom I had been discussing Indian humor and the appropriate patterns associated with razzing stated,

> You can usually razz another Indian about anything they've done, or said, or even make up something to razz them about. But if you razz somebody about

their family, then you better be ready to go to blows. If you want to get somebody to fight, then just say something about their family.

Although Indians avoid razzing someone about their family, they often razz each other about their tribal membership. For example, a common razz among interactants of different tribal groups is to accuse each other of favoring a specific canine delicacy, for example, roast dog or puppy and dumplings. That Indians enjoy razzing members of differing tribes with regard to the consumption of these delicacies is exemplified by a discussion I had with a woman from northeast Oklahoma who informed me that her home community had recently hired a new animal control officer, who happened to be a member of a southwestern Oklahoma tribe. The woman explained that the "dogcatcher," who was about her age, was often razzed about the duties associated with his position. She further related that whenever she would encounter the dogcatcher she would tell him, "Hey . . . quit picking up our dogs. I know you're taking them down south to use for your feasts. We don't have any watchdogs left. We're unprotected." In response to the razz, the woman informed me that the "dogcatcher" would reply, "It's not me. It's those Kiowas who are coming up here and taking your dogs. Besides, I heard that they were going to put on a big feast for you people and feed you your favorite meal."

Purpose in Razzing Rituals

Although razzing is enjoyed as humor, the communicative behavior also serves as a method to (a) determine cultural competency, (b) identify in-group and out-group members, and (c) as a form of instruction.

Determining Cultural Competency. If the interactants are unsure about the Indianness of each other, one or both of the participants tacitly engage the other in a razz to elicit the appropriate methods that a culturally competent Indian would enact in response to the razz. The use of humor, or "razzing" behavior, as a criterion of Indianness, is not displayed haphazardly but follows normative patterns with specific behaviors and strategies that must be followed. If one of the participants does not employ the appropriate methods, then that person's identity as an Indian will be suspect. Furthermore, if someone attempts to razz another and is not perceived to be an Indian, or if that individual does not use the appropriate methods, the other participant(s) will refrain from engaging that person in the razzing behavior and will be reluctant to engage that person in any future interactions. Moreover, that person's razz will be met with silence, which, in this context, an Indian would interpret as an indication of nonacceptance.

Identifying In-Group and Out-Group Members. Razzing, as an in-group process, is used to identify in-group members and as a device to exclude out-group members or those persons who self-identify as an Indian but who do not comport themselves in the appropriate manner. Because of the matters involved in knowing the appropriate behaviors, if a non-Indian or candidate Indian were to razz in an inappropriate manner, that person would be regarded as exhibiting offensive or rude behavior. For example, many non-Indians generally refer to an Indian male as "chief." Although the word *chief* may not be used in a derogatory manner, it is interpreted by most Indians as a racial slur. Nevertheless, it is not unusual for an Indian to razz another by referring to him as chief, nor would an Indian be offended by the sobriquet from another Indian. Many of the circumstances in which this razzing behavior is performed must be exhibited according to the culturally appropriate methods, otherwise misinterpretation could result in offense, hostility, verbally aggressive acts, and so forth.

That razzing is used as a method to determine the Indianness of another is illustrated by one informant, with whom I had been discussing the methods involved. The informant, in discussing the inappropriate razzing behavior of a candidate Indian, said,

> Most people don't accept . . . as an Indian. Whenever you talk to him he starts telling you about your tribe as if you don't know anything. He tries to razz everybody, but he usually winds up offending everyone he talks to. I don't think he means to offend anyone, but it's because he doesn't know how to razz. He thinks he's being funny but he usually winds up making everybody mad. That's one of the reasons everyone think he's just a white man. He doesn't have an Indian sense of humor.

Those, then, who do not employ the appropriate methods in razzing often offend those whom they are attempting to razz and are not perceived as socially competent Indians, for example, "he's just a white man."

Socialization. Finally, razzing is used as a method of socialization. Indian cultures are oral cultures and, as such, learning how to behave in an appropriate Indian manner is accomplished largely through observation and social interaction. By razzing an individual when he or she has been judged to deviate from accepted and expected social propriety, the individual is made aware of his or her social impropriety and also, through razzing, given instruction about what is expected of a socially competent member.

The Contextual and Reflexive Nature of Razzing Rituals

Razzing is contextual in the sense that the instance in which the razzing behavior is exhibited are dependent on the events that occur as the members begin to interact. The basis for razzing evolves from the situation itself, for example, if one participant were to commit a verbal error or exhibit a behavior that was in violation of some not-so-important social norm. Another example would be if one were called on to speak for another in a public setting and the speaker mispronounced a name or forgot the message he was to deliver. Or, if a person were to be "painted up" (a common practice among younger Indians in which one Indian falls asleep in the presence of others and his or her face is painted in a bizarre fashion by the others present), this would be grounds for what Indians call a "shame story" and would be recounted to others at a later date.

To say that razzing is reflexive points to the fact that the recounting of some out-of-the-ordinary or prior "deviant" behavior can be repeated in future encounters, with alterations and abbreviations, when something in that future situation elicits it.

Act Sequence in Razzing Rituals

Whenever Indians interact, razzing and shame stories are frequently topics of conversation. Whoever is present can engage the other participants in razzing, become the object of a razz, or expect to have a shame story about their past actions recounted to the others present. In addition, when real Indians recount a shame story, the original story is elaborated and embellished each time it is retold, with the final version faintly resembling the original occurrence.

The razzing ritual is usually initiated by a particular participant who recounts a supposedly true past occurrence and then proceeds to embellish the original story. The act-sequence structure of razzing bears resemblance to the model of "griping" in Israeli discourse, as described by Katriel (1990). In terms of Katriel's model, the initial interactional offering by one of the participants may be viewed as the "initiation phase" of a razzing ritual. Next the addressee(s) will elaborate on the initiator's statement, in an attempt to be more creative or to make the original story sound better. These elaborations function "as an acknowledgment phase, indicating the participants' willingness to enact the ritual (or else the attempt to enact it would be aborted)" (Katriel, 1990, p. 110). During this acknowledgment phase, other participants will elaborate on the statement of the initiator and the preceding addressor that creates a "chain-effect of individual contributions which are, by and large, 'more of the same' " (p. 110).

Generally the ritual will continue until it is terminated by switching to a different topic or until the participants run out of elaborations. That a shame story, with continued recounting, can lose its original context is exemplified by an incident that occurred while I was having dinner with several friends. One member of the dinner party, who apparently had had a tiring day at the office, yawned and uttered, "It's been a long day." Another member of the dinner party immediately quipped, "I-long-gay? What is that? A new Indian word? What does it mean? You're too full to eat anymore?" The other participants joined in and began razzing the person who uttered the phrase about the meaning of the "word" and what tribal language it reflected. On several later occasions, with the originator of the new "word" present, the story was recounted in several different versions, none of which resembled the original occurrence. The original incident finally deteriorated into a simple admonishment not to eat excessively or they would become "I-long-gay," with no further explanation offered.

The Setting of Razzing Rituals

Many situations and incidents provide grounds in which Indians razz each other, or engage in "humorous story telling" about the past actions of someone. The subject(s) of the "stories" may be present or absent and either known or not known to the participants.

During initial interaction, Indians who do not know each other often enter into this form of verbal sparring. The following dialogue, which occurred in the Native American Studies office at a midwestern university when two Indians were asked if they knew each other, serves to illustrate this point:

R: I don't think we've met before, but I heard your name mentioned a lot. I guess you owe a lot of people money.

B: No, it's probably because of my generosity and caring ways.

Although neither participant knew the other, both proceeded to engage in razzing to establish the Indianness of the other party. Nevertheless, if either of the parties would have become offended during this exchange in initial interaction, the episode would have ended immediately. That any occasion provides grounds for razzing is evidenced by a formal tribal dinner I had attended, in which the spokesman's remarks concerning the purpose of the dinner and subsequent prayer had exceeded the half-hour mark. The person sitting next to me leaned over and jokingly whispered,

> Boy, Uncle . . . sure is wound up. The grease on top of the chicken and dumplings is beginning to harden. When he gets through we might have to grab a ladle to break through that layer of grease so we can eat.

Although it would have been inappropriate for either of the participants to tease the spokesman about the length of his speech and prayer, humorous comments are often made to one another.

Razzing in the Form of Songs

Not only does razzing take place in face-to-face interactions, it also occurs in the form of songs that are directed toward other individuals or events. Razzing in the form of singing is best exemplified by "forty-nines." Traditionally, forty-nine singing was originated by the Kiowa tribe of Oklahoma, and as Kennan and Hill (1978) noted in a study of Kiowa forty-nine singing from a communication perspective, "Its function, in the days before tribal confinement to the Anadarko, Oklahoma, area, was a prelude, postscript, or celebration of past raiding parties" (p. 1). Although Indians no longer conduct "raiding parties" against other tribes or non-Indians, forty-nine singing still occurs but as a means of inter- and intratribal socializing. Forty-nines are generally held after a powwow (intertribal social event), are conducted out-of-doors, and are held not only in Oklahoma but in any state in which Indians may gather for powwows, conventions, and so forth. That forty-nine singing is used in razzing was further elaborated by Kennan and Hill (1978), who found that

> The event offers a kind of forum whereby individuals engage in a kind of friendly verbal dueling. Very often participants are well acquainted with each other and frequently singers direct barbs in the form of songs at one another. There is no real intent to seriously insult the object of such a song, rather the songs take the form of and are accepted as friendly, personal jokes. (p. 12)

That forty-nine singing can be directed as a razz toward a specific event is illustrated by a particular song that was adapted from an older song to razz an annual weeklong event—the American Indian Exposition or "Indian Fair"—held in Anadarko, Oklahoma. Indian fair goers are always cautioned against drinking the city's water, as it has been known to induce weeklong cases of diarrhea; therefore, the razz against the Indian Fair asserts, "I will see you next summer time, American Indian Exposition. Hope you don't get the diarrhea all week long."

Participants in Razzing Ritual

Age Status

Razzing is appropriately restricted to interactants of equal status, with status primarily referring to age groups. It is inappropriate to relate stories about others out of your status level. That is, younger individuals are required to exhibit respect for older individuals and are not able to razz those who are older.

That younger individuals are sanctioned for attempting to razz, or make light of the actions of someone who is older, was evidenced during an interaction I had observed in which one Indian male was recounting to another Indian male a not-so-pleasant event that the former had experienced. During the conversation, the son of one of the interactants began to razz the older individual concerning his not-so-pleasant experience and was immediately sanctioned by his father, who stated, "Be quiet. You're not supposed to talk to older people like that. You're supposed to be respectful to those who are older than you are." Although it would have been acceptable for the Indian males to razz each other over the unpleasant experience, it was unacceptable for the younger Indian to attempt to enter into the razzing behavior with those who are older.

Candidate Indians

It is also unacceptable for "candidate Indians," or those who are attempting to develop and maintain an Indian identity, to engage in the razzing ritual because they have not been afforded the status necessary to razz others. Candidate Indians are individuals who can provide proof of tribal lineage but have not been socialized in an Indian environment and are seeking an Indian and tribal identity. This person will seek out other Indians in an attempt to engage in frequent interaction. Although the candidate Indian may present himself or herself as a "competent member," his or her identity is not readily taken for granted, nor is competency immediately conferred.

I had been discussing this notion of candidate Indians with several informants and had asked about the identity of a person with whom I was not familiar. One informant explained,

You know, . . . wasn't raised around Indians, but he's been coming around and has been trying to learn Indian ways. He's trying to learn too fast and act like he's one of us. I told him it takes time. It's best just to be quiet and watch. You're not one of us yet, so kind of hold back until you learn how.

Gender

Even though razzing is generally restricted to participants of the same status and age group, razzing is not subject to any obvious gender restriction. Indeed, males and females can and do engage each other in this form of verbal sparring, with either serving as the initiator or the recipient of the razz.

Razzing: Distinctively Indian Humor

A final constituent of the use of Indian humor is its "closed-groupness." Understandable and amusing especially to Indians, most non-Indians would be unable to appreciate the humor. Indian humor, as are other forms of humor, is based on stereotypes that only members of the community are privy to. It is assumed that if you are truly one of us, then you can understand and will not have to ask what the meaning was, or what was humorous about a story or joke. For example, a common joke among Indians is, "Peter MacDonald was in the kitchen eating his breakfast and his wife hollered 'Peter what are you eating?' and Peter hollered back, 'Mutton, Honey.' " This joke assumes (a) that hearers know that Peter MacDonald was the infamous chairman of the Navajo Nation, (b) that Navajo people enjoy mutton as one of their staples, and (c) that hearers are knowledgeable of the Navajo stereotypes. Too, it is assumed that you have seen the commercial for Nut-N-Honey breakfast cereal.

That razzing has humorous appeal only to members of the Indian community was evidenced by one member, who was telling me of his experiences at a club that featured stand-up comedians, in which he stated,

They have amateur night over at this comedy club in Tulsa. We ought to put a table on the stage and let three Indian guys razz each other. They'd probably run all the white people out, because they wouldn't be able to understand what they were saying.

I had asked several Indian informants if they felt that only Indians could understand the humor used by Indians. All of the informants agreed that non-Indians seldom appreciate a humorous story and one informant in particular stated,

A lot of times I'll tell my white friends something has happened that I think is really funny or I'll tell them about a razz on someone else. After I get through telling them the story they'll just sit there like they're still waiting for the punch line. They really don't understand our humor. Also, if I try to razz them like I razz my Indian friends, they get upset and say that I tease too hard.

Although Indians take delight in razzing and relating shame stories about themselves and others, and find it witty, they regard it as distinctively Indian humor.

An Exemplar of Razzing

Let us take a closer look at the communicative behavior of humorous storytelling or razzing. This particular incident occurred at the culmination of a Native American Church (NAC) meeting (religious service) I had attended in north central Oklahoma. The razz centered around a meeting that was held on the Osage Indian reservation in northeast Oklahoma.

Native American Church meetings are most often conducted in tepees, are intertribal, and begin around sunset and continue until a few hours after sunrise. Following the completion of the church service a noon meal is served for all of the participants. During the time before the meal begins, the church members usually sit in the tepee, relax, share experiences, and, on almost all occasions when I have been present, relate humorous incidents that have occurred in previous meetings.

The conductor (minister) of this particular service related an experience that had occurred in which one of the members present had been requested to "fan a person off" (bless them with an eagle feather), which occurs when a person enters an Osage church house or tepee, a practice that other tribes do not engage in. The minister began this story by stating to no one in particular, "Did you all hear about that time when . . . was at that meeting over in Osage country and he tried to fan a dog off?" One church member stated, "We heard about that. What really happened?" At this point the "offending" person interrupted and stated,

Well, if you're going to tell the story I might as well tell it right. I was over there at Aunt . . . for their fall meeting and during the night a heavy rain storm hit and two of her dogs came inside of the tepee trying to find a dry place. The fireman ran the dogs out and . . . had the staff and he started shooing them with it. Later on one of the dogs came back and sat down just inside of the tepee door and acted like he was invited to this meeting. . . . was sitting on the crossroads and turned around and told me to fan that dog off. Well, I didn't know what to do because you know we never do that over here, but these Osages are different and maybe they do things like that over there. . . . said, "hurry up and fan that dog off." I thought, well my folks always told me that when I go around other tribes be respectful of their ways and maybe they do that over here so I guess I better fan that dog off, because I sure don't want to offend anyone. So I got into my feather box and got out this little feather and started smoothing it out and I started to get up and go over there and fan that dog off. Well, about that time Uncle . . . said kind of meanlike, "what are you trying to do," and I said I was going to fan that dog off. Well, he told me to sit down because we don't do anything like that over here. Everybody kind of laughed and looked at me like I was an idiot and I got real shamed out and wanted to say . . . told me to do it but I kept my mouth shut, but I told that guy he shouldn't be telling me to do stuff like that.

Following the completion of his story, the other participants began adding to the story. One participant stated,

Yeah I was there at that meeting and it was pretty shameful when . . . tried to fan that dog off. But you know when he went to fan that dog off, that dog put his paws up in the air as if he was ready to be blessed.

Another participant said, "I was at that meeting and I saw . . . try to do that. I thought that dog was going to take the staff and put a gourd in his paw and start singing church songs." One of the church members who had been to an Osage meeting stated, "You know those Osages sure do like to fan everybody off. I bet they would fan a dog off if one came in. But I sure wouldn't have tried to do that." Another jokingly commented to the narrator of the story, "You should have went ahead and fanned that dog off. I bet he was one of your relatives. They said you belong to the dog clan." Finally, one participant who was Osage explained,

We might fan each other off over there quite a bit, but at least we use good feathers. That was the stinkiest, most pitiful little feather I have ever seen. I don't believe we would use that on a dog. And you know, . . . sure likes to use that little feather. He's always trying to take it out of his feather box and use it.

At this point the others began to question him more specifically about the incident and eventually the event terminated. The topic then shifted to an account of another meeting.

The preceding episode demonstrates that it is presumed that those in attendance possess the necessary background knowledge to understand the story and to "fill in the gaps." The circumstances that are essential in understanding the story are not elaborated. It is taken for granted, by attendance at such an event, that participants are knowledgeable about how to appropriately engage and make sense out of what is going on. For example, no one explained that Osages "fan a person off" (bless them with an eagle feather) when they enter the church house or tepee, a practice that other tribes do not follow. Furthermore, animals are not allowed in the meeting and obviously would not be fanned off.

It is also assumed that the listeners know that the "fireman" is the person who builds the fire and tends it throughout the night and regulates when, and who, may enter or leave. Furthermore, the participants assume that the listeners know that the man who "sits on the crossroads" (a type of deacon) functions in an advisory capacity and if he told someone to do something it would be performed without question. Finally, on the basis of a person's attendance it is assumed that he or she is knowledgeable about the ritualistic procedures performed in the various Native American Church meetings.

By making light of the situation, the recipient of the razz was viewed as enacting the appropriate behavior. For those who engage in this ritual, a central rule of razzing is "one who razzes another must also expect to be the recipient of razzing." This rule is further exemplified by an exchange that I had witnessed between two Indians who were razzing each other. One of the participants became offended by a razzing remark and was quickly admonished by the other participant who stated, "If you can dish it out, you've got to be able to take it." The practice of relating such a story in a specific context is such that the "account-ability" (in the sense meant by Garfinkel, 1967) or competence of all who are involved in its telling is taken for granted. As Garfinkel puts it, "the practices are done by parties to those settings whose skill with, knowledge of, and entitlement to the detailed work of that accomplishment-whose-competence they obstinately depend on, recognize, use and take for granted" (p. 1). If someone were to have asked for further elaboration, then their cultural identity, competence, or both would have been suspect.

It is further understood among the participants who may legitimately initiate a razz and who may participate in its elaboration. The initiator must be one who is culturally acceptable—that is, viewed by the others as a competent member. If a person has been afforded marginal competence then it would be inappropriate for him or her to initiate such a story. Neither would it be acceptable for him or her to razz the subject of the story. Moreover, knowing that all settings provide an arena in which someone may razz another, the competent member realizes that the setting was not an acceptable place to play a practical joke. Finally, it is assumed that one who is afforded marginal acceptance understands it is best to refrain from interacting.

CONCLUDING REMARKS

It has been the purpose of this chapter to examine and explicate a particular speech event, razzing, which serves to communicate a type of cultural identity for the American Indian. For the "real" Indian, Indianness is not a material "thing" that can be documented, possessed, and displayed. Rather, it is achieved by comporting oneself in culturally appropriate manners. In this case, it is knowing how to appropriately engage others in episodes of humorous storytelling or razzing. The culturally competent member knows when and where it is acceptable to engage others in razzing, what is an appropriate topic, who may properly be razzed, and how to react when he or she is the focus of the razz.

Indianness, to the "real" Indian, is not something that one can simply be but is something one becomes, is, or both, which requires the participation of other culturally competent members. He or she knows that "the doing" of being and becoming an Indian is not a static affair and that his or her position as an Indian is not something that is ultimately achieved. That is, he or she knows that in the course of managing everyday affairs, an Indian must comport himself or herself in a manner that is consistent with the expectations of other Indians.

NOTES

1. Although it is considered "politically correct" to use the label *Native American,* I prefer the term *American Indian.* The term Native American is a label that is generally used, and ascribed to, by many researchers when referring to Indian people—"dominant groups can exercise power in naming others . . . it is often difficult for the less powerful groups to control their own labels" (Martin, 1997, p. 6)—and in many situations if an Indian fails to use this term in conducting research or in referring to his or her culture he or she will find himself or herself corrected for not using this term. On many occasions at SCA, ICA, and so forth, I find I am corrected by my colleagues for not using the appropriate term. Furthermore, in the course of my research, the term *Indian* is the label that is almost always used by tribal elders and the indigenous people that I observed, interacted with, interviewed, or both, and not Native American.

2. One anonymous reviewer of this chapter questioned my use of the term *Indian culture* stating that "there obviously are hundreds of Indian cultures, 'Indian community' when there obviously are numerous Indian communities." What I have tried to explain is that there are "obviously hundreds of Indian tribes and numerous tribal communities" each of which is distinguished by its own elements of language, rituals, and so forth.

Indian culture, on the other hand, is a cultural system that is eclectic, formed by many groups who have a shared history, a common heritage, a geographical proximity, racial characteristics, and ethnicity (Collier, 1997, pp. 37-38). Therefore, the phenomenon I describe is not specifically reflective of any one of the "hundreds of tribal cultures," but a behavior that functions as a form of interactive behavior for Indian culture, a culture made up of group members who have created a perceived commonality and a "community of thought and action based on what people say and do and think and feel as a result of their common history and origins" (Collier, 1997, p. 38).

REFERENCES

Abrahams, R. (1976). *Talking black.* Rowley, MA: Newbury House.

Basso, K. (1979). *Portraits of "the Whiteman": Linguistic play and cultural symbols among the Western Apache.* Cambridge, MA: Cambridge University Press.

Bogden, R., & Taylor, S. (1975). *Introduction to qualitative research methods: A phenomenological approach to the social sciences.* New York: John Wiley.

Collier, M. (1997). Cultural identity and intercultural communication. In L. Samovar & R. Porter (Eds.), *Intercultural communication: A reader* (pp. 36-43). Belmont, CA: Wadsworth.

Deloria, V. (1988). *Custer died for your sins.* Norman: University of Oklahoma Press.

Garfinkel, H. (1967). *Studies in ethnomethodology.* Englewood Cliffs, NJ: Prentice Hall.

Garner, T. (1983). Playing the dozens: Folklore as strategies for living. *Quarterly Journal of Speech, 69* (1), 47-57.

Giago, T., Jr. (1990). My laughter. *Native Peoples: The Arts and Lifeways, 3* (3), 52-56.

Hecht, M., Collier, M., & Thomas, M. (1988). *African American communication.* Newbury Park, CA: Sage.

Hill, W. W. (1943). Navajo humor: Methods for identifying the gifted and talented American Indian student. *Journal for the Education of the Gifted, 11D* (3), 53-63.

Hymes, D. (1972). Models of the interaction of language and social life. In J. Gumperz & D. Hymes (Eds.), *Directions in sociolinguistics: The ethnography of speaking.* New York: Holt, Rinehart & Winston.

Katriel, T. (1990). "Griping" as a verbal ritual in some Israeli discourse. In D. Carbaugh (Ed.), *Cultural communication and intercultural contact* (pp. 99-113). Hillsdale, NJ: Lawrence Erlbaum.

Kennan, W., & Hill, L. (1978). *Kiowa forty-nine singing: A communication perspective.* Paper presented at the Speech Communication Association Summer Conference on Intercultural Communication, Tampa, FL.

Kochman, T. (1981). *Black and white styles in conflict.* Chicago: University of Chicago Press.

Labov, W. (1972). Rules for ritual insults. In D. Sudnow (Ed.), *Studies in social interaction* (pp. 120-169). New York: Free Press.

Martin, J. (1997). Understanding whiteness in the United States. In L. Samovar & R. Porter (Eds.), *Intercultural communication: A reader* (pp. 54-62). Belmont, CA: Wadsworth.

McCall, G., & Simmons, J. (Eds.). (1969). *Issues in participant observation.* Reading, MA: Addison-Wesley.

Miller, F. C. (1967). Humor in a Chippewa tribal council. *Ethnology, 6* (3) 263-271.

Opler, M. E. (1938). Humor and wisdom of some American Inidan tribes. *New Mexico Anthropologists, 3,* 3-10.

Pratt, S. (1985). *Being an Indian among Indians.* Unpublished doctoral dissertation, University of Oklahoma, Norman.

Shutiva, C. (1994). Native American culture and communication through humor. In A. González, M. Houston, & V. Chen (Eds.), *Our voices: Essays in culture, ethnicity and communication* (pp. 117-121). Los Angeles: Roxbury.

Wieder, D. L., & Pratt, S. (1990). On being a recognizable Indian among Indians. In D. Carbaugh (Ed.), *Cultural communication and intercultural contact* (pp. 45-64). Hillsdale, NJ: Lawrence Erlbaum.

5

The Cultural Deprivation of an Oklahoma Cherokee Family

LYNDA DIXON SHAVER • *Bowling Green State University*

This chapter discusses the cultural deprivation of an Oklahoma Cherokee family. Their experiences are those of many native people who are forced to live in a different culture and who must learn to survive in two cultures. Using perspectival rhetorical analysis, I analyze the family's story as contextualized in the history of Oklahoma Indians to discuss the family's loss of Indianness and the family members' efforts to return to their Cherokee traditions in current times. The primary dilemma or site of conflict that emerges is the Euro-American sociocultural demand for family members to assimilate as revealed by their internal and external verbal and nonverbal communication. Loss of Indian land, loss of language, restrictions on association with other Cherokees, bias and prejudice against Indians, and sociocultural pressures to not be Indian are revealed by the analysis as the changes in communication that led to the family's assimilation, the loss of their Indianness. Nevertheless, the analysis also reveals that in the 1980s, the family had begun to reconstitute itself as an Oklahoma Cherokee family as it sought to regain its lost culture.

This chapter will tell the story of one Oklahoma Cherokee family's cultural deprivation and their attempts to regain that culture. Analysis of the family's story and parallel analysis of the history of Oklahoma Indians show that the family members' internal and external verbal and nonverbal communication was changed by the following: loss of their land, discontinued use of their language, restricted association with other Cherokees, bias and prejudice sanctioned by Euro-American government officials, and other sociocultural pressures.

The stories of the various indigenous people, in what is now the United States of America, are as different as are the cultures of hundreds of separate Indian nations. Many American Indians[1] today live more as Euro-Americans[2] than as Indians. This Oklahoma Cherokee family's

---

AUTHOR'S NOTE: An early version of this chapter was presented as part of a panel at the Speech Communication Association Conference, in Miami, Florida, November 1993. The author wishes to thank Dolores Tanno and two anonymous reviewers for their insightful and helpful suggestions for this study.

story, when told as part of the story of Oklahoma Indians, provides insight for intercultural communication researchers and others into the loss of culture for many Indian families from many nations.

The family's *Indianness,* a term from Pratt (1985), is a social construction through communication. Their Indianness was lost when family members were forced to communicate as Euro-Americans and compelled to conform to mainstream ways-of-doing. The family was deprived of its Cherokee ways.

THEORETICAL FOUNDATIONS AND METHODOLOGY

Using Edward Hall's position on the oneness of communication and culture, this study focuses on the communication of the Cherokee family and its ways and is informed by analysis of Oklahoma Indian history. The culture of a family is made evident by its communication—language and behaviors.

For this study, Bochner's (1982) definition of *assimilation* is used: a process that occurs when people adopt, by choice or because they have no choice, the customs, beliefs, folkways, and lifestyles of a more dominant culture. As assimilation of the Cherokee family into the Euro-American mainstream culture occurs, the phenomenon can be identified through analysis of the family history.

To understand the current dilemma of Oklahoma Cherokees who have been deprived of their culture, one must understand that, unlike immigrants or sojourners (Szalay & Inn, 1988), the experience of the Indians has been involuntary displacement by intruders. Folb's (1997) insightful discussion of subcultures who are "nondominant" (p. 141) in a nation of privileged Euro-Americans is useful because it reinforces that Indians have been forced to assimilate by their lack "of access to power and high status" (p. 141) and inability to influence the "dominate culture's social, political, legal, economic, and/or religious structures and institutions" (p. 141). The historical events and the communication of the family members in this study reveal their assimilation as they are forbidden to access social resources that are available to the dominant cultural group.

This study is premised on theoretical assumptions from rhetoric (Billig, 1987; Billig et al., 1988; Burke, 1969a, 1969b, 1970, 1979, 1985; Cherwitz & Hikins, 1986) and semiotics (Eco, 1990) that communication, broadly defined as verbal and nonverbal, occurs through interaction, consciously and unconsciously (Burke, 1966; Potter & Wetherell, 1987). Others in the field of communication have called for rhetorical analyses of intercultural communication (McKerrow, 1996; Monfils, 1980). People's discourse, or their language culture (L. Shaver, 1993; P. Shaver, 1991), can be accessed through their words, architecture, surroundings, colors, topics selected, movements, social groups, and homes, revealing the perspectives of the interactants.

This theory is informed by Billig (1987) and Billig et al. (1988) who have illustrated that human thought and social discourse are made up of oppositions—dilemmas—that are explicit and implicit. The dilemmatic insight provided by Billig (1987) and Billig et al. (1988) recognizes that the language culture of individuals is organized by positive and negative attributes. By using Burke's (1969b) theory that oppositional discourse structures the perceptions of participants by composing master contesting and combative agons, Billig's (1987) and Billig's et al. (1988) discussion of dilemmas, and the term *sites of conflict* (P. Shaver, 1991; P. Shaver & L. Shaver, 1992a), this study accesses the semiotic coherence (Eco, 1990) of the language culture of the family. This dilemmatic method facilitates the study because it allows the emergence of the sites of conflict from the ethnographic data.

Perspectival rhetorical analysis (P. Shaver, 1991) has been used in other studies to access human texts by examination of the language culture in several settings (e.g., construction companies; health delivery organizations; elementary, secondary, and higher education; state and federal government bureaucracies; etc., L. Shaver, 1993; L. Shaver & P. Shaver, 1995; P. Shaver, 1991; P. Shaver & L. Shaver, 1992a, 1992b, 1992c). In these studies, access to human texts was provided by analysis of rhetorically motivated perspectives of societal groups or organizations and their members and of the organizations' patients, clients, or customers. The rhetorical perspective of a person, a group, an organization, or in this case, an Oklahoma Cherokee family, is revealed by analysis of its communication and history. Perspectival rhetorical analysis allows the sites of conflict to emerge, thereby providing insight into the cultural world of the other.

In this study, the data are the family history and the Oklahoma Indian history. By its nature, ethnographic research provides the kind of holistic data necessary for revealing internal relationships that "[actualize] certain possible connections" (Eco, 1990, p. 148), allowing for acceptable interpretations by permitting the analysis of the text (i.e., the "speech" of the organization) as a whole, thereby controlling the "otherwise uncontrollable drift of the reader" (Eco, 1990, p. 149). Close analysis of the family's stories, movements, decisions, and ways of doing, combined with description and examination of parallel historical events, reveals the sites of conflict for this Cherokee family that led to its loss of culture.

HISTORY OF INDIANS IN OKLAHOMA

To understand contemporary Indians in Oklahoma, one must understand the past. The loss of land and language, restrictions on their gatherings, bias and prejudice, and sociocultural pressures were developmental, segmented, and generational. To see from the Oklahoma Cherokee perspective, one must know that no native people are indigenous to what is now Oklahoma.

In the 1800s, almost three centuries after the first recorded white contact in 1541 by the Coronado expedition, the land mass now know as Oklahoma was divided into two parts; the eastern portion was called Indian Territory and the western portion was called Oklahoma Territory. Chief Allen Wright's name for the state is from the Choctaw language: *okla* and *homa,* which means "home of the Red People" (Strickland, 1980, p. 6). Cohen (1942) notes that separate treaties, legislation, and federal policy created the two halves. The western half—Oklahoma Territory—became a nonreservation holding area for rebellious nomadic hunting tribes. A reduced Indian Territory, in what is now known as eastern Oklahoma, became one of the bargaining chips in the early 19th century as the woodland, agricultural tribes, known as the Five Civilized Tribes (i.e., Cherokee, Chickasaw, Seminole, Creek, and Choctaw), were forced out of their homes and off of their lands in the Southeast United States and moved to Indian Territory. The appellation—Five Civilized Tribes—given by the whites was in contrast to the name—Wild Tribes—given to the plains Indians who had been marched into western Oklahoma from the West (Bolt, 1990; Filler & Guttman, 1962; Wright, 1951/1986). Our discussion will be on Indian Territory, the eastern portion of Oklahoma.

During the early to middle parts of the 19th century, eastern Indians were ordered by the federal government to leave native grounds, previous federal holding centers, and prisons and were forced to go to Indian Territory. The few provisions that were made for the Indian death marches were tragically inadequate. Men, women, and children died of pestilence, starvation, and exposure during these forced marches, including more than 4,000 on the Trail of Tears[3] when the Cherokees were moved in 1838 (Bolt, 1990; Filler & Guttmann, 1962; Wright, 1951/ 1986).

After suffering the loss of native lands and familiar environments, these tribes suffered by the enforced proximity of incompatible tribes forced to live together after the death marches. Furthermore, treaty promises were broken by the opening of lands to more white settlers, including the famous or infamous Oklahoma Land Run of 1889 (Strickland, 1980; Washburn, 1971; Woodward, 1961; Wright, 1951/1986). The relationship of Indians to their lost lands and specifically, to their new lands are key elements for understanding Oklahoma Indians.

The Land and the Indian

To deprive Indians of their culture, developers of the federal plan for cultural genocide knew that they must be separated from their land. The greed of Euro-American neighbors and new waves of immigrants contributed to the success of stealing Indian land. Strickland (1980) writes that, after the loss of their lands, Oklahoma Indians had more contact with Euro-Americans and experienced "tribal disorganization" (p. 5), depression, and demoralization. They faced a choice between the white culture and their tribal culture.

Individual ownership of the land was not practiced by the tribes. The land nurtured all who lived on it. The relationship of the land to cultural and religious beliefs was vital to the Indian. The displacement of the Indian from native lands, the death marches to new lands, and the loss of contiguous tribal lands in Oklahoma, by the General Allotment Act (1887) and other federal policies, contributed to the cultural deprivation of the various tribes (Deloria, 1974/1985; Lujan & Glenn, 1989; McNickle, 1973). This cultural deprivation of the tribal units through the loss of the land was replicated in individual families.

Indians were given an allotment of land, according to each tribe (Cherokees received 110 acres and a 40-acre homestead; Bolt, 1990; General Allotment Act, 1887). Through legal and illegal means, most of the allotments eventually found their way into the hands of white settlers. The federal decision to use allotments had several purposes, listed as follows: (a) The Indians were alienated from their culture and religion; (b) they became powerless as a nondominant subculture; and (c) having no central land base, the tribes began to disintegrate (Bolt, 1990; Deloria, 1974/1985; Folb, 1988).

Wahrhaftig and Thomas (1970) note that in Oklahoma during the 1960s the "pervasive social fiction" included the following: (a) that Cherokees were a "vanishing breed," (b) "that real Cherokees [were] about 'bred out,'" and (c) that "in twenty years, according to white myth, the Cherokee language and with it the separate and distinctive community that speaks it will fade into memory" (p. 43). Berkhofer (1978) notes that the word *civilization* was a code word for cultural genocide. *Assimilation,* a word acceptable to most mainstream members of society, was also used as a euphemism for cultural genocide.

According to Berkhofer (1978), Bolt (1990), and Strickland (1980), several methods were used to accomplish the goals of cultural genocide, in addition to the loss of tribal contiguous land masses. Indian children were taken from their parents and sent to the Bureau of Indian Affairs (BIA) or religious boarding schools. While at these schools, children were forbidden to speak their native language, wear their own clothes, or practice any traditional cultural activity. They were physically punished when they broke these rules. By depriving the children of their parents' influence and by not allowing the children to practice their culture, the mainstream white society was able to produce a generation of Indian adults who had been rewarded for being white and punished for being Indian.

In addition, Indians have a unique relationship—unlike any other minority—with the federal government. Indians are federal dependents, bound by a multitude of laws, policies, and practices that control their present lives. They remain the only minority that must prove their status by documentation (Attneave, 1985; Glenn, 1991; Lujan, 1990; Lujan & Glenn, 1989; Stedmon, 1982; Strickland, 1980; Washburn, 1971). Government-sanctioned policies for identification of Indianness, by certificate of degree of Indian blood (CDIB), have resulted in more assimilated than traditional Indians on federal rolls; traditional Indians are unable to produce Euro-American legal proof of who they are.

As Wardell (1938/1977) notes, the quantum of people on the federal rolls and on those determined by CDIB is usually lower that what is accurate because of the manipulation of the rolls both by Indians and whites. Indians were fearful of reporting the accurate amount because it would restrict their rights; whites enrolled people without their knowledge, for their own nefarious purposes. For Cherokees, claiming more white was not to claim less Cherokee. Cherokee, unlike other tribes, has long determined that to be any part Cherokee is to be Cherokee (Wright, 1992). Indians could not in the past, and do not today, have the right to determine who is an Indian.

Nevertheless, the fear of the rolls remains. During July 1996, an incident occurred at the Cherokee Tribal Headquarters in Tahlequah, Oklahoma. I witnessed a member of a Cherokee family attempting to get her grandfather to sign up for his CDIB. He adamantly refused, and as he left his grandchild said apologetically to the patient clerk, "He is still afraid of the roll." The fear of the federal rules is still present for the older generation of Cherokee elders.

Recent Oklahoma Indian History and Government Policies

Federal policies contributed to the cultural deprivation of many Indian people in additional ways, by sanctioning bias and prejudice through restrictions on Indian gatherings, tribal meetings, and individual rights of Indians (Strickland, 1980; Wright, 1951/1986). The Thomas-Rogers Oklahoma Indian Welfare Act of 1936 resulted in the dissolution of the tribal governments with the loss of all rights previously held, rendering tribal activity to be negligible. Other decisions by the Bureau of Indian Affairs (BIA) are noted to have been negative to the Indian family (Berkhofer; 1978; Strickland, 1980; Washburn, 1971). Former Principal Chief of the Cherokees Wilma Mankiller (in a speech given at the University of Oklahoma, 1988) said that, during the 1950s the BIA began a program of relocation for Indian families. Indian families, with few job skills and who lived in rural areas, were moved from their homes and extended families to poor urban settings. The result was further fragmentation of families, tribes, and cultures. Chief Mankiller (1988), as a child whose family was moved to San Francisco under this act, said, "Urban poor is much harder than rural poor. At least in rural *Tahlequah* [Oklahoma], we could eat."

Current Status of Indians in Oklahoma

Understanding Indian Tribal Governments (1984) notes that the modern era of self-determination for Oklahoma tribes came from court decisions of the mid-1970s (Indian Self-Determination Act, 1975), which served to reinstate the "special relationship between *all tribes* and the federal government" (p. 41). Challenges to the breaking of numerous treaties heightened awareness of minority rights (resulting from the civil rights acts of the 1960s), and changing court decisions eventually led to self-determination by tribal governments (Cohen, 1942; Indian Self-Determination Act, 1975; Strickland, 1980; *Understanding Indian Tribal Governments,* 1984; Washburn, 1971). The reassignment of some lands and payments of damages marked a new era in Indian affairs and, particularly, a new era in identification of people with their lost culture. The federally recognized tribes in Oklahoma are now self-ruling, doing battle with the federal, state, and local governments when necessary but ruling themselves in ways last seen in the 19th century (Bolt, 1990; Deloria, 1974/1985; Deloria & Lytle, 1983;

Lujan & Glenn, 1989; Rader, 1978[4]). The 1990 census report (U.S. Bureau of Census, 1990) shows Oklahoma to be the state with the largest population of Indians, with 8% of the population or 252,089 out of a total population of 3,145,585. All Indian rolls have increased during the last 10 years. This is attributed to many causes, including the phenomenon of people seeking to regain their culture and to the poor economy in Oklahoma, causing people to attempt to benefit from Indian health, food, and employment benefits (Glenn, 1991; Sly, personal communication, July, 1993).

The Indians who are members of the self-ruling tribes live their lives in many different ways. Identification of self as an Indian, public identification in social settings, and legal identification of Indians are complex issues that have contributed to the cultural deprivation of all Indians, including Cherokees. The questions "Who is an Indian?" and "Are you Indian?" and "How much Indian are you?" can bring a variety of answers. The questions can be considered inappropriate, rude, or a part of in-group Indian talk. The answers often vary according to who is asking the question (e.g., another Indian, a non-Indian, a repre-sentative of a federal, state, or county government, or a tribal official; Wardell, 1938/1977). Indians may not have identifiable Indian racial features because of intermarriage; their names may not be traditional; or they may have an Indian name but not have documentation to prove their heritage. How is it then that one can identify an Indian or how is it that one can know if one is Indian? Pratt (1985) would say that the ultimate identification comes from the person who knows if he or she is Indian. Ironically, the U.S. census forms provide one of the few legal instances in which individuals are allowed to say that they are Indian, without documentation. Problems in self-identification of Indianness, self, and others, then, contribute to cultural deprivation.

To summarize, no universally accepted criterion is available to answer the question, "Who is Indian?" One is identified as an Indian in a multitude of ways: by oneself, one's family, one's peers, the federal government, the state government, and the tribe. The modern Oklahoma Indian has a position in society that is on a continuum, with polar positions from assimilated to traditional.

In general, both traditional and nontraditional, urban and rural, unaf-filiated and legally affiliated Oklahoma Indians perceive that there is racial bias against Indians (Kim, Lujan, Shaver, & Boyle, 1991; Rader, 1978). Wahrhaftig and Thomas (1970) say, " racist' perceptions and relationships are the 'motor' driving the system and are embedded in the very day-to-day relationships" (p. 32). Rader, in speaking of McIntosh County (a county south of Tahlequah with large populations of

Cherokee and Creek Indians and the home of the family in this study), notes that Indians and other nonmainstream groups are ignored and undervalued by the dominant Euro-American power structure.

Oklahoma Indians represent a nondominant subculture. Whereas each tribe has a unique history and culture, the tribal members are influenced by varying degrees and diverse ways as Indians are on a continuum of assimilation that ranges from total to traditional. Respondents to a statewide survey of Indians said that they live in two worlds or that they can walk both ways (Kim et al., 1991).

The story of one Oklahoma family shows how that family's communication reveals its cultural assimilation into the mainstream culture by the sites of conflict: loss of their land, loss of language, restrictions on associations with other Cherokees, bias and prejudice sanctioned by the government, and other sociocultural pressures.

TSALAGI[5]: ONE OKLAHOMA CHEROKEE FAMILY'S STORY

The time was 1985; the place was Tahlequah, Oklahoma. The event was the ceremony that named Wilma Mankiller as the first woman to be Principal Chief of the Cherokees. At that gathering of Cherokees, Lou Jane, 92 years old, was honored as the oldest living Dawes Commission (General Allotment Act of 1887) enrollee on the Indian roll. The event marked the reconciliation of Lou Jane with her tribe—a 75-year separation from all Cherokee culture. The story that explains why this woman and her family were deprived of their Cherokee culture parallels the history of Oklahoma Indians and the Cherokee tribe.

This legend of *Tsalagi* was reported in 1830 as a part of the southeastern Cherokees' petition (Woodward, 1963) as they attempted to resist forced marches to Oklahoma in the Supreme Court of the United States:

> That the Cherokees were the occupants and owners of the territory in which they now reside before the first approach of the white men of Europe to the western continent; "deriving their title from the Great Spirit [*Asga-Ya-Galun-lati*] who is the father of the human family and to whom the whole earth belongs." Composing the Cherokee Nation, they and their ancestors have been and are the sole and exclusive masters of this territory, governed by their own laws, usages, and customs. (p. 18)

From these early days of somewhat peaceful contact and trading with whites, the Cherokees chose the losing side in various conflicts. According to McLoughlin (1986),

> By 1790 the Cherokees were no longer sure of their place in the universe. Not only had they suffered many bloody and devastating defeats in battle . . . but ever since their first regular contact with Europeans . . . they had gradually lost touch with important aspects of their old ways of life. . . . Although they were one of the largest tribes east of the Mississippi in 1690, their population decreased by more than half by 1740—from over 20,000 to less than 10,000. . . . They lost more than 50,000 square miles . . . [and] thousands of their people were driven from their homes and forced to resettle further inland. (p. 3)

As McLoughlin (1986) continues with the story of the Cherokee renaissance from the late 1700s through the time of the death march, he discusses the amazing changes of the tribe. The Cherokees, of necessity, changed from a people united by "language, customs, and kinship" (p. xvii) to a nation that made the transition from a hunting to a farming economy and "accepted the 'civilizing' policy of the whites, pressing forward to adapt to the new situation" (p. xviii).

The Cherokee adaptation to white ways incorporated some of their own traditions and the parts of the ideology of the dominant culture (Bolt, 1990; Deloria, 1974/1985). By 1820, a portion of the Cherokees was a generation of Anglo-educated landowners of substance, who presented a formidable challenge to the U.S. government and the poorly educated settlers, who kept encroaching on their land. The legal pressure began to force out these successful landowners and Christian Indians who were more frightening than the "blood-thirsty savages" of earlier days.

The Cherokee Family and the Irish Family

During the 1600s, both sides of the Cherokee-Irish family were involved in the events that decided their ultimate and joined destinies. The Irish immigrants, who came by choice and moved farther west by choice, arrived in the late 1600s meandering from one southeastern state (e.g., Virginia, North Carolina, Tennessee) to another, looking for a permanent home. At the same time, the Cherokees, members of the Deer Clan, kept moving farther west, pushed out by the immigrant newcomers. Prior to the Trail of Tears in 1838, many of the Cherokees moved to Arkansas and some went to Texas. During preremoval and pre-Trail of Tears time, Cherokees were "encouraged" by small incentives of land or cash to move to Arkansas, Texas, Missouri, and Kansas by the federal government. Many Indians left because of coercive methods, which were more successful than the incentives. The government-inspired purpose was to get Cherokees out of mineral- and farming-rich lands in the Southeast (Bolt, 1990; Woodward, 1963; Wright, 1951/ 1986). One part of the Cherokee family left before the Trail of Tears, but another branch was on the forced march. Both branches settled in Arkansas and eventually moved into eastern Oklahoma. The Cherokees, who moved to Pope County in Arkansas along with many other Cherokees, intermarried, assimilated to a degree, and eventually moved to the eastern portion of Indian Territory now known as Checotah, Oklahoma, McIntosh County. Cherokees who left the South during this time were called the "Old Settlers" prior to the march (Woodward, 1963). Later federal decisions about counting Indians would prevent the Arkansas, Texas, Missouri, and Kansas Cherokees from legally affiliating with their tribes. Despite numerous federal court battles, these Cherokees remain separated from their tribe. Officially, they are not Indians because they were not counted in the Dawes Commission (General Allotment Act, 1887) census. They were forever labeled as "white." Branches of the Cherokee family, who went to Texas or stayed in Arkansas, and their descendants, therefore, are not legal Cherokees, unlike the branch of the family that moved into Oklahoma during the late 1800s.

Despite many problems, the Oklahoma Cherokees (a) rallied as a nation, (b) built schools and seminaries for males and females, (c) established economic stability, (d) organized agricultural societies among the men and homemaking skill groups for the women, and (e) in general, flourished as a nation, in a new land. The general prosperity resulted in the following, as told by Woodward (1963):

> [In] 1859 George Butler, the Cherokee agent . . . reported to the commissioner of Indian Affairs that the population of the Cherokee Nation was 21,000, 4,000 of whom were eligible to vote. Living among the Cherokees were 1,000 whites and 4,000 Negroes (including slaves). The Cherokees had 102,500 acres in cultivation. . . . There were, in 1857, 30 (public) schools in the Nation, attended by 1,500 pupils; and the teachers were, with the exception of 2, all Cherokee.
>
> Thus, the Cherokee Nation basked in the warm summer of achievement. Winter and want were forgotten. The war clouds that hung low over the North and South of the United States were, in the parlance of the Cherokees' slaves, "too heavy to tote themselves over the Arkansas [River]." (p. 252)

The war clouds and the war issues did cross the Arkansas River. The Cherokees, after much indecision, placed their allegiance with the Confederacy. Once again, the Cherokees were on the losing side; they lost almost everything, including much of their land. Not until the

Indian Self-Determination Act of 1975 did the Cherokee Nation begin to rebuild toward its national sovereignty.

In post-Civil War times, Creeks and Cherokees shared land allotments uncomfortably in McIntosh County along with Euro-American settlers who had the law on their side. Again, government policy privileged Euro-Americans and sanctioned prejudicial behavior toward Indians. New rules required a white guardian for each Indian who was one quarter or more on his or her CDIB to do any business. When required to legally respond to the Indian census, Indians attempted to register themselves and their children as less than one-quarter CDIB to ensure that family members wouldn't have to have a white guardian appointed to handle their business. White guardians often took unfair advantage of the Indian (Berkhofer, 1978; Bolt, 1990; Deloria, 1974/ 1985; Deloria & Lytle, 1983; Wardell, 1938/1977).

One Cherokee Family in Oklahoma

Separation from their land continued. The family, along with other Cherokees, left Arkansas after the Civil War and went into Oklahoma. Lou Jane was born in Oklahoma, and her mother, father, and siblings lived in sod houses and tents. In her last years, Lou Jane would talk about times when the Indians would try to meet as family or as nation members, but they were scattered by armed white men riding in on horses. The women and children would hide, and the altercation resulted in injury and death for the male members of the tribe. She remembered the death of an uncle in one such attack with white men, who had disputes with her family. She told stories about how the family would take food into the Cookson Hills for fugitive Indian youths and men who were the target of Euro-American government and personal attacks. The family, like others, was restricted in their relationships with other Cherokees and in their traditional ways-of-doing.

All the family spoke English and Cherokee. The younger children spoke Cherokee less as their contacts with other Indians decreased, when Lou's mother stopped going to Indian meetings because the Baptist minister said it wasn't "Christian" or "civilized." Lou went to public schools, one-room schools in the country, and attended a rural Baptist church with her family. The church and the local schools forbade Indian language and Indian ways, just as did the boarding schools that some Indian children were forced to attend.

After her father deserted the family, Lou Jane and her family were isolated from their tribe by distance and fear of public gatherings with their tribe. They were destitute, living off of their last resource and tie to their tribe—their land. When her mother Malinda became seriously ill, Lou Jane walked miles to the nearest rail trestle, jumped on a train, and rode to Checotah. She begged the white doctor to come see her very ill mother. The doctor refused, but he sent medicine and a piece of paper that her mother was to sign to pay for the medicine. The paper gave their land to the doctor, whose family owns it to this day. Once again, separated from their land, the family moved onto relatives' land, until Lou Jane and each of her siblings married. During the times of the Dawes Commission (General Allotment Act, 1887) census taking, this family, as did many others, lowered their quantum.

The Irish family members had arrived in Oklahoma in the late 1800s, and the Irish husband married the Cherokee woman named Lou Jane in 1910, repeating a pattern chosen by many men of Irish or Scot descent who married Indian women. Benjamin was an Irishman who was very different from many of the young men whom Lou Jane knew. He didn't carry a gun; he wasn't Indian; he worked with machines; and he wanted to live in town—the city of Checotah, county of McIntosh. Thus ended the Cherokee family's relationship with the land. Until her death, Lou Jane would go for rides in the country and point out the lost family land and tell stories about her childhood.

The loss of language and restrictions on association with other members of their Cherokee Nation are two additional communication changes that contributed to the loss of culture. After most of these marriages, the family was not an Indian family but a white family. With the demands of the Irish husband, in response to the continued prejudice against non-English language use, with restrictions on social gatherings of Indians, with obvious bias toward Indians who dressed, looked, or acted like Indians, many Indian women were forced to assimilate so that they appeared to fit the family of their husbands. To protect their children from public bias, to satisfy the wishes of the non-Indian husband, and in response to sociocultural pressures from social and church groups, many Indian women changed their language, dress, and religion and carefully chose their social gatherings. Their children were acculturated as non-Indian children, so that their mothers could make sure that their children were safe from biased and prejudicial attacks on Indians in their society. Ironically, because female Indian children were raised and protected as white children, they found that, when they were grown, they had lost the traditional roles that their mothers had, roles that have given respect to them (L. Shaver, in press).

Lou's mother Malinda moved in with Lou Jane's new Irish family, as was common in those days. She was the only public Indian in the family. She spoke Cherokee, wore the many long skirts and multiple petticoats of a Cherokee woman, tied a band around her head when she had "the headache," doctored the children with herbs and Cherokee remedies, made the soap, and furiously cleaned the "town" house just as though it were the old "sod" house or her tent on her Indian land. Lou Jane retained the more subtle Cherokee ways. She brewed the tonics and the remedies but did not call them *Cherokee.* She created a family environment that didn't challenge the Irish father's authority, but because Cherokee clans are matrilineal, she drew her family to her, gaining and keeping their respect throughout her lifetime (Wright, 1992). By her careful planning, she was able to keep the family together, through the family home, even after her death (L. Shaver, 1996). Malinda directly passed to Lou Jane Cherokee traditions for women and family; Lou Jane passed these traditions more subtly. Her children were taught to do the following: trust only family, support family, handle conflict through indirect means, keep the peace in the household, avoid strangers, protect the family, tell no outsider about the family business, and so on.

Malinda tried to teach Cherokee to Lou's nine children, but they were forbidden to speak it. She succeeded in teaching it to only one grandchild, the grandchild who was her constant companion until Malinda's death in 1936. The last Cherokee speaker is my mother, who was 12 when her grandmother Malinda died. Lou's daughter was forbidden to speak Cherokee after her grandmother's death or to attend Cherokee gatherings. Ironically, her best friend was Creek. Unknown to her folks, her only childhood rebellion was to attend Creek powwows and other Creek gatherings. At family gatherings, some of Lou Jane's grandchildren tried to get her to speak Cherokee; she always refused by saying, "I've forgotten."

Lou Jane patterned her married life and the raising of her children after the dominant culture—the Irish immigrant family into which she married. Her language, behavior, and practices were typical of her neighbors. Her children were raised to be white. Because she and her nation were separated from their land, forbidden to use its language in social, civic, and church activities, restricted in types of tribal gatherings, and legally restricted from certain business dealings and civic involvement (e.g., voting) during her childhood and young adult years, she waited 75 years to make her peace with her nation. Her children and her grandchildren did not hear her talk about being "Indian" until she was in the last decade of her life. Whereas family members knew that they were Indian, the knowing did not include living the culture.

Lou Jane's story is a common one. The story is a taken-for-granted tale of assimilation and the "civilizing" of the American Indian. The "Why?" of this family's story is that being Indian in Oklahoma was a dangerous way to live. The more that you looked and acted like an Indian, and the more Indian language that you spoke, the more likely you were to suffer discrimination, abuse, and punishment from the legal system and society (Rader, 1978). As Brislin (1991) discusses, the reasons for discrimination are many, varied, and multilayered; they are implicit and explicit. In everyday life and society, the sanctions against Indians in Oklahoma from the dominant Euro-American culture were and are strong, ongoing, economic, and often, violent. In the past and today, being a traditional Indian is considered to be antisocial and results in Indians and their families being ostracized and subject to attacks. Laws were different for Indians and whites (e.g., voting privileges and buying alcohol were restricted to whites). The white men who married Indian women often insisted that the women no longer be Indian. Many times, the women were never again public Indians. Many women like Lou Jane obeyed their husbands and followed a defensive pattern of behavior that left their Cherokee culture in their past and out of their descendants' future (Berkhofer, 1978; Bolt, 1990; Deloria & Lytle, 1983; Rader, 1978; Wardell, 1938/1977).

Why have many Cherokee families been deprived of their cultural heritage? Their communication in language and behavior was restricted by law and sociocultural pressures to conform to Euro-American ways-of-doing; that is assimilation. Many did this to protect their children, their spouses, and themselves.

The Family and Their Cherokee Culture

In 1985, the first Cherokee woman was elected as Principal Chief of the Cherokee Nation. One of Lou Jane's sons left his home in Texas to travel to Checotah. He broke a family tradition and talked about Cherokee matters to his mother; he broke another family tradition and told his mother what she was going to do. Even in her 90s, no one told Lou Jane what to do. His message was, "Mom, Wilma Mankiller is to be the next Cherokee chief. I am going to take you to the ceremony." The entire family was shocked and delighted when she agreed. And that day, when history was being made for the Cherokee Nation and the tribe was beginning a new era of prosperity and harmony, Lou Jane witnessed the ceremony for Chief Mankiller. Furthermore, she was cited and honored as the oldest living Dawes Commission enrollee present at the ceremony. After that day, she talked about her childhood memories, the Cherokee gatherings, and her mother's and grandmother's lessons in living. One Cherokee woman, culturally deprived of her heritage through sanctions from society, made her peace with her nation and herself before her death. Her peace was a gift to her family. She gave them permission to find their heritage.

Since 1980, which was 4 years after the new self-determination laws for Indian nations, the Cherokee-Irish family members have made annual trips from all over the United States to return to McIntosh County. Many family members—there are more than 100 direct descendants of Lou Jane—have obtained their CDIB. They have obtained their tribal membership cards. Family members are choosing to retire to their "home place." Some are attempting to buy back the original allotments, to be close to their original land. The Cherokee family members are returning to the land and to their culture.

In the years since the Indian Self-Determination Act of 1975 was passed, a Cherokee national revival has occurred that includes both economic and cultural issues. The tribe has begun programs of economical renewal, language and custom restoration, and education to ensure the everyday survival of the tribe among a modern society and the ancestral survival of Tsalagi (Fite, 1993; Mankiller, 1988). Former Chief Mankiller (Fite, 1993) says, "The state of the Nation is good" (p. A1). The new Cherokee Principal Chief Joe Byrd, speaking for the Five Civilized Tribes, spoke eloquently at the 1996 Democratic National Convention in Chicago about the role of Indians in government and in U.S. society. The Cherokee Nation survived white contact, losses of land and resources after unsuccessful conflicts, death marches across the southern United States, the Civil War, the General Allotment Act (1887) that resulted in the loss of tribal lands, the dissolution of the tribe as a legal entity, and other calamities. Since then, the tribe has reframed itself as the new Cherokee Nation, skillful in survival in current times but rooted in the bedrock of Cherokee beliefs.

This Cherokee family has begun to revive itself also. Both the nation and the family, through communication—language and behavior—have socially reconstructed themselves to their culture. The family members celebrate their Indianness; they are Cherokee, Deer Clan. They have learned what they lost, and in the learning they regained their culture. Their early years were culturally deprived; they have stopped the deprivation by their search for what Lou Jane lost for 75 years. They have defied the plan for cultural genocide by re-identifying themselves as an Oklahoma Cherokee family.

In 1826, Boudinot, who fought against the removal of his Cherokee people, said, "I can see my native country, rising from the ashes of her degradation . . . and taking her seat with the nations of the earth" (Buck Waite, also known as Elias Boudinot, 1826, cited in McLoughlin, 1986, p. 125). The tragedy for Cherokee families should not be the temporary cultural deprivation that they suffered; the tragedy would be if that the cultural deprivation were to be accepted as reality. This nation and this family appear to have chosen to change the future by embracing the past.

CONCLUSION

This has been the story of a culturally deprived Oklahoma Cherokee family. The perspectival rhetorical analysis of the family's communication in the context of the history of Oklahoma Indians and the Cherokee Nation provides insight to the dilemmas that changed the communication of the family, changes that led to the family's loss of its culture. This is also the story of an Oklahoma Cherokee family whose members have chosen to rediscover their culture—who have refused to let the past die—who have chosen not to remain deprived of their culture. The sites of conflict have been addressed by those seeking to regain their land, to discover their language, to associate with members of their nation, and to ignore the prevailing bias against Indians. They have chosen to be an Oklahoma Cherokee family.

NOTES

1. There is a general lack of agreement among Native people in the United States as to preferred group names. *American Indian, Native American, Native People, Natives, Indigenous People,* and *Indians* are among the many terms that are currently used. In Oklahoma, among many Indians, we use the term *Indians* or the name of our nation. For this chapter, I use the term Indians as an inclusive term because I am talking about Oklahoma Indians, particularly Cherokees.

2. *Euro-American* is a term used to indicate the mainstream culture that some refer to as *Anglo* or *white.* In this study, *Euro-American* is used to indicate the mainstream dominant culture in general; *Anglo* is used to refer to the primarily Scottish, Irish, and English cultures; *white* is used to refer to the legal and common terminology among Oklahomans, historically and contemporarily.

3. The Trail of Tears was the 1838 federally mandated death march of the Five Civilized Tribes from the Southeast to Indian Territory. Many thought that the defeat and dissolution of the Cherokee Nation was inevitable when more than 4,000 people died during their forced march, when the tribe suffered because of the unfulfilled promises of the federal government, and when the bitter in-fighting between the Ridge family and the Ross family caused Cherokee to fight Cherokee (Woodward, 1963).

4. Rader (1978) conducted extensive interviews and surveys in McIntosh County in both the rural areas and the towns of Eufaula and Checotah for his study of the "limiting framework that relegates Blacks and Indians to the role of outsiders" (p. 1).

5. The Cherokee word for their nation.

REFERENCES

Attneave, C. (1985). Practical counseling with American Indian and Alaska native clients. In P. Pedersen (Ed.), *Handbook of cross-cultural counseling and therapy* (pp. 135-140). Westport, CT: Greenwood.

Berkhofer, R., Jr. (1978). *The white man's Indian: Images of the American Indian from Columbus to the present.* New York: Vintage.

Billig, M. (1987). *Arguing and thinking: A rhetorical approach to social psychology.* Cambridge, MA: Cambridge University Press.

Billig, M., Condon, S., Edwards, D., Gane, M., Middleton, D., & Radley, A. (1988). *Ideological dilemmas: A social psychology of everyday thinking.* Newbury Park, CA: Sage.

Bochner, S. (Ed.). (1982). *Cultures in contact: Studies in cross-cultural interaction.* New York: Pergamon.

Bolt, C. (1990). *American Indian policy and American reform: Case studies of the campaign to assimilate the American Indians.* Winchester, MA: Unwin Hyman.

Brislin, R. (1991). Prejudice in intercultural communication. In L. Samovar & R. Porter (Eds.), *Intercultural communication: A reader* (6th ed., pp. 366-370). Belmont, CA: Wadsworth.

Burke, K. (1966). *Language as symbolic action.* Berkeley: University of California Press.

Burke, K. (1969a). *A grammar of motives.* Berkeley: University of California Press.

Burke, K. (1969b). *A rhetoric of motives.* Berkeley: University of California Press.

Burke, K. (1970). *The rhetoric of religion.* Berkeley: University of California Press.

Burke, K. (1979). Theology and logology. *Kenyon Review, 1,* 151-185.

Burke, K. (1985). Logology: Over-all view. *Communication Quarterly, 33,* 31-32.

Cherwitz, R., & Hikins, J. (1986). *Communication and knowledge: An investigation in rhetorical epistemology.* Columbia: University of South Carolina Press.

Cohen, F. S. (1942). *Handbook of federal Indian law.* Albuquerque: University of New Mexico Press.

Deloria, V., Jr. (1985). *Behind the trail of broken treaties: An Indian declaration of independence.* Austin: University of Texas Press. (Original work published 1974)

Deloria, V., Jr., & Lytle, C. (1983). *American Indians, American justice.* Austin: University of Texas Press.

Eco, U. (1990). *The limits of interpretation.* Bloomington: Indiana University Press.

Filler, L., & Guttmann, A. (Eds.). (1962). *The removal of the Cherokee Nation: Manifest Destiny or national dishonor?* Lexington, MA: D. C. Health.

Fite, R. (1993, September 7). Mankiller says tribe in good shape. *Muskogee Phoenix,* p. A1.

Folb, E. (1997). Who's got room at the top? Issues of dominance and nondominance in intracultural communication. In L. Samovar & R. Porter (Eds.), *Intercultural communication: A reader* (8th ed., pp. 138-146). Belmont, CA: Wadsworth.

General Allotment Act, 24-388. (1887).

Glenn, L. D. (1991). Health care communication between American Indian women and a white male doctor: A study of interaction at a public health care facility. (Doctoral dissertation, University of Oklahoma, 1990). *Dissertation Abstracts International, 51,* 2722B.

Indian Self-Determination Act, 93-638. (1975).

Kim, Y., Lujan, P., Shaver, L. D., & Boyle, A. (1991, November). *Cultural adaptation of American Indians in Oklahoma.* Paper presented at a meeting of the Speech Communication Association on Ethnic Identity, Communication Assumptions, and Intercultural Communication, a Competitive Panel, Atlanta, GA.

Lujan, P. (1990). [Characteristics of Oklahoma Indians]. Unpublished raw data.

Lujan, P., & Glenn, L. D. (1989). *History of the Indians in Oklahoma.* Unpublished manuscript.

Mankiller, W. (1988, October). Speech made to the members of the FINE Program, University of Oklahoma, Norman, OK.

McKerrow, R. (1996, April). *Presentation on rhetoric and the study of culture.* Lecture presented at Bowling Green State University, Bowling Green, OH.

McLoughlin, W. (1986). *Cherokee renascence in the new republic.* Princeton, NJ: Princeton University Press.

McNickle, D. (1973). *Tribalism: Indian survivals and renewals.* New York: Oxford University Press.

Monfils, B. (1980, November). *The critical perspective in intercultural communication.* Paper presented at the meeting of the Speech Communication Association, Action Caucus on General Theory-Building in Intercultural Communication, New York.

Potter, J., & Wetherell, M. (1987). *Discourse and social psychology: Beyond attitudes and behavior.* Newbury Park, CA: Sage.

Pratt, S. (1985). Being an Indian among Indians. (Doctoral dissertation, University of Oklahoma, 1985). *Dissertation Abstracts International, 46,* 1277.

Rader, B. (1978). *The political outsiders: Blacks and Indians in a rural Oklahoma county.* San Francisco: R & E Research Associates.

Shaver, L. D. (1993). The relationship between language culture and recidivism among women offenders. In B. Fletcher, L. D. Shaver, & D. Moon (Eds.), *Women in prison: A forgotten population* (pp. 119-134). New York: Praeger.

Shaver, L. D. (1996). A house as symbol, a house as home: Mamaw and her Oklahoma Cherokee family. In A. González, M. Houston, & V. Chen (Eds.), *Our voices* (2nd ed., pp. 136-142). Los Angeles, CA: Roxbury.

Shaver, L. D. (in press). The dilemma of Oklahoma Native American women elders: Traditional roles and sociocultural roles. In H. Noor Al-deen (Ed.), *Cross-cultural communication and aging in the U.S.* Hillsdale, NJ: Lawrence Erlbaum.

Shaver, L. D., & Shaver, P. (1995). Care givers in communication with HIV patients: A perspectival rhetorical analysis of health discourse. In L. Fuller & L. Shilling (Eds.), *Communicating about communicable diseases* (pp. 261-276). Amherst, MA: HRD Press.

Shaver, P. (1991). An analysis of political discourse elements supportive of the mass communication process in the United States with specific reference to arguments utilizing First Amendment principles. (Doctoral dissertation, University of Oklahoma, 1991). *Dissertation Abstracts International, 52,* 3477A.

Shaver, P., & Shaver, L. D. (1992a). Applying perspectival rhetorical analysis in intercultural consulting: The chromosomal bivalency model. *Intercultural Communication Studies, 2*(2), 1-22.

Shaver, P. M., & Shaver, L. D. (1992b). *"Icons" of bureaucratic therapy: An application of Eco's semiotic methodology.* Paper presented at the meeting of the International Communication Association, Miami, FL.

Shaver, P. M., & Shaver, L. D. (1992c). *Signs in the organization: Architectural changes as organizational rhetoric in a public health facility.* Paper presented at the meeting of the Western Speech Communication Association, Boise, ID.

Stedmon, R. (1982). *Shadows of the Indian: Stereotypes in American culture.* Norman: University of Oklahoma Press.

Strickland, R. (1980). *The Indians in Oklahoma.* Norman: University of Oklahoma Press.

Szalay, L., & Inn, A. (1988). Cross-cultural adaptation and diversity: Hispanic Americans. In Y. Y. Kim & W. B. Gudykunst (Eds.), *Cross-cultural adaptation: Current approaches* (pp. 212-232). Newbury Park, CA: Sage.

Thomas-Rogers Oklahoma Indian Welfare Act, 49-1967. (1936).

Understanding Indian tribal governments. (1984). Oakland, CA: American Indian Lawyer Training Programming.

U.S. Bureau of Census. (1990). *1990 United States census report.* Washington, DC: Government Printing Office.

Wahrhaftig, A., & Thomas, R. (1970). Renaissance and repression: The Oklahoma Cherokee. In J. Howard (Ed.), *Awakening minorities: American Indians, Mexican Americans, Puerto Ricans* (pp. 43-56). New Brunswick, NJ: Transaction Publishing.

Wardell, M. (1977). *A political history of the Cherokee Nation, 1838-1907* (with "In search of Cherokee history: A bibliographical foreword to the second printing" by Rennard Strickland). Norman: University of Oklahoma Press. (Original work published 1938)

Washburn, W. (1971). *Red man's land/White man's law: A study of the past and present status of the American Indian.* New York: Scribner.

Woodward, G. S. (1963). *The Cherokees.* Norman: University of Oklahoma Press.

Wright, M. (1986). *Indians of Oklahoma.* Norman: University of Oklahoma Press. (Original work published 1951)

Wright, R. (1992). *Stolen continents: The Americas through Indian eyes since 1492.* Boston: Houghton Mifflin.

6

Linguistic Agons

The Self and Society Opposition and American Quakers

NANCY WICK • *University of Washington, Seattle*

Speech codes—that is, culturally distinctive folk theories of communication—are not, according to Philipsen (1992), about communication as a merely technical matter. They also implicate what it is to be a person, how persons are and can be united in social relationships, and how communication can be and is used to link persons as social beings (see Philipsen, 1986). Carbaugh (1989) makes much the same point in his article about cultural terms for talk, saying that in such terms one can find information about personhood, sociality, and communication. Speech codes used by people, then, tell us something about the position of the individual vis-à-vis society within that particular speech community.

Although this position can be discerned in many ways, including "talk," one direct way it is expressed is through oppositional terms—terms that are played dialectically against one another—with one favored over the other. Philipsen (1986, 1987) spoke of the ideas of "self" and "society" in speech and proposed this opposition as a basic one in cultural communication. Placing a group on the self and society axis, he said, "reveals a partial truth about it, a kind of cultural snapshot" (Philipsen, 1987, p. 245). In his studies of the Teamstervillers, Philipsen (1975, 1976, 1986) found a group for whom *society* carried more weight than *self*. Katriel and Philipsen (1981) discussed the self and society opposition in relation to the *Donahue* television program. And Carbaugh (1988, 1988/1989) built on this in his studies of discourse on *Donahue,* in which "self" held the favored position. Both Philipsen (1986) and Carbaugh (1988/1989) called this an "agonistic" pattern—not agonistic in the sense of people in conflict with each other but agonistic within the language itself.

AUTHOR'S NOTE: An earlier version of this chapter was presented at the Western Speech Communication Association conference in 1995.

The idea of identifying oppositional terms is not new. Burke (1941), for example, suggested that the analyst approach literature by noticing "what went with what" and "what opposed what" (p. 20). Rueckert (1982) used Burke's method to analyze Wordsworth's *Tintern Abbey.* He noticed that "nature" was associated with terms such as *repose, pleasure, kindness,* and *love,* whereas "society" was associated with terms such as *weariness, loneliness, darkness,* and *joylessness.* For Wordsworth, then, there is an opposition between nature and society, and nature is favored over society. Burke's method has since been applied to nonfiction. Berthold (1976), for example, successfully applied it to the speeches of John F. Kennedy, showing how Kennedy opposed the terms freedom and communism, the former connected with words such as *diversity, self-determination,* and *openness,* and the latter with words such as *aggression, attack, threat,* and *oppression.*

Other researchers (e.g., Baxter, 1988) have chosen to emphasize agonistic terms as held in tension, rather than one term as favored over the other. Baxter described the major oppositional pair of autonomy and commitment and how these operated, together with two other pairs, in relationship formation. Carbaugh (1990) proposed that although *Donahue* speech highlights "self," there is a communal agreement that "self" is favored over "society"; therefore, society is important insofar as it enforces the importance of self. Nonetheless, when the dialectical pairs are directly expressed in the discourse, they are often given relative weight that points dramatically to the speech community's view of the positions of self and society. I believe that oppositional terms— the "agonistic patterns" or "agons"—are a rich source for discovering these relative positions, even if the actual words *self* and *society* are not used.

The self and society split is indeed an old one, dating at least to the beginnings of Romanticism in the 18th century. Nevertheless, the value opposition of "self" and "society" may not be sufficient to capture everything about the personhood and sociality beliefs of all speech communities. According to Rosenthal (1984), it was preceded by another linguistic agon, that between self and God. "Self" did not begin life as a noun but merely as a reflexive that indicated identity with something else. No sooner did it become a noun, Rosenthal says, than it received a negative connotation: "Oure own self we sal deny, And folow oure lord god al-myghty" is an instance from 1400 that she quotes. This view of self was still seen as late as the 17th century, but with the Renaissance, things began to change (Rosenthal, 1984):

> When God created man in His own image, did He therefore create man a creator like Himself? . . . If the divine was *in* man, did this mean that an external force (divinity) entered man and lent him its powers, while also remaining outside him; or that man himself contained *all* of divinity in himself? The Renaissance hedged and squirmed over this puzzle but tended to go with the first possibility, while Romanticism, with its two extra centuries of man-centered experience, leaned toward the second. . . . Filling each self with divinity, Romanticism set this divine self against society. This self/society opposition, formulated most influentially by Rousseau, places all natural goodness in the self and all evil in society. (pp. 16-18)

The value opposition has been a strong one. Among the white, middle-class, educated Americans who are aficionados of *Donahue,* Carbaugh (1988, 1988/1989) has shown, Romanticism's "self over society" reigns supreme. Philipsen (1975, 1976, 1986) has shown, in his analyses of Teamstervillers, that among some groups the opposite position is taken. He has further formulated (Philipsen, 1986, 1987, 1992) two codes—the codes of dignity and honor—that reflect these opposite positions. Nevertheless, for some modern Americans, the self or God opposition is still alive and well and impinges on the self or society opposition. In this chapter, I present instances of a particular linguistic agon among a group who are members of the Religious Society of Friends (Quaker), and show how this agon points to the group's position regarding self and society. Although the speech code of Quakers has been written about before (see Bauman, 1970, 1983), no scholar has, to my knowledge, addressed this particular question. Among Quakers, I will claim, the nature of personhood and sociality cannot be understood without a third term, *God.*

METHOD

The materials for this study come from participant observation with the four-person Nominating Committee of the Moss Island Friends (a pseudonym, as are all of the names of individuals in this chapter), a small (about 50 members and attenders) and relatively new Quaker Meeting located in a large city. At the time of this study, I had attended Moss Island Friends for about 4 years but was not a member. I had had no previous experience with Quakers. Although 4 years may seem like a long time, among Friends it is considered minimal. It is not uncommon for people to hang around meetings for as long as 10 years before feeling ready for membership, and there is never any pressure to learn more about the group or to join. Indeed, Friends often seem reticent to tell a newcomer about their faith; in Quakerism the emphasis is on individuals discovering for themselves that this is their spiritual home, rather than being converted by enthusiastic members. As I began my research, then, I retained something of a novice's eye and ear on the ways of Friends, at the same time being familiar enough with this group to gain access to important settings.

Moss Island Friends is an unprogrammed meeting. This means there is no minister and, because the group owns no building, no paid staff. Worship consists of one hour of silent waiting, punctuated by vocal ministry if Friends feel moved to give it (for a fuller description of this process, see Davies, 1988). Because of the lack of professional leadership, the meeting is run by its members and attenders. A presiding clerk runs the business meeting, whereas a recording clerk takes notes. Other jobs are handled by committees: the Finance Committee, Adult Education Committee, Children's Program Committee, and so forth.

Offices are filled once a year by a Nominating Committee, at this point chosen by the existing Ministry and Oversight Committee. The committee meets during a period of several months to propose names of people to serve in the offices and on committees. After the individuals' willingness to serve is confirmed, their names are presented at a Meeting for Business (a gathering open to everyone in the meeting as a whole) and held over for one month. During that month, anyone who has a concern about an individual must take it up with him or her. Unless there are strong objections, the slate proposed by the Nominating Committee will serve. At no point is a vote taken.

I began observing Nominating Committee meetings at the invitation of one of its members. Although I had been involved with Moss Island Friends in other ways, I had never served on a Nominating Committee and, thus, came to the scene with fresh eyes and ears. I attended four meetings—about 2 hours each—three of which I was permitted to tape-record. After the four observations, I conducted 60- to 90-minute interviews—also taped—with the four members of the committee. The committee later taped five additional meetings for me; I have listened to these tapes and transcribed portions of them. Although the committee was far from completing its task at this point, I found enough consistency in the nomination process of the meetings I attended and taped to be confident that what went on at other meetings would not be substantially different.

During the same period, I attended the weekly Meetings for Worship and monthly Meetings for Business of the Moss Island Friends. This gave me access to Nominating Committee reports to the larger meeting. My corpus of materials, then, consisted of four complete and five partial meeting transcripts, four interview transcripts, and field notes of other observations. As a supplement to these materials I read *Faith and Practice,* a publication of North Pacific Yearly Meeting (1986), (a regional Friends organization). *Faith and Practice* is a "guidebook to Quakerism" as it is practiced in the Yearly Meeting and contains sections on worship, the business meeting, decision making, and committee duties, among other things. Because each Yearly Meeting writes its own *Faith and Practice,* and members are expected to be familiar with it, it is a reliable description of how things are done among this particular group of Quakers. Of course *Faith and Practice* was used only as a supplement; no statement made in it was accepted without confirmation by observation or interviews. Nonetheless, it proved a valuable source for grounding me in the philosophy underlying the scene I was observing.

AGONISTICS AND THE NOMINATING COMMITTEE

In reviewing my materials from the Nominating Committee, I was struck at first by how often the group talked about its own ways of doing things. They had gathered for the purpose of proposing people to hold offices and fill committees, but they seemed to spend almost as much time talking *about* what they were doing as actually doing it. I began to pay close attention to this "metacommunication," and soon noticed that the word *process* was most often used to describe what was happening. Members spoke of "our process" or "Quaker process" or "spiritual process." Moreover, this was often contrasted—implicitly or explicitly— with "secular process." When the contrast was made, the implication was always that secular process was inferior to that being practiced by the Nominating Committee members—at least in this setting. The two symbols that I will call "spiritual process" and "secular process," then, form a linguistic agon according to Carbaugh's (1988/1989) definition: two classes of symbols and a system of contrastive meanings, with each contrastive meaning resolved in one direction.

Before I display some examples of the agon, it may be helpful to describe the nomination process these Friends are referring to as I witnessed it during nominations for several positions and committees: When nominations were to be made for a position or committee, one of the Nominating Committee members would read a description of the duties of the office or committee, along with the qualities needed by those who would serve. The group would then "go into silence." This was a meditation period in which members pondered the position or committee in question. When ready, a member would state the name of someone for the role. Others would follow suit when they felt moved to do so. Nominations would go on until the members decided they were finished. Then they would come out of the meditation period and raise concerns or questions they had about the nominees, after which they would simply talk until they had arrived at the final name or names to be placed in nomination. No vote was ever taken. Sometimes the process could be completed quickly; sometimes it required much talking and more than one meeting before a selection could be made.

I have said that members spent a great deal of time talking *about* their process, even in the midst of going through it. Here is one example of how the nomination process itself was discussed. In this excerpt, Doreen is reporting back to the committee about her meeting with Mitch, the committee's candidate for presiding clerk. It had been her task to approach Mitch to see if he would be willing to serve:

Excerpt 1

> Doreen: And he was able to say that after the process, he felt clear that he could move forward, that he was willing to accept the call that came through us. Very much, very clear that it was, that he respected the process and that he felt that he was called through us as opposed to a secular nomination process.
>
> Patrick: Us picking.
>
> Doreen: Yeah, it wasn't us chattin' around saying we wanted Mitch to do it but it was a spiritual process, that he felt we had discerned a call and that he felt open to responding to it.

Here, Doreen describes the committee's process even as she reports on its results. She says Mitch "felt that he was called through us." Because this is a spiritual process—the nominee names arrived at through a period of meditation—we can only assume the call came from God. In other words, in the members' view of things, the committee was just the medium; they were not making the choices. She goes on to say that this process is in contrast to a secular nomination process, which Patrick then defines for her: "us picking." In her next comment, Doreen expounds on the contrast, saying it "wasn't us chattin' around" but rather that the group "had discerned a call." Similarly, in the second excerpt, Will has been delegated the task of talking to a committee member who will not be renominated to her position for a second year. (Committee terms are normally 2 years, but each member must be renominated for the second year; it's not automatic.) Will is asked if he will find this task awkward or difficult, and he explains that it won't be because of the way the committee made its decision:

Excerpt 2

> Will: Because I think that I can talk to Donna and say, and explain the process and say, you know, this is a spiritual process, we go through this phase, we go through that phase, we go through this phase, and say your name didn't come forward in that final phase.

The implication of Will's comment is that he could comfortably talk to Donna about her failure to be renominated because he doesn't feel responsible for it. The committee went through a spiritual process and the choice was really out of their hands. As Patrick has already said, it wasn't "us picking."

In both of these instances, the committee members are talking about the actual nomination process when they refer to the spiritual process. The symbol, however, has a broader application. In the following excerpt, Ron is talking about another Friend he has worked with in the past and complaining about this person's lack of adherence to Quaker process:

Excerpt 3

> Ron: Allen simply went on and did his own thing and didn't want to define a clerk and didn't want, and wanted to simply make decisions without going through a process.

Ron is stating his disapproval of a Friend who was acting too much as an individual. This person wanted to make decisions "without going through a process." Because it is a spiritual process he is referring to, we must assume that it is based, as Doreen has said, on calls—or in this case messages—from God. When using spiritual process, people do not make decisions on their own; they seek "outside help." Likewise, during a discussion of the effectiveness of committees, Will and Doreen had this exchange:

Excerpt 4

> Will: And the question is whether those committees are actually doing anything, uh, with those problems. Have we effectively delegated them? Which I take to be the question that we're metaphorically asking when we ask "Does the emperor have any clothes?"

Doreen: Measured by whether or not the problems are solved?

Will: Measured . . . no . . . um, I'm not sure that's a . . . I mean I wish . . . that'd be a great secular process, it's one I'd use at work, but I'm not actually sure it's the right criterion . . . measured by whether they're being addressed in a way that we, uh, feel is appropriate. Depends on the problem.

Here, Doreen suggests that perhaps committees can be judged on the basis of whether or not the problems they were created to solve get solved, but Will objects to this notion. He says, to rely on results is a secular idea, but that in a spiritual process, one is more interested in the process itself. That is what he means by "whether they're [the problems] being addressed in a way that we, uh, feel is appropriate."

In both of the preceding cases, the process referred to is not the nomination process but a more general Quaker way of doing things. But from what I have seen, the broader Quaker context is, in many ways, an extension of the nomination process. The typical business meeting or committee meeting begins with a period of silence, after which proposals may be presented. Friends raise any concerns or questions they have about a proposal and are told to "season" it. This means, essentially, that they should meditate about it. Then, in the following month, the proposal is reconsidered, at which time it may be approved or held over for more seasoning.

But given that Quakers do not vote, how do they decide to approve a particular course of action? During Nominating Committee meetings, I have said, Friends talk until they have chosen their nominees. Here is an excerpt from one meeting that illustrates how the "spiritual process" the Friends have been talking about may proceed:

Excerpt 5

1. Doreen: My sense is that we're looking at
2. three names: Mitch, Will, and Melinda.

3. Patrick: They're the ones with weight.

4. Will: That's funny. I've always thought of
5. Melinda as light.

6. Patrick: Do you know about Melinda's note-
7. taking ability?

8. Doreen: She's a good note taker. She also
9. may have more time, since she's not
10. currently employed outside the home—not

11. that being a mother isn't a full-time job. And
12. they have things well-arranged so she can do
13. things that are important to her. If she's
14. willing to make the commitment it could be
15. arranged. What we don't have is a sense of
16. where Melinda and Mitch feel led. Could we
17. discreetly ask where they feel led? Is this
18. appropriate?

19. Patrick: It feels like we're going down a blind
20. tunnel. If folks aren't led to do these jobs

21. Ron: They may be surprised at the offer. I
22. wouldn't want to go down the slots and ask
23. them. Our perception of their journeys is
24. important.

25. Patrick: I don't know where Melinda is at. I
26. see her filling some role in the current term.

27. Doreen: I couldn't nominate her for either of
28. these jobs. Well, I know I couldn't for
29. presiding, don't know about recording. I
30. don't know if there's enough support for Will.
31. I'm getting clear that it's Mitch and Will as a
32. team. I don't know which is which—I'd even
33. be comfortable with them rotating. But as a
34. team they're the team with the most balanced
35. strengths.

36. Patrick: I need to go.

37. Will: The operational question is, what's our
38. homework?

39. (many people talking at once)

40. Will: I see Mitch as someone who is
41. spiritually deep and a superb listener. I don't
42. know if he's a good facilitator, how we'd
43. work out the driving. I have less need to ask
44. questions of Mitch than I do of Melinda. Of
45. course, before we go public, we have to talk
46. to the person.

47. Patrick: What leads me to Mitch and Will is
48. that they don't have an agenda. That's
49. important. It's up to the committees to come
50. forward with an agenda.

51. Will: One final thing to throw in the pot. We
52. don't know what's happening with the
53. proposal to make recording clerk 2 years.

54. Doreen: The purpose of that was to provide
55. continuity. If Will is in either role that would
56. serve. I'm hearing that we're leaning to Mitch
57. and Will. Do we need another meeting to get
58. clear?

One of the first things to notice about this excerpt is what is *not* there. No one argues directly for a particular candidate; no one attempts to convince another that a particular candidate is the best. Friends make comments about candidates: Mitch is called a "superb listener"; Mitch and Will are said to have "no agenda." They also ask questions about candidates: Patrick asks about Melinda's note-taking ability; Will wonders about Mitch's ability as a facilitator. But no one says, "I think Mitch is the best," nor do they give the others reasons why they ought to feel likewise. To do either of these things would be to engage in a secular process. Instead, committee members seek and give information about the candidates. Ron noted the lack of the push-pull of secular discussions in his interview:

Excerpt 6

I think the key is, you're aiming for the people involved in approaching this decision to all feel comfortable with it. So it's not a contention process so much. You know, it recognizes the perspectives of the different people in the meeting in the discussion and, as I say, it's also open to the sort of deeper perceptions, the more spiritual or more intuitive perceptions of how things may work. Language is a terribly limited process for explaining reality, and I think the objective of that process was to allow not just articulatable criteria to come forth but also perception and feeling and other intuitions.

Committee members also speculate about candidates' leadings ("What we don't have is a sense of where Melinda and Mitch feel led") and discuss the best way they, as a committee, should proceed ("Could we discreetly ask where they feel led?"). *Leading* is a Quaker word meaning, essentially, a call or message from God. When a Friend says "I feel led to participate in AIDS care," for example, it means she has meditated on this idea and has received the message that this is work she should do. Going back to the idea already stated, that the Nominating Committee is not really doing the picking, their choice must be confirmed by the chosen individual's leading. Earlier, Doreen said the committee had "discerned a call" for Mitch that he felt led to respond to. So the committee's spiritual process involves finding calls or leadings for others, who then—through their individual spiritual process—must confirm that this call is a true one. The process just described—what the committee calls "spiritual process"—is also called "discernment" by Quakers (notice Doreen uses this word). *Discern* comes from a Latin root word meaning "to separate." Friends say they separate their small selves from their larger selves—their "God selves," if you will, so that they may make judgments in line with the will of God.

Looking at Excerpt 5 in a more structural sense, we can see that Doreen leads the group to their final choice (confirmed at the next meeting) by stating what she sees as the group sentiment. First, she says, she senses that three names are on the table (lines 1-2), then that she's clear two of those names, as a team, are the right choices (lines 29-35), and finally, that people are "leaning" to the two names and perhaps another meeting is required to get clear (lines 56-58). What Doreen is stating in each case is what she thinks is the *sense of the meeting*. Friends use either this term or the term *unity* to describe what they are seeking in their decision-making processes. In her interview, Doreen had this to say on the subject:

Excerpt 7

For me, what we're seeking is a sense of the meeting. . . . I use the language *sense of the meeting* to distinguish it from consensus, which other people would use because consensus can be a secular process. A sense of the meeting means a sense of the people gathered of God's will, a sense of God's will as discerned by the community that's gathered.

Notice that Doreen once again distinguishes this process from a secular process, which she calls consensus. *Faith and Practice* (North Pacific Yearly Meeting of the Religious Society of Friends, 1986) describes unity in similar terms:

The unity which Friends seek and hope to capture in a recorded minute is God's will in relation to the matter under consideration. Assent to a minute, however, does not imply uniformity of judgment. Rather, it is a recognition that the minute records what the group feels is right at a given time. (p. 78)

In other words, unity and unanimity are not the same thing. Friends try to unite on what they think is best for the group, even if the decision is not their personal preference (see also Hare, 1973). So spiritual process, or discernment, has another aspect—the suppression of the individual will. Essentially, each individual seeks to give up the small self for the larger one, while conferring with others who are doing the same. The "sense of the meeting" represents the best judgment of the group about the will of God. This judgment must be considered superior to that of any one individual, although individuals are free to "stand in the way" of decisions if they feel strongly enough that their own leadings are right. I will have more to say about this in the sections to follow.

THE MEANINGS BEHIND THE SYMBOLS

If the symbols "spiritual process" and "secular process" do form a linguistic agon among this group of Quakers, what are the meanings attached to each symbol? The excerpts already cited provide some clues. In Excerpt 1, the exchange between Doreen and Patrick, for example, Doreen says that Mitch "felt that he was called through us as opposed to a secular nomination process." And in answering Patrick's comment, she says "he felt that we had discerned a call." Spiritual process, then, is about being called, as opposed to being chosen. It was not a matter of the members picking, as Patrick says, but the committee "discerning" a call. In other words, the call comes from somewhere else. Committee members recognize it; they don't create it. If the committee is seeking unity, they are seeking God's will for the community. Therefore, the call must come from God. One meaning we might attach to our symbol "spiritual process," then, is "seeking God's will," whereas "secular process" might mean "seeking the people's will." Interestingly, the word *God* is almost never used during Nominating Committee meetings. And although Doreen and Will used the word during their interviews, Ron and Patrick did not. Nonetheless, some variant of "seeking God's will" seems to accurately fit how Quakers see spiritual process. Asked directly about it in his interview, Will said,

Excerpt 8

It's a rough one. I . . . I am convinced that um . . . all the Quakers with whom I've spoken deeply believe in some unified force and believe in an idea of rightness and believe that rightness feels right . . . um and some people are very attached to the word *God* and some people don't care and some people are very offended by it and I've never found one word that worked for everybody.

The idea of feeling and intuition—as Will said, "feels right"—is also part of "spiritual process" and seems—for some people, at least—to be another way of talking about God. Ron, in Excerpt 6, talks about "deeper" perceptions, "the more spiritual or more intuitive perceptions," seeming almost to equate spiritual with intuitive. Toward the end of one meeting, the committee spoke rather directly about the way they experienced the nomination process:

Excerpt 9

Patrick: How do we go about what we're doing? All of a sudden you pulled the Finance Committee together. What's different between a secular and a spiritual process?

Will: Instead of weighing Allen—bookkeeping experience, and so forth— what I did on hearing his name suggested, I got a mental picture of him as treasurer and asked, "Does that feel right?" "Does that fit our meeting's path?" Was there a sense of rightness, fittingness, of it clicking?

Doreen: A sense of visceral satisfaction—satisfaction-in-the-heart space.

Patrick: When we were looking at Allen, I saw him standing up there with his individual shtick. What's so spiritual about this? One person comes up with a name.

Ron: What I like is you look at the name, you get a feeling, you don't analyze—like we're not running people through a filter.

Will: It's an item of faith-slash-discernment; it makes a personal sense of rightness by association with item of divinity. When I feel it because it's right in a greater sense, not logically making sense like that individual. You look in yourself for the same voice that in your personal history is the voice that other people turn to, the voice that has benefited your spiritual growth. I'm getting used to the sound of that voice. It's hard to describe in language.

Doreen: The other piece is surprise. If it surprises me but feels right, it's a leading. There's that sense of having it come to me whole rather than my piecing it together.

Patrick: That's reassuring. That's the same process I go through.

Doreen: You thought you were just muddling.

Will: Real clarity gets clearer to me in retrospect. It gets to fit more and more.

Running through this excerpt is the notion of intuitive versus logical process. Spiritual process is intuitive; secular process is logical. Will speaks of "getting a mental picture" as opposed to "weighing" a person; Ron says he "gets a feeling," he "doesn't analyze." Will comes back to the idea of God when he says the choice is "right in a greater sense," but he also says it doesn't necessarily "logically make sense." Each Friend here seems obligated to contrast the process with its opposite, which—one has to assume—is a secular process.

Closely related to logical versus intuitive is something I shall call "gestalt" versus "linear." In the excerpt above, Doreen says she recognizes spiritual process when an idea "surprises me but feels right," when it "comes to me whole rather than my piecing it together." The idea of surprise, of not arriving at a conclusion one step at a time, is prominent in these data. Several times during the actual nomination process, Friends have prefaced names they have placed in nomination by saying "I am surprised by. . . . " And Patrick, who is the least experienced and most skeptical Quaker of the four, said this in his interview:

Excerpt 10

The thing I've always objected to in the past and I guess it may still appear this way is, okay, I'm one of those guys out in the audience, whoever it was from Nominating would stand up there and talk about this process of choosing people to be on committees or positions and always seemed to wave their hands a lot, like the names rise to the top and we don't pick people based on *their* leadings. We pick them based on, you know, mystery. . . . And so you go in there and here's this process, and it's exactly as described, if you remember what is talked about, and what I find is that, so this stuff is not this weighty Quake kinda stuff that, I mean, you gotta be in touch with George Fox or somethin' in order to pull nominations out of your hat, but that it's a process which is actually pretty well in tune with how I make decisions myself. You know, I think about things, I go for a bike ride, I—as I read in a book today—close your eyes and listen and see what comes up and I don't—I like to think I'm kinda irreverent about it, so I'd like to say that a lot of these decisions aren't as nonsecular as I think we'd like to think but a lot of 'em are. You know, a lotta times I've been really surprised about uh . . . the names that come up—some of those names, you know, like the ones I said.

For Patrick the skeptic, then, the fact that he is surprised by the names he places in nomination is a key way in which he distinguishes this process from others he uses in his life. Clearly, this is not something he has figured out but something that has "come to him whole," as Doreen puts it. In fact, Patrick's whole speech nicely reflects the spiritual or secular agon as it affects identity. Before his service on the Nominating Committee, he has heard about this spiritual process and comes away thinking of it only as "mysterious." But when he joins the committee, he discovers one doesn't have to be a "weighty Quake" (an expression meaning experienced and wise Friend) or "in touch with George Fox" (the 17th-century founder of Quakerism) to understand what's going on. One closes one's eyes and sees what comes up. And when he says names that surprise him, he knows he has somehow entered into the mystery; he is doing spiritual process.

The fact that these Friends talk about process so much leads to another meaning of the agon: process oriented (spiritual) versus product oriented (secular). Ron's and Will's quotes in Excerpts 3 and 4 illustrate this point. Ron complains about a Friend, Allen, who "wanted to simply make decisions without going through a process." This is a cardinal sin among Quakers. Many times in business meetings, I have seen Friends wrangle for a considerable amount of time, not over *what* to do but over how to decide what to do. Furthermore, this goes on even when the point in question is a minor one. Will expresses the agonistic rather directly in Excerpt 4. He asks if committees are doing their assigned tasks, and Doreen questions whether this would be measured by whether the problems are solved. Will says that, whereas that would be a good secular process, it won't wash here. Rather, it is whether "they're being addressed in a way that we feel is appropriate." Doreen spoke even more directly to the point in her interview:

Excerpt 11

So I'm a believer that—I like decisions—but I'm also willing to take a pretty big leap of faith about the decision, the product itself because I have faith in the process, because I have faith in the way we come to where we come. And there are times when I think a decision is 100% correct but I'm uncomfortable in how we got there. And that feels to me—sacrilegious is much too strong a word—but it feels wrong to me. It feels like a failure on our part. If what I want to do is figure out what God wants me to do in my life, it doesn't matter whether I in retrospect chose the wrong thing. But if I chose it for the wrong reason, I am not doing what I feel my purpose in life is and that is to be obedient to God. So being obedient to the process is to me, I guess, I'd say more important than right outcome, decisions.

In a very real way, when Quakers join a meeting, what they sign up for is a process. There is no creed among Friends, because they believe individuals may receive new messages at any time; thus "scripture" is always evolving. What Quakers are expected to believe is that if they listen for and follow the leadings of God, they will be led in the right direction. And by extension, the meeting as a whole must seek together for corporate leadings, which are likewise to be followed.

Running through many of the quotes I have cited is the notion of "control." In spiritual process, these Friends are saying, they don't have full control over what happens, whereas in a secular process they would have. In the spiritual process they are seeking unity, which means the will of God as discerned by the people present—not their own will. In the spiritual process, they seek intuitive insights; they don't set up logical criteria to go by. In the spiritual process ideas come to them whole, as a surprise; they don't figure it out step-by-step. In the spiritual process they are called to simply be faithful to the process, and the product will take care of itself, whereas in a secular process they would be focused on bringing the product about. The language of the meetings in general also suggests lack of control. When participants place names in nomination, for example, this is most often done with an intransitive construction, such as "Joe Blow's name comes forward for me," or "Joe Blow's name comes to me," or "Joe Blow's name occurs to me." It's the exception for anyone to begin a nomination with the word *I*. Rather, the names seem to appear without being connected to a nominator. In fact, out of 36 nominations I recorded, only three included the word *I*. This is in sharp contrast to the typical *Robert's Rules of Order* for nominating, in which a person would usually say "I nominate Joe Blow."

Another very common expression found throughout the meetings has to do with being "led" or being "called." In Excerpt 9, Doreen says that if something is a surprise, it's a leading. The word *leading,* as already noted, is used by Quakers to indicate a message they have received during meditation, calling them to take a particular action. This refers once again to the idea of seeking the will of God. In Excerpt 5 (lines 15-20) Doreen and Patrick have an exchange about the possible leadings of nominees. The members of the committee also used the expression "Are we led" fairly frequently, in reference to themselves when discussing proposed actions, indicating that the final decision was not completely in their own hands.

THE SELF AND SOCIETY SPLIT REVISITED

The meanings behind the spiritual or secular process agon, as I have articulated it, look like Table 6.1. These meanings, taken together, point to a different view of personhood and sociality than the one posited by Katriel and Philipsen (1981) or by Carbaugh (1988) on the basis of the

TABLE 6.1 Meanings of Spiritual and Secular

Spiritual Process	*Secular Process*
Seeks the will of God	Seeks the will of the people
Intuitive	Logical
Gestalt	Linear
Process oriented	Product oriented
Giving up control	Having control

Donahue discourse. When members of the Nominating Committee speak of spiritual process, they speak of a process in which they give up personal control and seek the will of God, in which they don't analyze, in which they expect to be surprised and to have things come to them whole. In other words, the self is not in the favored position that it holds among *Donahue* aficionados. On the other hand, these Friends do not much resemble Philipsen's (1976) Teamstervillers either. The control they give up is not to another person whose role is higher on the hierarchy than their own. In fact, there *is* no hierarchy among them. They give up control to God in full expectation that their fellows will do the same.

What I have said thus far makes it appear that the crucial split for Quakers is not self and society but self and God. However, society is part of their thinking in the form of the Quaker group itself. I have said that Quakers seek unity in their decision making. Let's look again at the *Faith and Practice* (North Pacific Yearly Meeting of the Religious Society of Friends, 1986) description of this process:

> The unity which Friends seek and hope to capture in a recorded minute is God's will in relation to the matter under consideration. Assent to a minute, however, does not imply uniformity of judgment. Rather it is a recognition that the minute records *what the group feels is right* [italics added] at a given time. (p. 78)

Doreen says unity is "a sense of God's will *as discerned by the community that's gathered* [italics added]." In other words, when the group gathered collectively seeks God's will, the individual bends to the group, assuming that the group bends to God.

This is very different from the view of personhood and sociality among both *Donahue* fans and Teamstervillers—the two opposite sides of the spectrum. Carbaugh (1988, 1988/1989) says that on *Donahue*, people are encouraged to "speak their minds," that everyone "has a right to his/her own opinion," and people are expected to be "tolerant" of differing views (1988, pp. 28-29). For *Donahue* fans, society is made up of individuals who do not give up any rights to the group. When they speak, regardless of the topic, they fully expect the result to be dissensus. Philipsen (1975, 1976, 1986) says that among Teamstervillers, people are encouraged to "know their place" (Philipsen, 1976, p. 25), to be respectful of people with authority, and to carry on traditions. The person in Teamsterville counts only as he or she fits into established society; agreement is assumed and talk only reaffirms common beliefs.

In Quaker process, Friends are expected to first listen internally for their own leadings, which means consulting the God within. They then express what they have heard to other Friends, who have been doing their own listening. They do not assume that consensus is already there before they speak, as Teamstervillers do, nor do they assume dissensus will be the result after they speak, as *Donahue* fans do. They seek unity, a path the whole group can agree to, which is only possible when each one seeks God's will rather than his or her own will. And although one person has the right to block an action in Quaker Meeting, this is rarely done; indeed, I have never seen it done in 4 years of attending a "meeting" (see also Sheeran's 1983 account of a different meeting). If the group has collectively sought God's guidance and arrived at a decision, the individual is expected to stand aside, unless he or she feels very deeply that the decision is wrong. Quakers, then, when going through a spiritual process, value the group over the individual, but not just any group. They value the society over the individual when that society collectively seeks God's guidance. Quakers view what it is to be a person and how persons can be united in social relationships with reference to the fact that there is "that of God" in everyone, and people seeking God's truth together cannot fail to find it.

It is interesting to note that Quakers' two-step process for finding truth—that is, the individual search for leadings followed by a corporate search—grew out of its history. According to Quaker historians (Brinton, 1952; Cope-Robinson, 1995; Hubbard, 1974), early Quakerism stemmed from a highly ritualized church in which, the founders believed, too much emphasis was placed on outward symbols and not enough on inner truth. Thus it was a religion that encouraged individual action as opposed to following societal rules. But when early Friends saw fit to do some embarrassing things while following what they believed to be leadings, Quaker leaders decided that individual leadings should be submitted to corporate scrutiny, the better to discern the will of God.

It could be argued that any religious organization seeks God's will in its decision making, so that in any religious context the differing valuation of self and society might be found. However, Quakers are different in that the seeking after God's will is entirely an inside job. There is no authority vested in any external source. There is no minister, no written creed to which members subscribe, no ritual performed with prewritten prayers and hymns. Although some Friends read the Bible, it is not considered the authoritative word of God. Members believe there is "that of God" in each person. To engage in spiritual process is to seek inside for that God-like part, then to consult with others who are doing the same. Thus, spiritual process is deeply connected with identity. To engage in spiritual process is to invoke an identity in which the everyday self is set aside in favor of a greater self. The real meaning of the spiritual or secular agon, as I have presented it here, then, is that it plays two identities off one another, affirming one in favor of the other. Each Friend sees self and society from a Quaker identity and a secular identity, with the Quaker identity favored.

The Friends who served on the Nominating Committee are well aware of these two identities and talk about how one influences the other. In his interview, Will says,

Excerpt 12

When I do process facilitation at work, I am not particularly trying to find God's will, but then again—well, I probably come closer to it than I should admit to my boss . . . um, because I do . . . I do try to do um . . . I mean it's not about expedience. It's about allowing people to function in an environment of maximum honesty and my article of faith on that is that if people are being honest with each other and with themselves then correct decisions will get made and good business will happen and we'll be able to respect ourselves in the morning. Um, when I'm doing process facilitation in "meeting," I'm using most of the same skills, but I'm doing it to a different end. I'm doing it with a specific goal of finding God's will, which I think is something people are able to do, which is why I'm a Quaker. I have that belief that people are able to do that. Put another way, uh, I think people have insight into what's right.

And Patrick, in Excerpt 10, says the process is "in tune with how I make decisions myself." Thus, although a Quaker identity and a Quaker view of self and society are adopted in a Quaker context, they are not exactly forgotten in the outside context. When Friends talk about spiritual process versus secular process, what they are talking about is the dual identities they all hold. To do spiritual process is to invoke a spiritual identity in which—on the individual level—the self gives up control to God and—on the group level—the self yields to God and to the group in which others are yielding to God as well. The specialized language discussed in this chapter is one way of invoking the Quaker and spiritual identity. Spiritual process not only contains the five characteristics I have listed but is carried out through the use of a special vocabulary. Friends listen for leadings, "season" difficult decisions, and discern the proper course to take. These are words widely used within a Quaker context, rarely or never used outside of it. The contrasting of spiritual process with secular process is a way of separating the Quaker identity from the everyday one.

This does not mean, however, that Friends forget their Quaker identity when living in the "outside" world. On the contrary, Quakers are famous for being true to their leadings in the face of societal constraints. Many have refused to fight in wars, for example, and countless others have refused to pay taxes to support wars. *Faith and Practice* (North Pacific Yearly Meeting of the Religious Society of Friends, 1986) says,

> We value the part we have in shaping the laws of our country. It is our task to see that these laws serve God's purposes. Our aim is the building of a social order which works toward the kingdom of God. We affirm our unchanging conviction that our first allegiance is to God, and if this conflicts with any compulsion of the state, we serve our country best by remaining true to our higher loyalty. (p. 47)

Quaker process, on the individual level, requires the person to listen for the leadings of God. If these leadings conflict with the edicts of society, then society must be rejected in favor of a higher power. The Quaker, then, favors his or her own version of the truth over that of society—just as would any *Donahue* fan. But it's not quite that simple. First, any individual Friend would be encouraged to bring a leading to the meeting for corporate seasoning. This step is *required* only when the Friend seeks sponsorship of the meeting for his or her cause; nevertheless, it is always encouraged. Second, the split here seems to be not a pure self and society split but self-in-concert-with-God and society. As implied in the *Faith and Practice* excerpt, protesting the government is not taken lightly. It is done only when the Friend feels the choice is between obeying God and obeying society as represented by the government. For Friends, it seems, the Renaissance view of divinity entering humankind and lending its powers, yet also remaining outside of people, is still current. The Quaker expression that there is "that of God" in every person confirms this; there is "that of God," but not God himself or herself.

CONCLUSION

In this chapter, I have identified one linguistic agon in the speech of a group of Quakers studied over a period of a few months. By analyzing the discourse in which this agon is expressed, I have been able to isolate the meanings behind the symbols and to connect them with this group's view of personhood and sociality. Although these Quakers articulate a belief that they should set aside the self and its needs, their belief does not fall neatly on the "society" side of a self and society opposition, so their code cannot be said to be strictly a code of honor, favoring society; or a code of dignity, favoring the self. Rather, Friends views of both self and society can only be understood through a third term, God. The self contains "that of God," but God nonetheless remains separate from the self. Thus, the self is superior to society only when it consults with God. Conversely, society is superior to the self only when individuals in the society jointly seek the will of God. For these Friends, the terms *spiritual process* and *secular process* implicate two identities—a Quaker identity and a secular identity, the former favored over the latter.

REFERENCES

Bauman, R. (1970). Aspects of 17th century Quaker rhetoric. *Quarterly Journal of Speech, 56,* 65-74.

Bauman, R. (1983). *Let your words be few: Symbolism of speaking and silence among seventeenth-century quakers.* Cambridge, MA: Cambridge University Press.

Baxter, L. (1988). A dialectical perspective on communication strategies in relationship development. In S. W. Duck (Ed.), *Handbook of interpersonal relationships* (pp. 257-273). Chichester, UK: Wiley.

Berthold, C. (1976). Kenneth Burke's cluster-agon method: Its development and an application. *Central States Speech Journal, 27,* 302-309.

Brinton, H. (1952). *Friends for 300 years.* Wallingford, PA: Pendle Hill.

Burke, K. (1941). *Philosophy of literary form.* Baton Rouge: Louisiana State University Press.

Carbaugh, D. (1988). *Talking American.* Norwood, NJ: Ablex.

Carbaugh, D. (1988/1989). Deep agony: "Self" vs. "society" in *Donahue* discourse. *Research on Language and Social Interaction, 22,* 179-212.

Carbaugh, D. (1989). Fifty terms for talk. *International and Intercultural Communication Annual, 13,* 93-120.

Carbaugh, D. (1990). Culture talking about itself. In D. Carbaugh (Ed.), *Cultural communication and intercultural contact* (pp. 1-9). Hillsdale, NJ: Lawrence Erlbaum.

Cope-Robinson, L. (1995). *The little Quaker sociology book.* Melbourne Beach, FL: Canmore.

Davies, A. (1988). Talking in silence: Ministry in Quaker meetings. In N. Coupland (Ed.), *Styles of discourse* (pp. 105-137). London: Croom Helm.

Hare, A. P. (1973). Group decision by consensus: Reaching unity in the Society of Friends. *Sociological Inquiry, 43,* 75-84.

Hubbard, G. (1974). *Quaker by convincement.* New York: Penguin.

Katriel, T., & Philpsen, G. (1981). "What we need is communication": "Communication" as a cultural category in some Americans' speech. *Quarterly Journal of Speech, 48,* 301-317.

North Pacific Yearly Meeting of the Religious Society of Friends. (1986). *Faith and practice.* Corvallis, OR: Author.

Philipsen, G. (1975). Speaking "like a man" in Teamsterville: Culture patterns of role enactment in an urban neighborhood. *Quarterly Journal of Speech, 61,* 13-22.

Philipsen, G. (1976). Places for speaking in Teamsterville. *Quarterly Journal of Speech, 62,* 15-25.

Philipsen, G. (1986). Mayor Daley's council speech: A cultural analysis. *Quarterly Journal of Speech, 72,* 247-260.

Philipsen, G. (1987). The prospect for cultural communication. In D. L. Kincaid (Ed.), *Communication theory from eastern and western perspectives* (pp. 245-254). San Diego: Academic Press.

Philipsen, G. (1992). *Speaking culturally.* Albany: State University of New York Press.

Rosenthal, P. (1984). *Words and values.* Oxford, UK: Oxford University Press.

Rueckert, W. (1982). *Kenneth Burke and the drama of human relations.* Berkeley: University of California Press.

Sheeran, M. (1983). *Beyond majority rule: Voteless decisions in the Religious Society of Friends.* Philadelphia: Philadelphia Yearly Meeting.

7

Researching Cultural Identity

Reconciling Interpretive and Postcolonial Perspectives

MARY JANE COLLIER • *University of Denver*

This chapter presents a review of emerging issues and challenges facing cultural and intercultural communication scholars who choose an interpretive perspective to study how cultural identity is constituted through communication. Selected postcolonial critiques of interpretive approaches are overviewed, with a focus on ontological and epistemological issues. The issues and points of contention are then applied to one research program on cultural identity and intercultural communication. In particular, calls for broadening the context to acknowledge historical and social constraints, the effects of power and privilege on the process of inquiry, and the need for self-reflexivity and critique are examined, along with a description of future research directions.

Scholars who study cultural and intercultural communication are beginning to recognize and struggle with the multitude of epistemological and ontological challenges that must be managed for valid and coherent research to be accomplished. Among the most vocal critics of interpretive approaches to culture are scholars from postmodern and postcolonial perspectives.

This chapter is the result of a desire to understand and respond to concerns raised by critics of interpretive research in general (postmodern ethnographers, postcolonial critics, critical theorists, and cultural studies critics), as well as more specific issues raised by readers of my own work. My goal is to embrace the call for self-reflexivity and begin a dialogue about the intersections and possibilities for integration, as well as the points of contestation between postcolonial perspectives and interpretive perspectives of cultural identity.

As a newcomer to postcolonialism, I begin by sketching my preliminary understandings of postmodern issues that form a backdrop to what I am approaching as the more specific postcolonial critique. Then I describe postcolonial issues, or strands that I read to be ontological and epistemological problematics that need to be recognized and negotiated by scholars of cultural identity. In the second section of the chapter, I discuss the problematics in the context of my own research program on cultural identity. Finally, I address how my reconciliation of postcolonial and interpretive perspectives must incorporate a reflexive move to recognize my role as an intimately engaged observer or participant who has particular privileges, socialized background, and negotiated cultural identities.

THE POSTCOLONIAL CRITIQUE IN AN ERA OF POSTMODERN SKEPTICISM

Although postmodernism is a complex umbrella label for various approaches, there are certain overarching epistemological assumptions shared by those scholars who label their perspectives as postmodern. Postmodern scholars are primarily concerned with exploitation, power, empowerment, and the development of rhetorical tools to deconstruct and critique linguistically constructed and textually mediated social realities and provide alternative interpretations of texts. For example, Fiske (1991) proposes a conflictual theory to contest the consensual theory reading of *Donahue* discourse by Carbaugh (1991). Shome (1996) notes that postmodernists place their emphasis on the subject as constructed and constrained by histories and essentialist categorizations. Prus (1996) characterizes postmodernism as "extreme skepticism in the viability of all forms of knowing (and presumably all interpretation as well)" and also notes that "since no viewpoints are to be privileged over any others, postmodernist notions also may appeal to those pursuing themes such as liberalism, democratization, egalitarianism, and individualism" (pp. 217-218).

During (1995) describes postcolonialism in the following way: "Postcolonialism is regarded as the need, in nations or groups which have been victims of imperialism, to achieve an identity uncontaminated by universalist or Eurocentric concepts and images" (p. 125). The goal of postcolonial critique is to make visible the ways in which oppression occurs and to help people "invent a shared image through which they could act to liberate themselves from imperialist oppression" (p. 126). Shome (1996) adds that postcolonialists place emphasis on the processes of imperialism and the imperialist subject in global and local settings and examine many types of "colonized" or "marginalized" groups.

Under the heading *Power/Knowledge: The Politics of Social Science,* Cameron, Frazer, Harvey, Rampton, and Richardson (1992) summarize,

As many commentators have pointed out—perhaps the fullest and most insistent statement can be found in the various works of Michel Foucault—social science is not and has never been a neutral enquiry into human behavior and institutions . . . we may notice what an enormous proportion of all social science is conducted on populations of relatively powerless people. . . . Foucault observes . . . that the citizens of modern democracies are controlled less by naked violence or the economic power of the boss and the landlord than by the pronouncements of expert discourse, organized in what he calls "regimes of truth"—sets of understandings which legitimate particular social attitudes and practices (p. 2).

Delgado (1994) echoes the need for critics (and presumably interpretive researchers as well) to interrogate their own work. Openness to criticism is "a positive step, representing both interest and reflective inquiry that potentially can lead to more and better scholarship" (p. 77). Conquergood (1992) describes contemporary ethnographers as recognizing that anthropological discourse benefits from reflexivity, criticism, and a recognition of the rhetorical strategies involved in creating a voice of authority. Interpretive scholars can similarly benefit from acknowledging that the politics of language is "real politics" and adopting an academic voice and using "expert discourse" carries with it a moral imperative for attention to consequences of that discourse.

In the remainder of this chapter, I intend to begin a dialogue, a process of critical reappraisal, reflexive questioning, and response to contestable issues in my research program on cultural identity. To organize the specific discussions of both postcolonialism and my interpretive perspective to cultural identity, I propose an analytical framework based on ontological and epistemological problematics.

PHILOSOPHICAL PROBLEMATICS

Criteria for a strong theory of understanding, or knowledge accounts, are the appropriateness of, and consistency among, ontological and epistemological assumptions toward the goal of inquiry. Ontological and epistemological assumptions describe how researchers characterize interlocutor approaches to coming to be who they are and knowing what to believe, as they constitute their membership in a myriad of cultural groups. Such assumptions also state researcher orientations about how their own identities may affect the research process and how they will build knowledge about the respondents' construction of cultural identities.

In essence, each researcher holds two sets of ontological claims: a set of claims about how respondents "do" the "being" of their cultural identities and a set of claims about his or her own identity construction within the academic, historical, socioeconomic, and disciplinary milieu. In addition, the researcher makes two sets of epistemological claims: a set of claims about how respondents come to believe and know about their cultural identities and another set about how she or he, as the researcher, should best develop methodological orientations and justifications that lead to knowledge about respondent construction of cultural identities.

Ontology and epistemology are interdependent, interpellated sets of assumptions, just as the relationship between researcher and researched, subject and object, colonized and colonizer is interdependent and interpellated (Minh-ha, 1995). Nonetheless, researchers have particular cultural identities as academics and are socialized with particular norms and preferences for epistemological paradigms, and these are often transparent and taken for granted. I attempt, therefore, to view researchers and respondents separately, the writer "here" attempting to capture the written about "there," as well as to discuss the intersections and overlap in ontologies and epistemologies.

POSTCOLONIALISM

Ontological Claims

Inquiry about cultural identity includes attention to the complexity of and interrelationships among such social constructions as race, ethnicity, and sex. Cultural group members use race, sex, and class as markers of group identity and status within the broad context of historical structures, ideologies, and current social practice. Cultural identities are multifaceted and intersecting. McClintock (1995) asserts that race, gender, and class are not separate realms of experience but "come into existence *in and through* relation to each other—if in contradictory and conflictual ways. In this sense, gender, race and class can be called articulated categories" (p. 5). She also notes that, just as social conduct may not be best understood by privileging one identity over another or thinking of them as separate, there are multiple ways in which group members define their ability to influence others and the environment. Thus, the implication is that researchers should recognize and engage subjective and collective interpretations of power and resistance and "a more diverse politics of agency, involving the dense web of relations between coercion, negotiation, complicity, refusal, dissembling, mimicry, compromise, affiliation, and revolt" (McClintock, 1995, p. 15).

With regard to assumptions about how respondents learn to be or do sex and gender identities, McClintock (1995) asserts,

> Indeed, one of the most valuable and enabling moves of recent feminist theory has been its insistence on the separation of sexuality and gender and the recognition that gender is as much an issue of masculinity as it is of femininity. (p. 7)

In other words, postcolonial scholars recognize that males and females enact, negotiate, challenge, and confirm their cultural identities in the presence of each other.

Researchers also have a set of ontological assumptions about their identities as researchers and academics. Hall (1995) notes that scholars and critics speak from particular cultural, social, and historical places that include, but are not limited to, one or multiple ethnic backgrounds, classes, and educational ideologies. Postcolonial scholars call for making the sometimes implicit ontological assumptions explicit and opening them to examination and critique. For example, Foss (1997), in her summary of the works of bell hooks, describes types of dialogue and dialectical struggle with insiders and outsiders, which may contribute to decolonization of the mind. More specifically, hooks argues that others can provide "concrete counter-examples" that "disrupt the seemingly fixed (yet often unstated) assumptions" (hooks, 1994b, p. 130) as well as indicate "whether our words act to resist, to transform, to move" (hooks, 1989, p. 16). In addition, hooks also calls for dialogue with "those who exploit, oppress and dominate us" (1989, p. 129) because, as Foss (1997) points out, this opens up spaces for greater understanding of the structures and functions of domination. Delgado (1994) calls for researchers to critically examine their identities and ontological assumptions when he discusses the importance of being open to critiques of implicit privilege and alternative interpretations of texts.

To summarize, postcolonial scholars recognize that the identity groups that are the object or subject of study are formed and socially constructed in historical and ideological contexts in which power is consistently experienced, used, and negotiated. Furthermore, power and privilege inequities constrain the field of choices for interlocutors. Race, sex, and class are identity groupings experienced by interlocutors as multifaceted and overlapping, and there are diverse forms of agency and strategies of empowerment that are enacted by group members. Postcolonial scholars also acknowledge the need to consistently interrogate their work. For instance, hooks (1990), among others, advocates dialogue between the "oppressors" and the "oppressed" to examine racism, sexism, and oppression at all levels, to enable growth.

Epistemological Claims

Race is an academic, governmental, and political categorization system that has been used throughout history by representatives of those institutions to identify outsiders, or abjections (McClintock, 1995) to exert and maintain power. Scholars such as hooks (1990), McGoldrick (1994), and van Dijk (1987) argue that the traditional categories of race, based on biological or genetic conceptions of people, are inaccurate due to intermarriage, changes in the number of racial categories over the years, and arbitrary and changing definitions of how the categories are constituted. Furthermore, such categories are examples of "regimes of truth" created by empowered groups to maintain their own distinctiveness, difference, and status.

Hall (1995) points to the "immense diversity and differentiation of the historical and cultural experience of black subjects" (p. 225) that lends support for recognizing that race in general, and "black" specifically, is a politically, culturally constructed, and oversimplified category. González, Houston, and Chen (1994) also describe the need to represent the heterogeneity and within-group differences among members of ethnic groups.

McClintock (1995) explains that the categories of race, ethnicity, and class were fundamental constructions of Western, industrial modernity, becoming central to the middle-class self-definition and what she calls the "policing" of the working class, Irish, Jews, prostitutes, feminists, gays and lesbians, criminals, and militants. McClintock also argues that race and ethnicity are not synonymous with black or colonized, though many past researchers seem to assume such an equivalence. She agrees with hooks (1989) that scholars need to begin a discourse on race that interrogates whiteness.

McClintock (1995) points to the compelling feminist critique of scholarship in the social sciences and humanities, to stress that researchers should recognize the interrelationships among gender, race, and class. She stresses that this critique is largely from women of color who challenge Eurocentric feminists claiming "to give voice to an essential womanhood (in universal conflict with an essential masculinity) and who privilege gender over all other conflicts" (p. 7). Her contentions that gender should not be studied as if it is synonymous with women, and that feminism is as much about class, race, work, and money as it is about sex, is consistent with ontological assumptions about the heterogeneity and complexity of cultural identities.

Hall (1995) asserts that a significant shift is occurring in black cultural politics with the recognition of the positive aspect of ethnic differences. He notes, "ethnicity acknowledges the place of history, language and culture in the construction of subjectivity and identity, as well as the fact that all discourse is placed, positioned, situated, and all knowledge is contextual" (p. 226). He also points to the development of a new conception of ethnicity: "a new cultural politics which engages rather than suppresses *difference* and which depends, in part, on the cultural construction of new ethnic identities" (p. 226).

In addition to a call for reconstituting such constructs as race, ethnicity, and sex, postcolonial scholars argue that categorizing groups into dualistic extremes of the "powerful" or "imperialist" versus the "powerless" and "colonized" is an inappropriate oversimplification and that there is no center or "standard" to which "outsiders" or the "marginalized" should be held. For example, Ashcroft, Griffiths, and Tiffin (1995) describe the binarism of settler or colonized, or center or margin, as a fallacy and argue that all cultures change, adapt, affect and are affected by one another. If ethnicity is defined as the social construction of group identification, on the basis of ancestry and origins preceding or outside the present nation-state of residence (Banks, 1987), an important question raised by Ashcroft et al. is whether some ethnic groups and not others are entitled to be called "ethnic." They argue that Euro-Americans should be defined and studied as ethnics, rather than as the "center" that is nonethnic and to which others should be compared. Parry (1995) makes a similar argument by proposing that Spivak (1990) may underestimate the power of the subaltern, in that hegemony is inseparable from counterhegemony. She points out that hybridity challenges colonial authority by the continual and mutual development of independent cultural traditions, the interweaving of new cultural forms and practices with the maintenance of established cultural forms.

In summary, postcolonial scholars hold that constructs such as race, ethnicity, class, and sex are overgeneralized categories, used by groups to classify and come to know about others, and are used to maintain power and status. Race, sex, and class should be interpreted in contexts of unequal power and privilege and should be recognized as interpellated. Finally, dichotomous and essentialist assumptions about imperialists or colonized, men or women, or ethnic or nonethnic, misrepresent the heterogeneity within groups and the multiple ways in which groups create and respond to agency and power.

Postcolonial Critique of Ethnographic Traditions

Emerging postmodern and postcolonial critiques of ethnographic research incorporate intersecting ontological and epistemological assumptions. Most of the critiques center on the "crises of representation." Prus (1996) reviews Clifford and Marcus (1986) and Marcus and Fischer (1986) and describes concerns

> ranging from allegations that anthropological ethnography represents a form of cultural domination, to questions concerning people's abilities to inform others about their lived experiences, to matters of propriety regarding forms of representation, to explicit calls for poetic license and fiction in the development of ethnographic accounts. (p. 222)

Calls for research accounts that make explicit the limitations of the ethnographer and the process of doing ethnographies, and greater voice and characterizations of the ethnographic other, are indeed constructive, and making such moves could improve validity of research as well as limit the voice of the privileged ethnographer.

Prus (1996) outlines his interpretation of postmodern criteria for valid accounts or knowledge claims:

> the study of situated, interpretive, interactive, emergent features of human lived experience, emphasis on the necessity of attending to the other in a thorough, careful, open-ended manner, use of concepts that are built up through sustained encounters with the life-worlds of ethnographic others, and a concern that ethnographic others be accorded fuller participation in representations of their life-worlds. (p. 226)

In addition, "good (i.e., postmodernist)" ethnography should include "greater representation of the researcher's background and personal experiences throughout the ethnographic text, and encourage extensive, open-ended, polyvocal (researcher presence diminished) textual representation of those being studied" (pp. 227-228). Conquergood (1991) points out that most ethnographers have already begun a "radical rethinking of the research enterprise" (p. 180) consistent with these themes.

As researchers, ignoring our academic power and privilege and the effect of our multiple identities on our ontological and epistemological assumptions may have the far-reaching consequences of promoting and continuing racism, sexism, and classism, as well as maintaining an "us versus them" opposition in our writing. An additional consequence is the disrupting of everyday practices and contributing to change of the cultural patterns of the observed. Finally, our academic and media texts contribute to the social construction of identities and can influence the basis on which resources are distributed. It is critical that researcher positionality, race, class, sex, and ethnicity, as well as academic training, be acknowledged as constraints and continuing constructions. Ontological and epistemological assumptions about respondent identities and communication need to be reframed to incorporate the power of counterhegemony, legitimize the power of the "margins" or the "colonized," and reject the binary, dualistic assumption that power is exerted by one group in one-way fashion.

AN INTERPRETIVE PERSPECTIVE
TO CULTURAL IDENTITY

The cultural identity theory (CIT) originally proposed by Collier (1988) and Collier and Thomas (1988) is one of many emerging theories of cultural identity (e.g., Carbaugh, 1990; Kim, 1995). This theory was expanded by Hecht, Collier, and Ribeau (1993) through the explanation of several features, or properties, of cultural identities that were then applied to research of African Americans and has been modified and extended in a series of studies on various ethnic groups within the United States and South Africa. Because my goal in this chapter is to be self-reflexive and interrogate my own work, I focus my comments on research in which I was directly involved.

In an interpretive approach, the goal of the researcher is to build understanding of how respondents come to do, or be, or know (Sachs, 1984) their cultural identities. Thus, ontological and epistemological claims about how respondents construct their identities are critical. Whereas the thrust of postcolonialism is the critique of the imperialistic or colonial construction of structural, historical, institutional, and aesthetic discursive practices, the thrust of interpretive approaches has been the negotiation and enactment of cultural identities in particular interactional contexts. Power inequities and history are acknowledged to some degree in interpretive approaches, and individual agency and contextual negotiation are acknowledged to some degree in postcolonial approaches. Nevertheless, each perspective alone may present a somewhat limited view of how people come to know and do or be cultural identities.

To reconcile the critiques of existing research outlined above with past and current research of CIT, in the remainder of the chapter, the points of contention are applied to the conceptual, ontological, and epistemological assumptions, which form the foundation of my work with CIT. As well, findings from selected studies that confirm and challenge the evolving metatheoretical assumptions are overviewed. Future research moves are also suggested.

In the discussion to follow, there are notably brief references to several studies. Although I am aware that limited information on the respondents, methods, and results makes it very difficult for the reader to understand and judge theoretical appropriateness, the descriptions are provided to illustrate ontological and epistemological assumptions and choices. I refer the interested reader to the published versions of the research for more thorough discussions and specific rationale.

Ontological Assumptions

To overview, one of the major premises held by CIT scholars is that cultural identities are historical, contextual, and relational constructions. Cultural identities have enduring (historical) as well as changing properties (Hecht et al., 1993) and are commonly intelligible and accessible to group members (Carbaugh, 1990). Cultural identities emerge in everyday discourse and in social practices, rituals, norms, and myths that are handed down to new members. Being a member of a cultural-identity group occurs when interlocutors demonstrate their ability to use and understand the language code, symbolic forms, and interpretations; share worldview premises and sense of history; enact normative practices; and are accepted and judged as "real members" by "insiders" (Wieder & Pratt, 1990).

More specifically, primary ontological assumptions about interlocutor identity that I hold include one that humans negotiate identity contextually (Brown & Levinson, 1978; Ting-Toomey, 1988). Cultural identities are broad, and potential identities may become more and less salient for individuals throughout conversations, relationships, contact with other groups, and development of social histories. National cultural identity is one of many such cultural identities as ethnic, sex, and corporate, which may emerge or be avowed over other identities in a particular situation. My research acknowledges the heterogeneity within self-identified groups and the overlapping nature of identities (Collier & Thomas, 1988; Hecht et al., 1993). The assumption that U.S. Americans or South Africans are similar in their conduct within groups, and different across groups, oversimplifies and inappropriately privileges the role of one identity, national affiliation, in encounters with one another. Also, national identity may not always be a valid frame with which to understand how individuals define themselves or orient toward others. We (Collier & Bornman, in press) for example, conducted focus group interviews in 1992 in South Africa and found that Afrikaners featured their ethnic distinctiveness by referring to themselves as Afrikaner and used racial labels to point to others, such as blacks. Blacks, on the other hand, featured race in their descriptions of self and other, whereas coloreds, when speaking about others, pointed to race and language, by making a distinction between Afrikaans-speaking or English-speaking whites.

In the cultural identity theoretical framework, researchers assume that individuals belong to many cultural groups, and different cultural identities may become salient depending on who is present, the history of the group, topic and type of encounter or episode, language game in use (Wittgenstein, 1974), and interpersonal and intergroup dynamics such as power, control, inclusion, and affiliation dynamics. Cultural identities emerge out of class differences, ethnic differences, regional differences, sex differences, and the intersections among them. Nevertheless, particular cultural identities are enacted and become salient and contested in particular historical, political, economic, and social contexts. As well, variations in the political or ideological form of the ethnic identity manifest in the situation may change, depending on the topic and relationship with the other conversational partner. As Conquergood (1991) aptly notes, "borders bleed as much as they contain . . . boundaries are now understood as criss-crossing sites inside the post-modern subject" (p. 184).

Tajfel (1978) points out that individuals construct their (multiple) cultural identities as in-group members, in comparison to out-group members. An ontological assumption in CIT is that people enact identity to distinguish themselves, the "insiders," from others, the "outsiders," and that some groups construct boundaries that are tighter and others that are looser. In my research I found that discourse about cultural and intercultural communication commonly includes experiences of being stereotyped negatively by others and is often accompanied by counterexamples of the in-group to "set the record straight" and express pride in the in-group (Collier, 1994; Collier, Thompson, & Weber, 1996).

In-group cultural identities and relationships with out-group members are constructed contextually through avowal and ascription. Avowal consists of the perceived identity enacted by the self or group members in a given communication situation. In other words, avowal is, This is who I am (we are) as a member(s) of my (our) cultural group here and now. Avowal occurs as "front stage" enactment with others

(Goffman, 1959) and is similar to the construct of "self-face" that Ting-Toomey (1988) applies in her model of intercultural conflict.

Ascription of identity consists of perceptions of others' identities and self's perception of identities attributed to self by other: This is how I see you seeing me as a member of my cultural group here and now (Collier & Bowker, 1994). Brislin (1986) argues that stereotypes and prejudices are maintained because they serve positive functions for group members. Allport (1954) found that ascribed stereotypes are linked with the formation of prejudice and such extreme attitudes affect not only constitutive ideas of self and other but also approaches to interaction and relationships. Consistent with the research findings of van Dijk (1987) I found that racism did characterize white South African descriptions of the conduct of blacks and seemed to function to reinforce in-group similarity of experience and solidarity (Collier, 1994). Mimicry, jokes, and stories may be additional forms through which insiders critique outsiders and thereby constitute their membership as insiders. In 1992 when the data were gathered, the groups with the highest socioeconomic power in South Africa also expressed the most frequent and most intense forms of prejudice in focus group discussions with other members of their in-group (Collier, 1994).

The difficulties in pinpointing distinctions between insiders and outsiders become apparent in that avowal and ascription are interdependent and occur with in-group members and out-group members. In dyadic conversations, both interlocutors avow and ascribe potentially many identities. Avowal and ascription processes can affect the relationship tone, content, and talk about substantive issues in conflict, ideas about what rules and procedures should be followed in the discussion, and ultimate judgments of others' competence and desire to continue the relationship. One person's avowal is affected by his or her impressions of the other's ascriptions. I found that when a South African Afrikaner and a Zulu were discussing the possibility of opening a community center to blacks in the Afrikaner neighborhood, the negotiations were affected by the Zulu's perception that the Afrikaner viewed him or her as a member of a low-class, criminal, angry group (Collier, 1994).

It is essential to underscore my ontological claim that some individuals have more options to enact or conceal cultural identities than others. More specifically, Martin (1997) argues that privilege and power come from having options to feature or not feature an ethnic or racial identity. For example, in interethnic conversations between African and European Americans in the United States, African Americans do not have the option of downplaying their racial identity to feature a national or individual identity, because ascriptions about them are so strongly race based, and avowals by groups with lower sociopolitical power can be more easily discounted than the ascriptions by the more sociopolitically powerful other. White ethnic U.S. Americans, on the other hand, have the option of featuring an ethnic identity (as German or English for instance) or putting their national identity front stage, or may feature their individuality and expect that such avowals will be honored by the other.

Identity enactment occurs not only in a context of sociopolitical power but also in the context of relationship co-construction. I have found that discussion with a relational partner or another group member may change an individual's conclusions about descriptions of contested issues related to identity constitution or descriptions of normative practices. For example, I examined identity problematics among intra- and interethnic friends in the United States (Collier, 1996). I found that individually, some friends said there were no rules of appropriate conduct that applied to their sex as male or female or their ethnic identity, but when friends were given the opportunity to jointly discuss their impressions of rules for each sex and ethnic identity in their friendship, many pairs came up with detailed examples (Collier, 1996). Not only does conversation about identities and norms affect identity enactment but also the relationship with other, context, and topic. Respondents who described themselves as being "Mexican American" at home with grandparents and parents, told interviewers that they may enact more of a "Chicana or Chicano" identity with peers at a Mecha meeting of students at the university (Collier, 1988).

In summary, identities are multiple, overlapping, and contextually constituted and negotiated. Sociopolitical power and group histories constrain options for identity enactment, and relational dialogue may change impressions of norms and contested issues. The salience of the identity depends on such processes as avowal and ascription, as well as interaction with other in-group members and interaction with and discourse from out-group members. A dialectic tension between me or us and you or them is apparent as individuals negotiate their individual, group, and relational identities (Collier, in press).

Epistemological Assumptions

Certain assumptions about the nature of empirical inquiry are fundamental in my interpretive approach and interactionist ethnographic (Prus, 1996) approaches to cultural identity. First, "*Science is a thoroughly hermeneutic or intersubjective inquiry*" (Prus, 1996, p. 213). In both approaches, dialogical intersubjectivity, based on hermeneutics, is a primary epistemological assumption. "A central objective in interactionist ethnography is to provide a careful, balanced, open, and representative voice to the participants" (Prus, 1996, p. 225). Whereas postmodern ethnographers such as Denzin (1990) or cultural-studies scholars such as Fiske (1991) emphasize the centrality of structuralist factors such as class, race, and gender, Prus notes that concentrating on such factors exclusively is "apt to be of limited utility for readers who wish to learn about the life-styles of others in a careful, through, reliable and open manner" (p. 226).

One approach to building scholarly knowledge about cultural identity is to focus on respondents' processes of coming to know who they are in relation to one another. I am primarily interested in studying the problematic process of how persons affiliated with cultural groups who have different histories, practices, and premises, cocreate and make sense of such group identities in social contact with one another. Such an approach is consistent with defining and researching identity as constituted in and by conversation. Cronen and Lang (1994) argue that meaning as use (Wittgenstein, 1953), a constructionist view of communication, may be one useful way to build knowledge about communication and identities. They are concerned with "the relationship between episodes of lived experience and the stories that people tell us in such episodes" (p. 7). They point out that the individual stories shared by people reflect their understanding of the rules (Pearce & Cronen, 1980) and grammar (Wittgenstein, 1974) that emerge and change and constitute their identities and relationships with others.

A constructionist view is consistent with the interactionist ethnographic approach outlined by Prus (1996). Although postmodern critics suggest that all perspectives and theoretical approaches are open to question and deconstruction requires a constant search for alternative interpretations, CIT does privilege the interpretive perspective over others, because this perspective is consistent with the goals of research inquiry and the ontological and epistemological assumptions of CIT.

My intent in inquiry has been to recognize and feature the voices of respondents by involving them in the interpretive process and focusing on their accounts of racial, ethnic, and gender identities in particular contexts of interaction. In my current work I am attempting to increase respondent involvement in the research design and application of results to their communities, a trend in participatory research and among many feminist scholars (Wolf, 1996).

My research on cultural identity has been based on discourse texts, with focus group discussions, dyadic and individual interviews, and open-ended questionnaires. Group members are asked to describe such communicative constructs, processes, and interactions as salient group identities; labels; histories and socialization; norms or rules of appropriate conduct; membering processes; how they learned normative practices; in-group, out-group, or both differences; reactions to and impressions of others' conduct; and conflict management. More recently, to break down the arbitrary barrier between scholar or object of study, I have begun to ask respondents to confirm or provide alternative interpretations (Collier & Bowker, 1994). In this way, respondents play an active role and the researcher or interviewer and respondent or interviewee creates intersubjective interpretations of the discourse. In addition to recalled conversations or interactions between friends, I have recently begun to supplement my interpretations by examining media portrayals of different culture groups and probing label preferences, norms, and views of history and the future, in varied social conversations across varied contexts (Collier & Bornman, in press).

To increase the role of the respondent in interpretations and to increase intersubjectivity in a study of intercultural relationships among women (Collier & Bowker, 1994), we used the following procedures: Initial interviews with respondents were videotaped and a draft of interpretations and thematic categories was written. The draft was shared with the respondents, who provided editorial suggestions, modifications, and additional examples. The additional comments from respondents were then incorporated by the authors into a final draft.

Often, CIT research teams have been composed of what Mirande and Tanno (1993), among others, call insiders and outsiders. For example in a study on intra- and interethnic communication, coauthors included an African American and two Euro-American researchers (Collier, Ribeau, & Hecht, 1986) and a study of intercultural conduct in South Africa (Collier & Bornman, in press) was coauthored by an Afrikaner South African and an ethnically European American from the United States.

Epistemological approaches should be consistent with ontological assumptions. I previously articulated that one of my ontological assumptions is that an important way of knowing and being a member of a cultural group is by aligning with insiders and distancing self from outsiders. I also propose that this orientation and practice should be recognized by researchers and what is attended to epistemologically should include insider or outsider constructions by respondents. Whereas I concur with postcolonial critics who caution us to recognize the dangers of overgeneralizing and overlooking heterogeneity within groups, it is inappropriate to conclude that insider or outsider dichotomies are not relevant to respondents' experiences. The self is a "polysemic site of articulation for multiple identities and voices" (Conquergood, 1991, p. 185), and insider- or outsiderness as well as the boundaries and margins are places in which identities are constituted. Because humans create a social reality based partly on insider and outsider judgments, I incorporate those terms in my work, with the caveat that some individuals are both insider and outsider, and there are degrees of acceptance among, and distance between, group members.

In research on African American ethnic identity, we articulated an ontological property of cultural identity about how identities are negotiated by individuals across situations, in relationships and in groups, that points to the need for different research perspectives and methods to inquiry about cultural identity (Hecht et al., 1993). People experience their identities as contextually bound; that is, some identities are personal and unique to the individual, others are dyadic, such as in friendships, and others are communal or group oriented. Consequently, researchers may focus on individuals, on friends or family members as they are together, or on group members during rituals or community gatherings. Although much of my early research on CIT is from the individual frame, in which I ask individuals to describe impressions of their cultural identities, more recently I have used a dyadic frame to view the joint negotiation of norms and critical points among ethnic friends (Collier, 1996), and we used focus group discussions to view cultural identity enactment and in-group negotiation in South Africa (Collier & Bornman, in press).

It is important, within an interpretive perspective to cultural identity construction, to recognize the utility of different frames of analysis. Avowal and ascription processes may be compared and contrasted and additional normative patterns and constitutive beliefs described. For instance, we found that respondents were easily able to move from recounting individual experiences and interpretations of conduct to descriptions of out-group conduct and resulting in-group reactions (Collier et al., 1996). Cuban Americans, Iranian Americans, American Indians, and Chinese Americans articulated some similar norms for each ethnic group, including respect for elders and primary language; differences emerged in intergroup norms regarding language and use of such nonverbal cues as silence. Comparing the in-group and intergroup frames, we analyzed the discourse by noting ontological and epistemological dialectic tensions. Chinese American and Iranian American discourses were based on clearer status hierarchies and higher power distance than the other two groups, whereas the urban American Indians described the use of high power distance in community contexts with elders present and an orientation toward equality with an out-group member.

Coding and interpretive procedures have evolved over the course of the CIT research program to involve insiders and outsiders and dialogue among the coders. For example, in the study of South African friendship norms and constitutive categories, we used focus group discussions (Collier & Bornman, in press). Focus groups place the emphasis on socially negotiated interpretations, rather than researcher interpretations, of observed patterns (Morgan, 1988). Consequently, we made the choice to study in-group dialogue and see whether patterns emerged in descriptions of friendship communication and experiences with out-group members.

Because one coauthor, an Afrikaner, was from the ethnic group with the most socioeconomic power when the data was collected, the focus groups were facilitated by the "outsider," a U.S. American. Anderson (1992) points out that, whereas it is not appropriate to assume that "white scholars are unable to generate research with people of color as research subjects," "white scholars must work in ways that acknowledge and challenge white privilege and question how such privilege may shape research experiences" (p. 51). Frey and Fontana (1993) also influenced us in their recommendation to obtain polyphonic accounts and minimize the role of ethnographer or participant observer, to diminish author bias and influence. In an attempt to acknowledge the biases that are inherent in our race and class backgrounds, interpretations of the transcripts were gathered from insider members of each cultural group, blacks, coloreds, Asian/Indians, Afrikaners, and British, in South Africa.

Finally, in a recent study, I combined insider-outsider interpretations of the intersections between ethnic and friendship identities (Collier, 1996). I asked an insider from the African American, Asian American, European American, and Latino ethnic groups, and an outsider from one of the above groups, to independently code open-ended questionnaire descriptions of friendship norms and patterns. Then the insider and outsider were paired and, through dialogue together, reached consensus about emergent thematic categories. In that study, not only did friends talk together to see if intersubjective agreement could be reached about rules for their friendship as the initial procedure, but then, coders had to reach intersubjective agreement for a category to be described in the final draft.

RECONCILIATION AND THE NEED
FOR CONTINUED DIALOGUE

Within the CIT approach, race, ethnicity, and sex, as well as contextually enacted identities, are social constructs. Respondents in my study of South African experiences with discrimination (Collier, 1994, p. 22) called race, sex, nationality, and ethnicity "involuntary affiliations" and many, when asked to describe instances of prejudice and discrimination, talked about the power of ascriptions from others in affecting them negatively. Several respondents, who identified themselves as black or colored, noted that race was a categorization based on genetics or biology and did not represent, as one respondent said, "my heart or my thinking" (Collier, 1994, p. 22). I am now beginning to acknowledge the paradoxes and complexities of interpreting the role of race and identity, given respondent preferences and avowals of a racial identity as black South African and, later in the conversation, describing the limitations of race as a social category. Clearly, race as a category of identity must be interpreted as interpellated in political, economic, and historical context, to understand the preference for avowing an identity of black South African, as well as in relational context, to understand the preference for seeing beyond race to individual character and heart.

Using the CIT framework, my colleagues and I (Collier, 1991; Collier & Bornman, in press; Collier et al., 1996) have examined the relationship between respondents' self-identified affiliation with national, racial, and ethnic groups and the extent to which respondents share such identity patterns as in-group norms, experiences with out-group discrimination and prejudice, and constitutive ideas and strategies for managing conflict. In each study, an overall pattern of in-group differences has been found, as well as individual differences, lending support for the power of historical ascriptions, colonial and imperial influences on identity formation, and the power of individuals to contextually negotiate and cocreate emergent identities. Adding greater depth to "how the categories of whiteness and blackness, masculinity and femininity, labor and class came historically into being in the first place" (McClintock, 1995, p. 16) can facilitate our understanding of the ontological and epistemological processes of interlocutors.

Postcolonial claims that race, class, and ethnicity are socially and historically constrained, paradoxically involuntary or voluntary, and socially constructed (hooks, 1990; McClintock, 1995; McGoldrick, 1994), are consistent with my assumptions and approach to CIT. I have studied the interpellation of membership constructions and identity enactment in multiple configurations of identity as in-group, out-group and in intergroup contexts. One example is the recent study in which I and my colleagues examined the dialectic tensions between ethnic and national identities among members of four ethnic groups in the United States (Collier et al., 1996). I have just begun, however, to appreciate the historical and contextual complexities of race and power and the interaction moves featuring individual differences in some intercultural contexts and featuring race groups as cultural groups in other intercultural contexts. Incorporating the role of power, privilege, history, and ideology in the social construction of group identities will strengthen the validity and coherence of our knowledge claims.

I am attempting to increase the recognition of individual and group agencies and the multiple strategies that are used by in-group and out-group members as they negotiate their boundaries and peripheries. For example, I am working on a collaborative project examining how adolescents in a particular school in London maintain, challenge, and negotiate different national, ethnic, and gender identities in intercultural friendships, within an educational context that is oriented toward reinforcing traditional English values and norms of conduct (Collier & Thompson, 1997).

I have consistently recognized the power of naming (Tanno, 1994) and asked respondents to provide their own group label preferences (if any) in in-group and out-group contexts. More recently, I asked respondents to talk about what the in-group and out-group labels mean to them in their contexts of use. I found that many more respondents describe themselves as multiethnic and use such terms as "being on the margin" (Collier et al., 1996, p. 22) or "having two faces" (Collier et al., 1996, p. 30). Thus, I am attempting to lessen the essentialism apparent in some anthropological approaches (Bhabha, 1995) cross-cultural, and intercultural approaches to cultural identities. I have defined European Americans as ethnic in my work in CIT; there is no "center" that is nonethnic (Bhabha, 1995).

My current research reflects my recognition of the power of interaction and the value of a phenomenological approach (Langsdorf, 1994). The starting point or focus, for me, has become the interaction between intercultural friends or discussion of group members, informed by notions of history, socialized values, and normative practices. My goals are generally consistent with the four major concerns of phenomenologically oriented researchers outlined by Langsdorf (1994): to focus on the constitution of cultural identities as they are enacted in historical and social contexts, commitments to reflexivity and multiple interpretations, and an approach to meaningfulness as "culturally specified, morally attuned, socially negotiated, and locally applied" (p. 8). Given those goals, I need to pay much more attention to historical, as well as power and social class issues, to inform my interpretations and understand the local occurrences of interaction. I also see that much of my work lacks discussion of competing interpretations, let alone reflexive discussions of my role of privilege as it might affect the dialogue that emerges.

Concerns regarding the "crises of representation" raised about ethnographic research apply equally to the interpretive approach to CIT. I have incorporated several new procedures into the design and data gathering, for an ongoing series of studies on intercultural relationships as interpersonal alliances and the paradoxes and dilemmas of cultural identity difference in friendships, to answer such critiques. Interviews have been designed as more open-ended and collaborative, and multiple sessions with respondents are planned. Data on interethnic friendships will be gathered through dyadic interviews and focus groups of pairs of friends to compare the social construction of identities from dyadic and group frames. Such a move will also increase the polyphonic voices of the respondents. With regard to issues of "Who can speak for the group?" and the "myth of authenticity" (Griffiths, 1995), questions and dialogue with respondents will be incorporated to probe them.

As well, respondents are being asked to select labels, describe norms, and talk about what they consider to be "authentic" and how they know when someone is a "real or recognizable group member" (Wieder & Pratt, 1990, p. 48) and when someone is an outsider. Persons who identify themselves as outsiders are being asked to describe their experiences. Individuals with multiple identities and those who consider themselves marginalized can all be involved to compare and contrast different levels of insider or outsider or middleness. In the focus group context, such discourse can reveal a great deal about what is considered to be authentic, appropriate, and salient and to identify the force of particular norms of conduct.

Future research can be more participatory; Wolf (1996) outlines a series of feminist studies based in such a tradition. In CIT research, respondents can be asked to edit and add questions to the interview guide as well as add questions to the focus group discussion. They can also be solicited in follow-up meetings to talk about ways in which the findings of the research can be applied and used in their own communities and friendships.

Finally, I am moving away from studying intercultural communication competence, as a process of negotiation of mutually appropriate and effective conduct, to competence as problematic and the social construction of intercultural relationships as interpersonal alliances. Such alliances are based in dialectic tensions between being individual and having a cultural group identity or identities, constructing separate cultural identities and a joint relationship, managing power and status differences, in-group support or challenges, and confirming each other's cultural identity as similar and different (Collier, in press). The qualities and enactment of alliances are co-constructed and situated communicative processes.

I have come to see that competence, a central issue in my early work, is a construct that is based on implicit privilege. On the basis of my argument on ethnographic traditions, I maintained in the past that acceptance into a cultural group is contingent on the ability to demonstrate competent communication conduct. Relevant questions from postcolonial critics include, "Competence and acceptance from whom? Who decides the criteria? Who doesn't? Competent or acceptable on the basis of what social and historical context?" To assume that ontologically interlocutors negotiate mutual rules of appropriate conduct is to deny the power of ideology, historical structures, and limitations in the field of choices.

I am learning the value of approaching cultural identity enactment in the context of historical and social relationships. As well, I am coming to appreciate the value of viewing interpretation in the context of critical theory and ethnography as performance-based. "Identity is more like a performance in process than a postulate, premise, or originary principle" (Conquergood, 1991, p. 185). Conquergood (1991) explains that the "performance paradigm privileges particular, participatory, dynamic, intimate, precarious, embodied experience grounded in historical process, contingency and ideology" (p. 187).

Although some of the goals of ethnographic and interpretive research are similar, my specific goals and methodological choices are also different. I am convinced of the value of asking respondents to "make mindful" processes that have become invisible or transparent and describe conduct that they oftentimes do unconsciously. When probed, respondents are readily able to reflect on their experiences and perform interpretations and tell stories about selves and others in ways that may not emerge in ethnographic observations. Whereas I concur with Conquergood (1991) when he argues that cultural knowledge is embodied in the gesture, action, and specific context of doing the identity, and that discursive descriptions on questionnaires or in interviews miss out on this richness, I also hold that a part of being human is to reflect on and evaluate the doing or being of their cultural identities throughout everyday activities. Consequently asking respondents, as well as researchers, to share their sense-making processes and analytical frames is a move toward recognizing how our identities get co-constructed.

RECOGNIZING MYSELF AS
INTIMATELY ENGAGED PARTICIPANT

The relationship between researcher and respondent deserves more attention in my future research of CIT. To focus on this relationship is to focus also on the relationship between researcher ontology and researcher epistemology. As a European American, middle-class white female, I have a great deal of unearned privilege and sociocultural power. In my past research, I have tended to de-emphasize the power of the context and its attendant history and ideology, partly because I have relatively high privilege and power. In my everyday conduct and my academic projects, I can and do take for granted such factors. My academic training and role models, who were primarily European American upper-middle class males, taught me to assume that individuals have choices in conduct and can mutually negotiate relationships and rules of appropriate behavior and obtain positive outcomes. Early scholars in intercultural communication taught me that the best theorizing included explanations and predictions of interpersonal conduct based on culture-general variables.

I have just begun to realize the power of transparency and invisible assumptions, the taken-for-granted presuppositions, that form my own identity as a Euro-American woman in the academy. One method by which groups who have sociocultural power keep their power is by reinforcing those assumptions until they become invisible to insiders. They become the taken-for-granted norm or standard to which everyone else is held. To insiders, the use of the label "American" to designate national identity as citizens of the United States is an acceptable and common normative practice that is unconsciously followed. To a Canadian or Latin American, it can be a presumptuous and ethnocentric label. Postcolonial critics appropriately call for such invisible assumptions to be interrogated and the "insider" normative standard to be open to question, just as international feminists call for recognition of the voices of women, heretofore the silent majority of victims of economic, political, and social oppression worldwide (Morgan, 1996).

I find it is much easier (and familiar) in the academy to be what I now recognize as imperialist and colonialist, to focus on developing more sophisticated ways to argue the merits and advocate the utility of my approach to cultural identity theory as if it is a commodity that I own and must strategically market and sell. This process is rather diametrically opposed to inviting conversation about possible invisible assumptions, hegemonic tendencies in my work, or unrecognized sources of privilege and power. With this chapter, I hope to create the beginning of a dialogue among researchers from a wide array of perspectives, oriented "to understand, appreciate, and value the worlds and perspectives of the others" (hooks, 1994a, p. 54). I am not dismissing my responsibility to continue to interrogate my own assumptions and be reflexive, nor do I wish to place the burden of critique on others; I am calling for the kind of dialogue that hooks (1989) describes as central to growth and transformation and moves against domination (Foss, 1997).

A final observation is that although I was enculturated with the need to write in an "objective" style, eliminating any references to works that would allow the reviewer to pinpoint my identity, I have chosen to articulate and begin to question my positions and biases and places of privilege. "Blind review" procedures are not consistent with interrogating one's own race, sex, ethnicity, nationality, and academic training, nor are they consistent with applying critiques to one's own research program. In this chapter, I have chosen to move from third person to first person, from the objective overviewer of postcolonial scholarship to the intimately engaged participant in research on cultural identity. With self-reflexivity comes the need for change.

REFERENCES

Allport, G. W. (1954). *The nature of prejudice.* Garden City, NY: Doubleday.

Anderson, J. A. (1992). On the ethics of research in a socially constructed reality. *Journal of Broadcasting and Electronic Media, 36,* 353-357.

Ashcroft, B., Griffiths, G., & Tiffin, H. (1995). Ethnicity and indigeneity: Introduction. In B. Ashcroft, G. Griffiths, & H. Tiffin (Eds.), *The post-colonial studies reader* (pp. 213-214). New York: Routledge.

Banks, J. A. (1987). *Teaching strategies for ethnic studies* (4th ed.). Boston: Allyn & Bacon.

Bhabha, H. K. (1995). Cultural diversity and cultural differences. In B. Ashcroft, G. Griffiths, & H. Tiffin (Eds.), *The post-colonial studies reader* (pp. 206-209). New York: Routledge.

Brislin, R. (1986). Prejudice and intergroup communication. In W. Gudykunst (Ed.), *Intergroup communication* (pp. 74-85). London: Arnold.

Brown, P., & Levinson, S. (1978). Universals in language usage: Politeness phenomena. In E. N. Goody (Ed.), *Questions and politeness: Strategies in social interaction* (pp. 56-89). Cambridge, UK: Cambridge University Press.

Cameron, D., Frazer, E., Harvey, P., Rampton, M. B., & Richardson, K. (1992). *Researching language: Issues of power and method.* New York: Routledge.

Carbaugh, D. (1990). Intercultural communication. In D. Carbaugh (Ed.), *Cultural communication and intercultural contact* (pp. 151-176). Hillsdale, NJ: Lawrence Erlbaum.

Carbaugh, D. (1991). Communication and cultural interpretation. *Quarterly Journal of Speech, 77,* 336-342.

Clifford, J., & Marcus, G. E. (Eds.). (1986). *Writing culture: The poetics and politics of ethnography.* Berkeley: University of California Press.

Collier, M. J. (1988). A comparison of conversations among and between domestic culture groups: How intra- and intercultural competencies vary. *Communication Quarterly, 36,* 122-124.

Collier, M. J. (1991). Conflict competence within African, Mexican, and Anglo American friendships. In S. Ting-Toomey & F. Korzenny (Eds.), *Cross-cultural interpersonal communication* (pp. 132-154). Newbury Park, CA: Sage.

Collier, M. J. (1994, July). *The forms and functions of recalled instances of prejudice and discrimination among cultural groups in South Africa.* Paper presented at a meeting of the International Conference for Language and Social Psychology, Brisbane, Australia.

Collier, M. J. (1996). Communication competence problematics in ethnic friendships. *Communication Monographs, 63,* 314-336.

Collier, M. J. (in press). Intercultural friendships as interpersonal alliances. In J. Martin, T. Nakayma, & L. Flores (Eds.), *Readings in cultural contexts.* Mountain View, CA: Mayfield.

Collier, M. J., & Bornman, E. (in press). Intercultural friendships in South Africa: Norms for managing differences. *International Journal of Intercultural Relations.*

Collier, M. J., & Bowker, J. (1994, November). *U.S. American women in intercultural friendships.* Paper presented at a meeting of the Speech Communication Association, New Orleans, LA.

Collier, M. J., Ribeau, S. L., & Hecht, M. L. (1986). Intercultural communication rules and outcomes within three domestic cultural groups. *International Journal of Intercultural Relations, 10,* 439-457.

Collier, M. J., & Thomas, M. (1988). Identity in intercultural communication: An interpretive perspective. In Y. Kim & W. Gudykunst (Eds.), *Theories of intercultural communication* (International and Intercultural Communication Annual, Vol. 12, pp. 99-120). Newbury Park, CA: Sage.

Collier, M. J. & Thompson, J. (1997, May). *Intercultural adaptation among friends: Managing identities across contexts and relationships.* Paper presented at a meeting of the Social Psychology of Language, Ottawa, Canada.

Collier, M. J., Thompson, J., & Weber, D. (1996, November). *Identity problematics among U.S. ethnics.* Paper presented at a meeting of the Speech Communication Association, San Diego, CA.

Conquergood, D. (1991). Rethinking ethnography: Towards a critical cultural politics. *Communication Monographs, 58,* 179-194.

Conquergood, D. (1992). Ethnography, rhetoric and performance. *Quarterly Journal of Speech, 78,* 80-123.

Cronen, V., & Lang, P. (1994). Language and action: Wittgenstein and Dewey in the practice of therapy and consultation. *Human Systems: The Journal of Systematic Consultation & Management, 5,* 5-43.

Delgado, F. P. (1994). The complexity of Mexican American identity: A reply to Hecht, Sedano and Ribeau and Mirande and Tanno. *International Journal of Intercultural Relations, 18,* 77-84.

Denzin, N. (1990). Researching alcoholics and alcoholism in American society. In N. D. Denzin (Ed.), *Studies in symbolic interaction* (pp. 81-101). Greenwich, CT: JAI.

During, S. (1995). Postmodernism or postcolonialism. In B. Ashcroft, G. Griffiths, & H. Tiffin (Eds.), *The postcolonial studies reader* (pp. 125-129). New York: Routledge.

Fiske, J. (1991). Writing ethnographies: Contribution to a dialogue. *Quarterly Journal of Speech, 77,* 330-335.

Foss, S. K. (1997). bell hooks. In S. K. Foss, K. A. Foss, & C. L. Griffin (Eds.), *Feminist rhetorical theories.* Manuscript submitted for publication.

Frey, L., & Fontana, A. (1993). The group interview in social research. In D. L. Morgan (Ed.), *Successful focus groups* (pp. 20-34). Newbury Park, CA: Sage.

Goffman, E. (1959). *The presentation of self in everyday life.* Garden City, NY: Doubleday.

González, A., Houston, M., & Chen, V. (1994). Introduction. In A. González, M. Houston, & V. Chen (Eds.), *Our voices: Essays in culture, ethnicity, and communication* (pp. xiii-xxi). Los Angeles: Roxbury.

Griffiths, G. (1995). The myth of authenticity. In B. Ashcroft, G. Griffiths, & H. Tiffin (Eds.), *The postcolonial studies reader* (pp. 237-241). New York: Routledge.

Hall, S. (1995). New ethnicities: The myth of authenticity. In B. Ashcroft, G. Griffiths, & H. Tiffin (Eds.), *The postcolonial studies reader* (pp. 223-227). New York: Routledge.

Hecht, M. L., Collier, M. J., & Ribeau, S. (Eds.). (1993). *African American communication.* Newbury Park, CA: Sage.

hooks, b. (1989). *Talking back: Thinking feminist, thinking black.* Boston: South End.

hooks, b. (1990). *Yearning: Race, gender, and cultural politics.* Boston: South End.

hooks, b. (1994a). *Outlaw culture: Resisting representations.* New York: Routledge.

hooks, b. (1994b). *Teaching to transgress: Education as the practice of freedom.* New York: Routledge.

Kim. Y. Y. (1995). Identity development: From cultural to intercultural. In H. B. Mokros (Ed.), *Information and behavior: Vol. 5. Interaction and Identity* (pp. 347-369). New Brunswick, NJ: Transaction Books.

Langsdorf, L. (1994). Why phenomenology in communication research? *Human Studies, 17,* 1-8.

Marcus, G. E., & Fischer, M. (1986). *Anthropology as cultural critique.* Chicago: University of Chicago Press.

Martin, J. (1997). Understanding whiteness in the United States. In L. Samovar & R. Porter (Eds.), *Intercultural communication: A reader* (pp. 54-62). Belmont, CA: Wadsworth.

McClintock, A. (1995). *Imperial leather.* New York: Routledge.

McGoldrick, M. (1994). Culture, class, race, and gender. *Human Systems: The Journal of Systemic Consultation & Management, 5,* 131-153.

Minh-ha, T. T. (1995). No master territories. In B. Ashcroft, G. Griffiths, & H. Tiffin (Eds.), *The postcolonial studies reader* (pp. 215-219). New York: Routledge.

Mirande, A., & Tanno, D. V. (1993). Understanding interethnic communication and research: A rose by any other name would smell as sweet. *International Journal of Intercultural Relations, 17,* 381-388.

Morgan, D. L. (1988). *Focus groups as qualitative research* (Qualitative Research Methods, Vol. 16). Newbury Park, CA: Sage.

Morgan, R. (Ed.). (1996). *Sisterhood is global.* New York: Feminist Press.

Parry, B. (1995). Problems in current theories of colonial discourse. In B. Ashcroft, G. Griffiths, & H. Tiffin (Eds.), *The postcolonial studies reader* (pp. 36-44). New York: Routledge.

Pearce, W. B., & Cronen, V. (1980). *Communication, action, and meaning.* New York: Praeger.

Prus, R. (1996). *Symbolic interaction and ethnographic research.* Albany: State University of New York Press.

Sachs, H. (1984). On doing "being ordinary." In J. M. Atkinson & J. Heritage (Eds.), *Structures of social action: Studies in conversation analysis* (pp. 413-429). Cambridge, UK: Cambridge University Press.

Shome, R. (1996). Postcolonial interventions in the rhetorical canon: An "other" view. *Communication Theory, 6,* 40-59.

Spivak, G. C. (1990). *The postcolonial critic: Interviews, strategies, dialogues.* New York: Routledge.

Tajfel, H. (1978). Interindividual and intergroup behaviour. In H. Tajfel (Ed.), *Differentiation between social groups* (pp. 27-60). San Diego: Academic Press.

Tanno, D. (1994). Names, narratives, and the evolution of ethnic identity. In A. González, M. Houston, & V. Chen (Eds.), *Our voices: Essays in culture, ethnicity, and communication* (pp. 30-36). Los Angeles: Roxbury.

Ting-Toomey, S. (1988). Intercultural conflict styles: A face-negotiation theory. In Y. Kim & W. Gudykunst (Eds.), *Theories in intercultural communication* (pp. 213-238). Newbury Park, CA: Sage.

van Dijk, T. (1987). *Communicating racism: Ethnic prejudice in thought and talk.* Newbury Park, CA: Sage.

Wieder, D. L., & Pratt, S. (1990). On being a recognizable Indian among Indians. In D. Carbaugh (Ed.), *Cultural communication and intercultural contact* (pp. 45-64). Hillsdale, NJ: Lawrence Erlbaum.

Wittgenstein, L. (1953). *Philosophical investigations.* Cambridge, MA: Blackwell.

Wittgenstein, L. (1974). *Philosophical grammar.* Cambridge, MA: Blackwell.

Wolf, D. L. (Ed.). (1996). *Feminist dilemmas in fieldwork.* Boulder, CO: Westview.

8

"Diversity" Versus "National Unity"

The Struggle Between Moderns, Premoderns, and Postmoderns in Contemporary South Africa

ERIC LOUW • Charles Sturt University, Bathurst, Australia

South African society is characterized by conflict and turmoil. In the wake of apartheid's collapse, social sense making is in a state of flux. A struggle is underway over what it is going to "mean" to be South African. This chapter aims to rethink South Africa by moving beyond the more traditionally used categories of race and class,[1] and delves, instead, into the cultural discourses that underpin the conflicts within what Lash (1990) calls a "cultural economy" (p. 5).

New ways of looking at South Africa emerge by focusing attention on the conflicts between premodern, modern, and postmodern discourses or cultures. These three cultures complement South Africa's three modes of production of a prefordist rural subsistence sector, a fordist industrial sector, and a postfordist "information" sector. These three cultural discourses and modes of production are, of course, not discrete. Rather, modernity, premodernity, and postmodernity blur into each other at their margins and interpenetrate and influence each other in a complex intermeshing process.[2] Furthermore, in South Africa these three "cultures" overlap and intersect with race, class, and political allegiance in a particular way because of how South Africa underwent a skewed modernization process—a process skewed due to the influence of the National Party's (NP) apartheid logic, which aimed for the production of a modern white state in Africa.[3] This skewed development left millions of (black) South Africans outside of the modernization process, and those blacks who were incorporated into this development process were given as few resources as the system felt it could get away with. The result is that today many black South Africans are premodernites or "semi"-modernites (i.e., only half integrated into modernist discourse). In other words, apartheid society skewed the allocation of media and education resources—hence, one's position in the race pecking order (white at the top, then Indian, then colored, then black) played a significant part in deciding one's class position and, hence, one's access to resources. This, in turn, has affected whether one is likely to be a postmodernite, modernite, or premodernite today. Political allegiance, in turn, strongly correlates with race and class position and which of the above three discourses or cultures one is comfortable with.

South African premoderns are those rural blacks who remain rooted in a traditional African culture. The 10 black homelands or *bantustans* created during the apartheid era are where this way of life has survived. Economically these areas are prefordist, with subsistence agriculture forming the basis of economic life. Nevertheless, most males from these areas do have experience with fordist relations of production, because virtually all homeland men have at some stage been migrant laborers in South Africa's cities or mines (Wilson & Ramphele, 1989, pp. 199-200). The money sent back to the homelands by these migrants, to support their wives and children, forms a significant input into these rural economies (Wilson & Ramphele, 1989, pp. 62-63). Most premodern South Africans now also have family members who have permanently relocated to the cities (usually to the squatter areas) with whom they continue to interact. Hence, South Africa's black rural population constitutes a premodernism that has been "modified" by contact with the modern sector. Nevertheless, premodern discourse has proved to be remarkably resilient in the face of the modernist onslaught. Hence, the old premodern Gnosis remains intact—wherein the sacred and profane remain undifferentiated and where autocratic strongmen (i.e., chiefs or *inkosis,* and headmen or *indunas*)[4] and medicine men (*nyangas*)[5] continue to hold sway over village life. The boundary between chief and medicine men is not always clearly delineated (Hammond-Tooke, 1975, p. 30). The black rural population is, in general, deeply conservative. They are generally motivated by a desire to acquire more land (and cattle) and a wish to preserve their traditional way of life (although this becomes less true among the rural youth).

The media play a rather marginal role in the lives of these people. In fact, the only media penetration of any real significance into these traditional rural areas is radio. Currently there are nine (state-controlled) radio stations broadcasting in black South African languages. This "black" radio service was born of the apartheid system in 1952 as "Radio Bantu" (Tomaselli, Tomaselli, & Muller, 1987, p. 51). The objective of Radio Bantu was to encourage the reproduction of premodern African society as an adjunct to the Bantustan policy—that is, separate tribalisms were encouraged as a modified form of the old British "divide-and-rule" policy. Each tribe was given its own homeland government, education system, radio station, and so forth. One of the consequences of apartheid, therefore, is that premodern tribal groups not only survived into the late 20th-century South Africa, they actually had power bases from which to operate. For those with a modernizing agenda (e.g., the African National Congress, the ANC) this has constituted a potential problem. The tension between the ANC and Chief Buthelezi's Inkatha Freedom Party (IFP) are a case in point.

South Africa's large lumpenproletariate population constitutes a transitional group that, although located in urban areas (in squatter shack settlements or hostels), is often more at ease operating within premodern discourses. Nevertheless, as members settle into city life and find work (usually in highly insecure, piecemeal jobs no one else wants) they are inducted into the world of fordism. They constitute a population in transition and, hence, under great stress, battling to survive in a world that premoderns find confusing, as they make the transition from one discourse or mode of production to another (Worsley, 1984, p. 190). Lines of cleavage and conflict in South Africa often slice right through these transitional communities—the more elderly lumpenproletariate often support conservative traditional groupings (as the IFP), and their children (who are being modernized by the urban experience) support the ANC. Hence, the squatter areas and the hostels are often at the cutting edge of violence in the country.

South Africa's industrial modernization process (especially in the 1960s) was unique, giving South Africa's modern population a distinctive character derived from its birth in a racial-capitalist context. South Africa's modernists are rooted in the cities, especially in black townships (such as Soweto). This (modern) township culture was a creation of apartheid's particular brand of fordist development. The NP, during the heyday of apartheid (1950s to 1970s), consisted of modernites. The NP's apartheid policy was constructed on a particular vision of a differentiated, bureaucratized, and industrialized nation-state. Apartheid social planners took modernism's predilection for autonomous, differentiated spheres (Lash, 1990, p. 9) to extremes. In many ways apartheid was but an extreme version of the Dutch modernist social organizing principle of *verzuiling* (pillarization), wherein society was ordered into separate self-regulating social spheres.

Apartheid constituted a mammoth attempt at social engineering in accordance with the logic of rationalized planning (Davenport, 1977, pp. 257-276). Significantly, the NP preferred to refer to their plan as "*separate development* [italics added]," that is, each ethnic group was to "develop" separately (in autonomous spheres from each other). The heart of the exercise was to build a modern (fordist) industrial state in so-called "white South Africa," surrounded by 10 black (homeland) states. The social engineers who built apartheid operated within a realist ontology that (over) stressed ethnicity as the key principle in terms of which social "reality" was to be structured and bureaucratized.

What these apartheid modernizers achieved, however, was (contrary to their original plan) not an industrialization on the basis of white labor but an industrialization dependent on a black working class (Lipton, 1985, pp. 403-404). Hence, by the mid-1970s South Africa's moderns were overwhelmingly an urban black working class. During the second half of the 1980s a black middle class emerged. This black middle class has expanded rapidly during the 1990s. Nevertheless, this new middle class has retained many links with the black working class and continues to share the same modernist world view. Ultimately, the black working and middle classes earn their living from a mass production urban industrial economy. It is a world with which they are comfortable, in a way that parallels the way in which 1950s modernites in the United States were content. These black township moderns tend to consume mass media (mostly radio and television) in a way that parallels media usage in the Western world during the 1950s and 1960s. Black township dwellers still constitute a coherent "mass" and so have not as yet entered the "demassified" world of fragmented media usage. By and large, these black moderns support the ANC. Indeed, they constitute the unshakable core of the ANC's support base and virtually its entire leadership core. Not surprisingly the ANC sees itself as a "mass" organization.

The ANC developed an alternative (anti-apartheid) vision of society, but ironically, it is a vision that remains a product of apartheid's modernizing and realist principles (a sort of inverse mirror image).[6] The ANC's leadership core are black urban dwellers, modernized by the apartheid state's industrialization drive and educated within Bantu Education programs—an education system that disseminated an ideology designed to serve racial capitalism. This ANC constituency may challenge the way apartheid structured "reality," but at a deeper ontological level modern "industrial realism" and instrumental logic are not questioned. In fact, the ANC glorifies mass society and industrial modernization (ANC, 1994): The ANC does not aim to fundamentally change South Africa's existing modernist infrastructure. Rather, the ANC's own policy guidelines say its program is aimed at the "better organization and rationalization of existing systems and resources" (ANC, 1994, p. 6) to facilitate a "redistribution" (Mboweni, 1992, p. 205) of the wealth and opportunities generated by the existing order. Like the NP before them, the ANC believes in development via a national bureaucratically implemented plan (ANC, 1994, p. 10). In short, the

ANC fundamentally operates within a realist worldview, although some premodernist (and hence prerealist) ideas, derived from the ANC's lumpenproletariate and rural supporters, are intermixed into the ANC's generally modernist vision of development (ANC, 1994). The ANC's addition of premodern ideas into its program commenced only 18 months before the 1994 election, when the ANC suddenly realized that it was going to need the votes of rural black people. To achieve this, the ANC made deals with traditional leaders and some homeland leaders (who had previously worked for the apartheid system).

Ultimately, the ANC's leadership core are the products of the NP's modernization program. As such, not only have they imbibed the instrumental logic of industrial realism but they now have a vested interest in maintaining the basic outlines of socioeconomic order created by racial capitalism over the past 40 years (but stripped, of course, of the white supremacy component). This has led the ANC into a modern etatized corporatism built around a deal negotiated between the ANC and NP. In terms of the ANC and NP corporatist settlement, the modern industrial state built by NP modernizers is now to be stabilized by an ANC government. The NP realized that they could not stabilize this socioeconomic order alone because they had insufficient "legitimacy." De Klerk's reform package, and the deal struck with the ANC, was premised on the NP's (conservative) desire to stabilize South Africa.

The ANC's grand vision and large-scale planning (ANC, 1994) exudes an optimism derived from an unquestioned secular (enlightenment or modernist) faith in the inherent rationality of the world. As modernizers their goal is to build a brave new world on the basis of realist metanarratives. With regard to the ANC's discourse, the most easily discernible metanarrative is that of Marxist realism, although the collapse of Soviet communism has resulted in the ANC modifying its policy into a neosocialist "mixed economy" program (Mboweni, 1992, p. 206; McMenamin, 1992, pp. 248-249). Generally though, the ANC still has faith in the capacity of a centralized state to act as the key agent of socioeconomic reconstruction and development (ANC, 1990, p. 66). This leads to an emphasis placed on "mass mobilization" and "mass action" leading toward the capture of the state's bureaucracy so that state power can be mobilized for the modernist development of "the masses of the people" (ANC, 1994, pp. 69-74).

Even a cursory look at South African postmodernites alerts one to a seemingly strong correlation between postmodernity and the penetration of postfordist ("Information Age") media technology. This is not to propose a simplistic McLuhanesque media determinism. But the South African instance does appear to corroborate the view that some correlation exists between a population's immersion in postfordist media and the growth of postmodernist thinking (and discourse)—a correlation that has fascinated many postmodernist thinkers (Harvey, 1989, p. 49). Simply put, in apartheid South Africa different sections of the population were given differential access to postfordist technology or texts (in terms of the race and class positions).

South African postmoderns are those urbanites who were not educationally or economically disadvantaged by apartheid—that is, those people who were able to gain full access to the mediacentric world of the Information Age. In general, a high percentage of white and Indian South Africans were affluent or middle class and thus "information rich." Hence, a very high percentage of whites and Indians—especially those under the age of 35—have been integrated into the global postmodernist discourse. Coloreds have traditionally occupied an intermediary position between whites and blacks, and their economic status has reflected this: Affluence in the colored community is very rare, with coloreds being divided almost equally into a middle-class and working-class group. Hence, a much smaller percentage of coloreds gain access to this postmodern experience. Only a really minuscule number of black South Africans were exposed to the hypersignifications of the postfordist mediacentric world. Essentially two subgroups of black South Africans did gain access to this postmodern experience: first, those black people who learned to use and/or benefit from racial capitalism (such as collaborators administering the homelands and black businessmen) and, second, exiles and students who lived in North America and Europe. (Those exiles who went to African and East European countries—i.e., the bulk of the ANC cadres—were, of course, not exposed to the postmodern experience.)

There is, consequently, a strong correlation, in South Africa, between being postmodern and being part of the country's highly skilled, mostly white or Indian (professional, managerial, information, and financial), postfordist sector. The younger one is, the stronger the correlation.

These postmoderns are, in general, somewhat negative about the ANC's totalizing theme of a state-centered modernization project. Their responses range from bemusement to fear—bemusement because the ANC's belief in Enlightenment metanarratives seems so naive from their postmodern "schizoid" perspective (Harvey, 1989, p. 53) and fear because the ANC's instrumentalist program seems set to undermine postfordist infrastructural needs (of a sophisticated information infrastructure, high-grade education and knowledge production infrastructure, and the debureaucratization of society). This group's postmodern "demassified" worldview and eclectic use of media resources does not sit easily with the ANC's "massified" vision of the world and drives toward a media that will "complement" development needs (see ANC, 1993, pp. 338-339). Consequently, the bulk of this post-modern group appeared to vote for the NP in the 1994 elections. Many, it seems, did so not because they actually supported the NP's polities but, rather, because they hoped the NP would act as a breaking mechanism on the ANC's policies, which they feared would produce "falling standards" and see South Africa slip backward, relative to the rest of the world.

RETHINKING THE SOUTH AFRICAN STRUGGLE

The conventional understanding of South Africa as a society characterized by ethnic, linguistic, racial (Schlemmer, 1977; Van den Bergh, 1967), and class conflicts (Stadler, 1987; Wright, 1977) all have great explanatory power. Ethnic, class, and language divisions are palpably explosive in South Africa. Nevertheless, these conventional categories each miss an important feature of the present sociopolitical struggle—namely, that there is a struggle over the issue of modernization. Modernites are striving for an enhanced modernization process. Many premodernites and postmodernites, on the other hand, are fearful of these modernites and their plans. It is a "fear" often conflated or intertwined with ethnicity and class in the minds of the players. But in any case, in South Africa, ethnicity, language, and class are generally good indicators of premodernity, modernity, and postmodernity anyway. A few examples should suffice to illustrate the intertwinedness of these categories.

As explained earlier, apartheid's race hierarchy influenced one's likely access to media and education resources. This, in turn, has played a large role in influencing one's access to modernity or postmodernity. Furthermore, there are strong correlations between race and class in South Africa.[7] Until 1994, most affluent South Africans were white or Indian. Most of the white and Indian population are middle class, with only a small white and Indian working-class population. (A poor white population first made a reappearance in the late 1980s.) The colored population is divided between a middle and working class. Black South Africans have generally fallen into the category of the rural poor, lumpenproletariate, or working class (although, since the mid-1980s the black middle class has been growing rapidly). In general, those at the top of the South African class hierarchy are largely postmodernites because of their access to postfordist media resources, and so forth. The middle classes of all races, on the other hand, form a transitional category—some are modern, others postmodern, depending on the level and length of their exposure to postfordist technology or texts. The black middle class is relatively new and hence have had only limited exposure, whereas a higher percentage of the white middle class has had more extensive and sustained exposure. Therefore, the black middle class remain overwhelmingly modernites, whereas many of the white middle class (especially the youth) are now at ease within the global postmodern discourse. South Africa's working class operates within fordist relations of production and generally has not been exposed to postfordist technology and its texts. Hence, not surprisingly, workers are almost exclusively modernites: The white working class prefer a neofascist modernity and the black working class, a Marxist modernity.

Language also influences the likely exposure South Africans will have had to modernity or postmodernity. For example, those using English as their home language are more likely to be postmodernites, first, because English is spoken by whites and Indians, who are, in general, more likely to be higher up in the class hierarchy. (During the British colonial era, 1795-1948, there was a strong correlation between being English and occupying a high status position. This correlation weakened after 1948 but never entirely dissipated.) Moreover, English is very much the language of global postfordism, hence English speakers have a natural advantage in accessing the global discourse. At the other extreme, the inability to use either English or Afrikaans means one has had no access to postmodern discourse and almost no access to modern discourse. Hence, those who speak only one of South Africa's indigenous black languages have been effectively "trapped" within premodern discourse. The transitionals between premodernity and modernism tend to be those who are at home with an indigenous black language but who also have a limited knowledge of either English or Afrikaans. South Africa's modernites are able to effectively use either English or Afrikaans (even if it is not their home language).

Rethinking South Africa's crisis and conflict in terms of a struggle for and against modernity does not, therefore, require that one abandon the more conventional categories of ethnicity, language, and class. Rather, it requires that the categories themselves be rethought in terms of a deeper-level ontological dispute over the question of being modern or antimodern.

The ANC constitutes South Africa's new ruling elite. The ANC represents the interests of those South Africans who are modernites or who aspire to being modern. As such, its central project is to build a modern industrial state. Given the value of the nation state as an administrative unit for modern industrial society, it is not surprising to find that the ANC consequently places a very high premium on realizing the etatist project of "nation building"—a unified South African nation is to be built where none currently exists (ANC, 1994, pp. 3, 69). This ANC project is premised on a modernist etatist worldview that is, at heart, a hybrid of the discourses of Third World modernization and Marxist modernization, although modified by the basic pragmatic need to not overly offend the United States and the World Bank. (It is, in part, this pragmatism that has led the ANC into a corporatist settlement with the NP. The worldwide crisis of etatism is simply ignored by the ANC because, as convinced modernists, they have an unshakable belief in rationalist planning, a faith that a better future can be built on the basis of their state-directed national plan. That the South African state is in crisis, is blamed entirely on apartheid. As modernites, those in the ANC have no conceptual framework to even begin contemplating the possibility that the local crisis may be part of a wider postmodern crisis of the state; Janicke, 1990.)

Two sections of the South African population feel threatened by the ANC's vision of state-directed nation building tied to an imposed modernization project. First, the premoderns fear that an ANC development program will crush their traditional African lifestyle because it will force them into a "one-stream" nation-building or modernization program. The ANC's plan as a single dimensional program that eschews lifestyles inimical to modernity will inherently allow no space for "diversity" in the form of premodern communities. The premoderns intuitively recognize this and, therefore, hold a deeply conservative antimodernism.

The postmoderns, on the other hand, fear that the ANC's neosocialist etatist development will effectively channel resources away from postfordist infrastructural needs for four main reasons. First, postfordist infrastructural needs are regarded as "elitist" by the ANC's constituency. Resources are rather to be allocated to those solidly fordist development projects from which the ANC's modern and aspirant modern constituency can directly benefit. Second (tied to the above anti-elitism) a deep anti-intellectualism exists in the ANC's constituency. Postmoderns fear this will lead to a downgrading and leveling downward of educational facilities, which would seriously undermine postfordism's requirement for a highly educated workforce. Third, the ANC's affirmative action program is geared toward enforcing the rapid promotion of black people—that is, creating posts for a population who, because of apartheid, generally only possess fordist and prefordist skills. In such circumstances, enforcing race quotas on employers will, therefore, effectively slow (stop?) postfordist growth. Fourth, because of the above three factors a "brain drain" is rapidly developing in South Africa; those already possessing postfordist skills are leaving, because they believe that an imposed fordist development program is antipathetic to their postmodern interests. The emigration, of course, reinforces the trend toward the emergence of a solidly modernite postapartheid society. These postmoderns are driven by an essential progressive antimodernism.

Hence, one finds the strange situation in post-1990 South Africa that these two widely divergent worldviews on (conservative) premodernity and (progressive) postmodernity have found themselves drawn together into a strange "coalition." It is a coalition born of the perceived common threat that a state geared up to modernization and nation building poses to both. Premoderns and postmoderns want a society that allows for pluralism and "diversity" to provide a "space" for their own differing (nonmodern) interests. The moderns, on the other hand, see "diversity" as a luxury that will detract from the requirements of postapartheid development. The battle lines between those advocating "nation building" and "diversity" have been drawn.

THE LEGACY OF APARTHEID 1:
A MODERN "FORDIST" RULING ELITE

The NP's fordist modernization program resulted in the creation of Africa's largest black working class during the 1960s and 1970s. Simultaneously, the administration of apartheid required a corps of black bureaucrats and security personnel, with the result that a small black middle class was in existence by the end of the 1970s. Following the 1976 Soweto uprising, the business sector launched a program to create a larger black middle class to counterbalance what was seen as the threat of a growing black working-class radicalism. Consequently, the country's black middle class was significantly expanded through the injection of business and government funding in the 1980s.

Nevertheless, a common characteristic shared by South Africa's black middle and working classes is that both groups are urbanites familiar with, and most comfortable within, fordist work practices. Class differences aside, they share the same modern outlook on life. Ultimately, this thorough-going modernism is a function of the way in which black South Africans, because of apartheid, acquired virtually no access to either postfordist technology or postmodern significations.

This has resulted in the survival of a large group of South Africans who are committed to "modernization," "nation building," "nationalization," a strong (centralized) interventionist state, and "mass" politics. What is of real significance is that it is this modern group that constitutes the heart of South Africa's ANC ruling elite. Hence, by skewing the penetration of postfordist technology in favor of whites, Indians, and coloreds, apartheid's legacy now looks set to have significant long-term implications for South Africa's sociopolitical and economic future because future decision making is going to be located in black hands. Perhaps the most significant legacy of apartheid will thus prove to be its creation of a postapartheid modern ruling elite. What is more, it is a modernist group with an emotional attachment to the realist grand narratives of Marxism and social democracy.

If one unravels the ANC constituency, one finds three different sets of interests that, for different reasons, coalesce around the theme of a neosocialist modernization project. First, the black working-class modernites want to "stabilize" (Lash, 1990, p. 16) modern industrialism, such that working class power is strengthened in society. This group also hopes that at least some of their children may improve their lot by succeeding in joining the middle class administrators of the development project. Second, the lumpenproletariate aspire to becoming modern and so want the fordist economic base expanded so as to create jobs for themselves. Third, black middle-class members see their role as administering the modernization and development project, from which they can enrich themselves. This black middle class has consequently adopted a vanguardist approach to development—members see themselves as an [apparatchik] elite who can create and administer the development plan on behalf of the rest of the black population. During the 1980s the working class was the dominant component within the ANC and UDF.[8] During the 1990s, however, the influence of the black middle class has been growing rapidly within the ANC. Hence, by 1996 a senior ANC politician, Jabu Moleketi (Economic Affairs MEC [a provincial cabinet member] in the Gauteng provincial government) could say that ANC government's policy was "to build a patriotic black bourgeoisie" (Malala, 1996). Current trends already indicate that it will be this (growing) black middle class that will be the key beneficiary of postapartheid restructuring in South Africa. The process, described by Fanon, of how this modernist comprador middle class took control in Africa in the 1950s and 1960s, replacing white functionaries with black functionaries (Fanon, 1963, pp. 149-156), is currently being repeated in South Africa.

The South African modernizing elite phenomenon parallels the continued dominance of "modernist" discourse—linked to a deep suspicion, hostility, or both toward postmodernism—among all of Africa's ruling elites. Significantly, a common feature throughout Africa is the low penetration of postfordist technology. Africans consequently remain, for the most part, cut off from the world's information highways and the postmodern significations flowing through these information networks. The majority of Africans live in a premodern world, whereas Africa's ruling elite live in modern cities.

Frantz Fanon's description of the African modernizing elite serves to define the emerging South African pattern as well (Fanon, 1963, pp. 178-179). These African ruling groups are simply comprador administrators of the old neocolonial relations of production put in place during the colonial period (Fanon, 1963, p. 152). Their modern urban lifestyles depend on the maintenance of the expert-driven economies of Africa, which were designed by the colonialists to service the needs of European and North American fordism. A growing problem for African countries is that, as the developed world reorients toward postfordism, there has been a decline in the demand for many of those African products previously required by developed fordist economies. African elite have simply not adapted to these changes, largely because as modernists they have generally failed to even recognize that any shift is underway. The African elite inherited a modern infrastructure from the now-departed settlers whose positions they filled (Fanon, 1963, pp. 155-156). Under the guidance of these comprador modernites, these existing infrastructures have simply been maintained: Africa's peripheral economies have continued to churn out the same old products originally demanded by core fordist industries of the 1940s, 1950s, and 1960s. In consequence, Africa's economies are not only stagnant, they are in decline as the demand for the raw materials of fordism has shrunk. In a sense the failure of Africa's modern ruling elite to adapt to postfordism confirms Fanon's view of their inherent "intellectual laziness" (Fanon, 1963, p. 149).

Examination of the ANC's plans and policy statements reveals that South Africa's new ruling elite espouses the same modernizing aims that have characterized Africa's ruling elites for the past four decades. In essence, the worldview of the ANC elite can be summed up as follows:

- A fordist industrial vision underpins their economic policies (ANC, 1994; Mboweni, 1992). There is no sustained consideration of postfordist developments, and when postfordism is considered, it is in terms of luddite negativity. Postfordism and postmodernity are seen as merely the concerns of the "developed world" and South African whites.

- The ANC has an unshakable faith in state intervention and bureaucracy as mechanisms for implementing development and modernization plans (ANC, 1994, p. 41; Mboweni, 1992, p. 207). And although the ANC has moved away from centralized socialist state planning since the collapse of the East European economic model, there remains a strong commitment toward state intervention to effect the redistribution of wealth from whites to blacks (McMenamin, 1992, pp. 249-252). There is little acknowledgment in ANC policy of the wider world trend toward state shrinkage associated with postfordist postmodern developments (Janicke, 1990).
- For South Africa's black moderns, capturing and using the state to effect economic redistribution plus the development of a patronage system to dispense jobs (Fanon, 1963, pp. 155-156) is the central goal. The objective is to capture the old established fordist positions in society—removing whites from these positions and replacing them with the new aspirant black bourgeoisie. This transfer of personnel is to be effected through an affirmative action policy (McMenamin, 1992, p. 252).
- The inherent etatism of South Africa's moderns is closely intertwined with a strong commitment to creating a "nation-state" through a nation-building program (ANC, 1994, p. 3). Harvey has noted the modernist predilection for wanting to rationally order space and time and their need to create "spaces of power" (Harvey, 1989, p. 258). Within the modernist project the "production of space" is a "political and economic phenomenon" (Harvey, 1989, p. 255). Nation-states have formed "natural" administrative units for fordism. The modernite need for rational control has manifested itself, spatially, as the exercise of political power within the framework of a geographically defined nation-state (Harvey, 1989, p. 275). Through social management, coercion, and education, those within the boundaries of these states are "inducted" into membership of "their nation." For the ANC modernites, "nation building" is a national adjunct to "development."
- As moderns, the ANC have adopted the logic of "mass"-based organization. Concomitantly, class-based politics and trade unionism remain a central feature of the South African political scene. Social movements (such as the Greens) that are such a feature of politics in the developed world (Dalton & Kuechler, 1990) are fringe players in the South African context.
- As modernists, the ANC believes that cultural production has to be organized; that is, cultural production must complement the modernization program. In journalistic terms, this has led to the call for the New World Information Order (Masmoudi, 1979), a media policy that has made an appearance at the South African Broadcasting Corporation since a pro-ANC Board was appointed in 1993. In a similar vein, the resolutions

emerging from a 1989 ANC cultural conference spelled out clearly the themes of planning and organizing culture production (Campschreur & Davendal, 1989, pp. 214-223) and of organizing cultural workers to carry out this task (Masekela, 1989, p. 254). These cultural workers are to restructure cultural "reality" in accordance with the needs of the "social plan." The ANC's is thus a "commanderist" and production-driven "mass" cultural form, designed to complement the needs of nation building (ANC, 1994, pp. 25-36)—a far cry from postmodernism's individualistic consumption-driven culture, with its multiplicity of choices.

- Education and knowledge are also to be subsumed into the nation building and modernization project (ANC, 1994, pp. 30-32). The ANC modernizers place a high premium on building a state education system for the production of technicists in accordance with the needs of development plan (see Wa Thiong'o, 1981). Linked to this, there is an implicit faith in "science" (as realist "grand narrative") as a key to development. Furthermore, of course, compulsory education is the quickest way for a modernizing elite to destroy a premodern sector.[9] The skepticism with which postmoderns view "science," scientifically planned development, and instrumental reason has not as yet entered the consciousness of South Africa's moderns.

- As modernites, they have a linear teleological view of development: For them, modernity is superior to premodernity. Premoderns are "primitive" and need to be "developed."

For both pre- and postmoderns the above modernist or nationalist worldview, if concretized into socioeconomic policy, means oppression. Implementing the ANC's modernization project would seem to require that these two nonmodern groups will have to be compelled to conform.

THE LEGACY OF APARTHEID 2: CONSERVATIVE PREMODERNS

Resistance to the ANC's modernization and nation-building plans arose even before any attempt was made to implement them. Buthelezi's IFP and the Zulu amakosi (traditional leaders) became the key players at formulating premodern resistance from 1990 (the ANC's unbanning) to 1994 (when the ANC came to power). It is resistance that is continuing.

The central feature of the IFP position was its call for federalism as a means for ensuring that "spaces" would remain where a premodern lifestyle could continue. Federal "diversity" was seen as the mechanism for curtailing the ANC's drive toward the creation of a strong (modernizing) centralized state. The ANC's response was that this would per-petuate apartheid's divisions and tribalism.

Modernizing elites are threatening for premoderns because, as Harvey (1989) notes, "modernity can have no respect even for its own past, let alone that of any pre-modern society" (p. 11). From a premodern perspective the ANC modernizers are South Africa's Jacobins, embody-ing the spirit of "creative destruction" (Harvey, 1989, p. 16). As Harvey says of this spirit, "how could a new world be created, after all, without destroying much that had gone before" (p. 16). Hence, many South African premoderns fear what they see as the threat to traditional African society emanating from the modernist impulse toward nation building. For premoderns, nation building translates into the decon-struction of their lifestyle.[10] Not surprisingly then, the IFP's hold over its rural heartland has remained unchallenged (72% voted IFP in the 1996 Kwa Zulu-Natal provincial elections), but former IFP constituents in urban areas are switching to the ANC (*Financial Mail,* 1996, August 5).

The main problem faced by ANC modernizers is that South Africa's premoderns were given power bases by apartheid. A core feature of apartheid was the creation of 10 black homelands. (The idea behind this was that black people were to be "removed" from the South African political scene because they would exercise their political rights in these homelands.) In the process, apartheid empowered tribal premoderns who captured these homeland spaces. In the rest of Africa the premoderns has no means to resist the modernizing elites who assumed control at the end of the colonial period. But in South Africa, premoderns entered the 1990s with their own (homeland) government and patronage structures and their own armies and policy forces. This meant that real premodern resistance to modernization and nation build-ing was possible in a way that it had not been in the rest of Africa.

One of the ways that the ANC has attempted to deal with this problem parallels the approach used by other African modernizing elites, name-ly, buying tradition into a government patronage system. In other words, the ANC seems intent on taking over and using the British-created chieftainship system (just as the NP took it over). This system buys the allegiance of chiefs and headmen by effectively making them civil servants. (They are to be paid by the central state to administer or con-trol rural black areas on behalf of the central government; Davenport, 1977, p. 100.) It is a patronage system designed for the benefit of modernites—the chiefs are paid to ensure an uninterrupted labor supply for the modern economy. As premoderns, these traditional leaders are treated in a condescending fashion by their modernite bosses. (The British treated them in this way, the NP did so, and now the ANC modernites are doing the same.) The ANC created an organization called Contralesa (Congress of Traditional Leaders of South Africa) to take this "patronage message" out to the rural areas before the 1994 elections. Contralesa was remarkably successful in some areas (e.g., Transkei) and very unsuccessful in others (e.g., Kwa Zulu). Prior to the 1994 election, Mandela invested much energy visiting traditional leaders to assure them that their position was not threatened by an ANC government—and promised them that an ANC government would continue to pay their salaries. (Traditional leaders would generally be able to "deliver" their communities *en bloc* as voters, hence buying their allegiance is crucial.) Where persuasion and patronage have not worked, coercion and intimidation have been mobilized by the moderns.

Since 1994, the ANC government has not fared well in its dealings with premoderns. First, the ANC failed in its bid to break the IFP by getting the Zulu king Zwelethini to shift his allegiance from the IFP to the ANC. Second, the ANC failed in its attempts to shift the payment of traditional leaders away from the (IFP controlled) Kwa Zulu-Natal provincial government to the (ANC controlled) central government. The ANC did succeed in buying King Zwelethini into the ANC patronage network, but they completely failed to grasp the full complexities of premodern politics and so they failed to win over the rest of the Zulu amakosi. In the process, Zwelethini was broken politically (Anonymous, 1996). Furthermore, the ANC failed to shift payment of the amakosi to the central government, when the constitutional Court ruled to uphold the Kwa Zulu-Natal Amakosi and Iziphakanyiswa Amendment Bill of 1995 and the Payment of Salaries, Allowances and Other Privileges Ingonyama Bill of 1995 (Naidoo, 1996). As modernists, the ANC have shown an ineptitude in playing premodern politics in their battles with the IFP.

But even more serious for the South African government has been the way in which the ANC has been losing the support of even those premoderns who were aligned to the ANC during the 1994 elections. The loss of support of the Transkei's (Xhosa) traditional leaders is especially galling for the ANC because the Xhosa are generally regarded as constituting the very heart of the ANC's traditional (ethnic) support base. In 1996 the ANC lost the support of Contralesa and the Transkei traditional leaders. The president of Contralesa (who was, at that time, also an ANC member of Parliament), Chief Patekile Holomisa, actually joined the IFP's Butheleze in a protest march against the ANC government's perceived discrimination against traditional leaders (Makhanya, 1996a). Holomisa ultimately resigned as an ANC Parliamentarian and Contralesa formally broke with the ANC. Contralesa also challenged the ANC's new constitution in the Constitutional Court for "inflicting irreparable harm to the entrenched cultural values of the indigenous peoples of South Africa" (because the concerns of traditional leaders were being ignored) (Makhanya, 1996a). By July 1996, the conflict between ANC "modern civic activists" and "traditional chiefs" in the Transkei was being described as constituting a "political challenge to stability" in South Africa (Streek, 1996).

But premodernity is not only a rural issue. Although the premoderns are overwhelmingly rural, they have also spilled over into the urban areas as a lumpenproletariate that has congregated in squatter shack settlements on the fringes of the main cities and as migrant laborers (in hostels). A struggle is going on between the ANC and IFP for the allegiance of this transitional population. The ANC promises an urban modernization program that will provide jobs and houses. This appeals especially to the young lumpenproletariate who wish to settle permanently in the cities and learn to be modern. The IFP promises to fight for spaces where a traditional lifestyle can survive. This appeals to those who see themselves as temporary migrants to the cities; that is, they ultimately wish to have a traditional home base to return to. Because the lumpenproletariate constitute a population who are transitional between premodernity and modernity, the struggle between the modernizers and traditionalists cuts right through this population. Furthermore, the squatter settlements and hostel sites tend to abut directly onto black formal townships, which creates geographically visible modernite and premodernite boundaries. Not surprisingly, much of the bloodiest fighting of the 1990s has taken place in and around the squatter settlements and around hostel sites.[11]

For the ANC modernizers, taming the shack settlements is likely to prove more difficult than imposing control over the traditional rural areas or hostels, because the lumpenproletariate constitute populations in turmoil: Normal social (disciplinary) mechanisms are weak and fragile (with even basic family structures having generally broken down and where no traditional leaders exist to control the area for the central government), the cleavages are raw, the levels of (poverty-induced) desperation are high, and huge population concentrations exist in situations that make policing such areas nearly impossible (e.g., no proper road system exists). For South Africa's nation building and modernizing planners, the rural premoderns and their lumpenproletariate cousins are a serious challenge. Failure to solve this challenge could easily derail their modernization project (as well as the corporatist settlement). In consequence, a high percentage of the country's limited resources will need to be allocated for a military solution to this problem. But the costs of repression, in turn, mean less resources available for meeting the aspirations of the core of the ANC constituency of black modernites.

"NATION BUILDING": A NEW SITE OF STRUGGLE

In the unfolding South African struggle over meaning (and resources) that is shaping up, the discourse of nation building will be central, given that this concept serves as a foundation upon which the ANC has built its modernizing vision. As the modernist nation-building plan is implemented, negative socioeconomic effects for some groups will be concretized. The intervention of coercive state machinery presumably will be required to contain the likely counteraction.

The point is, the ANC's nation building and modernist development program will not complement either the interests or worldviews of all South Africans. The black middle class is set to derive the most benefit from this program (just as this group benefited disproportionately in the rest of postcolonial Africa). The black working class and black aspirant moderns should also derive some benefit from the ANC's program so long as their requirements do not compete (for resources) with the emerging black middle class. Nevertheless, the expectations of the aspirant moderns almost certainly exceed the capacity of the ANC's modernization program to deliver in the short-to-medium term. Consequently, coercion may well need to be applied to control this sector to serve the interests that existing modernites have in a stable socioeconomic order.

The modern unified nation that the ANC seeks to construct will, of necessity, benefit certain sectors more than others. South Africans most likely to benefit will be, for example, those (a) familiar and comfortable with urban fordism and its "mass" infrastructures, (b) most able to mobilize the English language, (c) designated worthy of being recipients of "affirmative action" (blacks and women), and (d) designated as members of "the majority" group (i.e., black). On the other hand, building the ANC's modern unified nation will, of necessity, disadvantage other sectors, for example, those (a) comfortable within the Old Gnosis, (b) only familiar with black African languages, (c) designated as the (nonblack) beneficiaries of apartheid who must now be "penalized," and (d) designated members of "the minority."[12]

Within the context of the tension that will arise from the above state of affairs, the concepts of "nation," "nation building," and "national unity" serve as useful ideological tools to complement the modernist's development program. The concept of "building a unified nation" can help to conceal the new socioeconomic tensions and cleavages emerging in society. First, the modernizing black middle class elite can disguise for themselves the existence of these cleavages (and their own privileged position) by collapsing everyone into the collective rubric of the "South African nation." Second, the ideology of nationhood can serve (if the elite are lucky) to inspire the nonelite to accept their less privileged lot as a form of sacrifice in the task of building and developing their nation. Third, those opposing the new order can, from the perspective of those inside the discourse, be legitimately repressed for opposing the "needs of the nation" (and development). Of course, from within the rationalist instrumentalism of modernity, such opposition is not only unjustified but irrational. Crushing such opposition is not merely necessary, it is sensible.

Three sectors of the population unlikely to embrace the ANC's modern nation-building project are those wishing to remain premodern, postmoderns, and many nonblack moderns.[13] Nevertheless, when it comes to resistance, the responses from these groups are likely to differ. Postmoderns are unlikely to resist because, with their skills, they are highly mobile. The most likely postmodern response will be emigration, not struggle. Premoderns, on the other hand, are highly immobile. Their choice becomes acquiescence or resistance. The ANC and IFP conflict indicates that many premoderns do not intend to acquiesce. Nonblack moderns are the sector whose responses are not easy to predict.[14] In ontological terms, they should have little difficulty in joining a modern nation-building project. Furthermore, nonblack modernites have the skills to benefit from the ANC and NP corporatist deal. Nevertheless, in the South African context, race is a complicating factor. For this reason, many white moderns, in particular, see no place for themselves in a "unified" nation on the basis of ANC majoritarianism. Hence, after premoderns, white moderns are the group most likely to engage in armed rebellion against the ANC nation-building program. Likewise, race complicated the response of many premoderns during the 1994 election. Premoderns turned out in huge numbers in the homelands to vote for the ANC, in response to the ANC's black nationalist discourse and because they believed the ANC would give them white-owned farmland.[15]

The exact alliance of forces that will emerge against the ANC's nation-building project (and the tactics they will use) is not yet clear, but signs of a growing alliance between traditional leaders in Kwa Zulu (IFP) and the Transkei (Contralesa) must be of grave concern to the

ANC government. But whatever shape it takes, it seems assured that there will be resistance (and repression) in the future.

THE LEGACY OF APARTHEID 3: RULING ELITE "RESISTANCE" TO POSTMODERNIZATION

Postmodernism stands in a relationship of incompatibility with organized capitalist structures; that is, postmodernity has a relationship with the disorganization of capitalist economy and society (Lash, 1990, p. 18). This argument can be taken further. Postmodernism is incompatible with, and threatening to, modernists and modern industrial economies in general. Neither capitalist nor socialist modernizers will feel comfortable with postmodernity. In fact, postmodernity appears to be even more threatening to socialist modernites than capitalists, because it does not merely disagree with the (surface) details of socialist planning, it challenges (at a deeper ontological level) the very instrumentalism of planning itself. For the ANC's neosocialist planners a postmodernite vision is at best bizarre, at worst dangerous.

For the ANC's modernist constituency, the postmodern worldview is incomprehensible. The ANC's constituency operates simultaneously within two "fixed meaning systems," namely, a neosocialist grand narrative and a black nationalist narrative. From within these "fixed positions" the world "makes sense"; "the enemy" is clear; that is, the ANC's constituency understands, and is opposed to, "the older established (white) bourgeoisie" (Lash, 1990, p. 20). These "old bourgeoisie" are understandable to the ANC modernizers because, ultimately, they operate in the same ontological realm of (seemingly) "fixed" fordist-derived meanings and identities.

But the new postindustrial middle classes construct their identities "along lines of difference, with looser group, looser grid and classifications whose valuative component is minor . . . a habitus which is on the basis of principles of toleration of difference in others" (Lash, 1990, p. 23). Their meanings are "nomadic" (Harvey, 1989, p. 44)—that is, postfordists

> have a whole range of different sources of identity than the older groupings and are likely to perceive their own "ideal interests" in terms of a whole different range of symbolism and a whole different range of cultural objects than do the older grouping. (Lash, 1990, p. 23)

These new identities and interests, and the appeal that "difference" has for postmoderns, does not sit easily with the ANC's nation-building project. A centralized, modernizing nation-state does not serve their ("transnational") postfordist interests. As postmoderns they must inherently have difficulty accepting centralized plans, grand-narrative-derived "truths," and corporatist settlements.

Not surprisingly, South Africa's postmoderns deploy the discourses of "pluralism," "market force," "strong local government," toleration for "others," "differences," and "decentralization." For the ANC, this sounds like support for everything they oppose—capitalism ("market forces"), apartheid ("pluralism" and "difference"), and the principle of homelands for Zulus and Afrikaners ("strong local government"). This is, of course, not what the postmoderns are saying, but cross-discourse readings almost inevitably lead to misinterpretation.

For South Africa's postmoderns, the threat posed to themselves by modernization is not of the same direct nature that it is for the premoderns. Postmodernites are not an ANC "target" per se, except in the wider sense that "the elite" are generally to be "penalized" within the ANC's plans (ANC, 1994). The threats posed by "redistribution," "rectifying imbalances," and "affirmative action" are rather diffuse. In fact, a key feature of the ANC "reconstruction" planning, namely, affirmative action, is not a direct threat to postmodernites, because few of the ANC's constituency (for whom posts need to be created) currently have the skills to occupy postfordist jobs (even in "token" roles). The threat is, rather, posed to those occupying the old fordist bourgeois posts (Lash, 1990, p. 20), especially those in parastatal enterprises. The threat that is posed to postmodernites is more circuitous. A danger is that, if the wider economy is forced into a narrowly conceived fordist development framework, the existing postfordist infrastructure may effectively atrophy. None other than a former ANC Minister of Telecommunications, Pallo Jordan, recognized this when saying, "South Africa is in the ironic dilemma of engaging in nation building when [other] nations were facing the dilemma of globalisation" (Anonymous, 1996c). What is likely, is that the ANC's modernization program may kill the postfordist sector by accident, rather than by design. The effects of changed policies in the areas of education, research funding, telecommunications, and taxation (intended to channel resources away from "elite" concerns) pose the greatest threat in this regard. For example, if the education system is restructured, so as to encourage the production of modernist technocrats, the intellectual resources, computer literacy, and so forth, required for the production of postmodern knowledge may well be undermined. The new ruling elite (as modernists) are likely to resist appeals by South Africa's postmodern "elite" that "spaces" be created and maintained for the exercise of their postmodern lifestyle; after all, creating and maintaining such spaces requires resources that modernists will believe can be better spent elsewhere. Ultimately, the ANC government will need to steer resources toward the needs of its modernist constituents, and this is almost certain to undermine postfordist infrastructural needs. This was acknowledged by none other than the man responsible for technological infrastructure provision in Johannesburg and Pretoria (the head of the Gauteng province's Information Technology Department, Michael Kahn) when he said that "community needs in developing states" were more important than "the business needs of the technologically developed world . . . it is a political question. We have a social commitment to development" (Anonymous, 1996b). This resource allocation threat to postmoderns can also be seen in South Africa's telecommunications policy. The Minister of Telecommunications, Jay Naidoo, has dealt with postfordist or globalization pressures by adopting a compromise position. He opted for a "five year period of exclusivity" during which resource allocation at Telkom (the state-owned telecommunications parastatal) will go toward "development" needs of the ANC's modernist constituency (Anonymous, 1996a). Only thereafter will postfordist issues apparently be considered.

The level of threat posed to South Africa's postmoderns will be decided by how the ANC intervenes to determine the allocation of societal resources. The ANC has made rather extravagant promises to the black constituency in terms of providing jobs, housing, land, and health facilities within a modern industrial framework. If the now high expectations of this constituency are not met, major social turmoil is likely to follow. Understandably, the ANC constituency's modernizing needs will be put first, followed by the needs to co-opt, pacify, or tame the premoderns and marginals. In consequence, postfordist infrastructural needs are the most likely to be starved of resources. Funds are unlikely to be allocated to pay for the hardware and software required for educating postfordist workers or for building the required information highways. Furthermore, ANC policies are unlikely to encourage the flow of private capital in these directions either.

An ancillary threat is that posed by the emigration of South Africa's skilled population, due to the perception that the ANC's policies will undermine the postfordist sector and, hence, undermine their postmodern interests. Postmodern "resistance," in fact, appears to be taking the form of emigration (rather than the "direct engagement" seen in the premodern sector). If current emigration trends continue, South Africa's postfordist economic sector may simply bleed away.[16]

QUO VADIS?

It appears that the world's most advanced societies are shifting toward postfordism. Fordist realists are no longer hegemonic, and the modern era is fading into postmodernity.[17] The question is, what happens to any society out of step with these trends? What are the consequences of rejecting the postmodernization process with its tendencies toward "centrifugal" pluralist diversity, social and linguistic fragmentation, postrealist breakdown of the metanarratives, and the expansion of mediacentricness experience? For South Africans, these are important questions, because the ANC and NP corporatist deal has seemingly entrenched a solidly fordist modernist program of action.

Will the ANC's neosocialist modernizing nation-building program impede the postmodernizing of South Africa? And if a modernizing South African regime attempts to go against the postmodernizing trends apparent in much of the world, would this then exact a heavy socioeconomic penalty for being out of step with wider world developments? Can a society afford to step outside those modes of discourse and relations of production that are (or are becoming) globally hegemonic?

Each era has its main modes of mobility and key communication conduits through which that era's economic and cultural life has flowed. When these conduits were blocked or shifted, the consequences have often been dramatic, for example, the decline of cities and societies in central Asia and the Middle East when the rise of Islam disrupted old land trade routes.

Modernists, with their preference for materially tangible phenomena (such as railway lines and heavy industry), generally have difficulty coming to terms with the seemingly intangible and ephemeral conduits of electronic information. Modernist development plans consequently have difficulty recognizing the importance of connecting into the proliferating global information highways that constitute the heart of postfordism. A neosocialist modernization program will thus, when making resource allocation decisions, channel funds toward creating an industrial infrastructure (and working-class jobs) in preference to creating a postindustrial infrastructure. Likewise, modernist development (and "national unity" programs) will inherently stress an education system on the basis of the linear logic of book-based texts rather than the more eclectic learning that will come from electronic texts. Communication within a postfordist electronic-information system is difficult (if not impossible) to control—and this undermines the predictability that modernist planners desire. So South Africa's new elite seem likely to block (mostly unintentionally but, occasionally, willfully) the growth of the infrastructure required for postfordism.

South Africa's corporatist settlement, which has congealed around the theme of a neosocialist modernist nation-building plan, offers South Africans a stability that racial capitalism could not. But in true South African fashion, this settlement may turn out to be a highly conservative venture when measured against trends in the rest of the world. It seems as if South Africa may now be steered into a modernist cul-de-sac, substantially isolated from global postfordism and its related postmodernization trends.

NOTES

1. This chapter is an exploration of shifting the debate on South Africa beyond the more traditional race and class categories—that is, the information era introduces new elements, hence, additional cleavages now need to be considered. This is not to suggest that the race and class categories are to be abandoned.

2. The notions modernity, premodernity, and postmodernity should not been seen to refer to neat watertight categories. Rather they refer to "structures of feeling" within a rather "messy" continuum. The intention is not to seek neat "fits," nor to categorize every South African into an appropriate "box." That would belie the incredible complexity of South Africa and its population.

3. The NP aimed to build a modern industrial state as a white African power base. An ironic unforeseen consequence was to produce a modernist black working class that formed the backbone of the 1980s anti-apartheid uprising.

4. Chiefs and headmen became important administrative agents of the apartheid system. The British originally developed the technique of stabilizing their rural domains by incorporating local hereditary leaders into colonial administrations as paid civil servants. The apartheid state merely continued this practice. Hence, many chiefs and headmen were unhappy to see the demise of apartheid.

5. "Nyangas" [medicine men or women] have enormous influence in rural South Africa, and even in the urban areas many "nyangas" have established themselves to meet the demand for "muti" [magic potions]. During periods of social tension the "muti" business booms. Hence, nyangas-led witch burnings and ritual killings for "muti" (made from human body parts) have become particular social problems in 1980s and 1990s South Africa.

6. The NP's original apartheid policy was a modernist national socialism geared toward furthering the interests of one South African group ("nation"), namely white Afrikaners. The apartheid state intervened to create a modern industrial society within which wealth was channeled toward Afrikaners. This was justified on the grounds that British colonists had economically suppressed white Afrikaners. The ANC's policy has become a mirror image of this logic: The ANC state intervenes to develop a modern industrial society within which wealth is to be channeled toward blacks. The justification is that whites have economically suppressed blacks (see Louw, 1994, pp. 33-34).

7. The British created South Africa (Benyon, 1980). Not surprisingly, when British colonial authorities constructed South Africa's social, economic, and political

infrastructures, the strong class differentiations of British capitalist society were transplanted. Class-based society was, however, given a particular form in Britain's African domains; that is, the British added a racial slant to their imperial class structure. Race and class were read together into a complex Imperial pecking order. Apartheid was merely the systematic codification of the race-class hierarchy created by the British, with one modification: During the British colonial period, British-born whites and then colony-born Britons were at the top of the pecking order. Apartheid tried to remove the distinction between Britons and white Afrikaners, who were not jointly to be at the top.

8. The United Democratic Front (UDF) was the internal wing of the ANC.

9. Every child from a premodern background who passes through the state's modernist schooling program represents a gain of one person for Africa's modernizing elite sector, plus, simultaneously, a loss of one person from the premodern sector. Hence, Africa's modernizing elites have placed great emphasis on "education" as a means of bolstering their position by expanding their numbers.

10. African modernizing elites have commonly shared a contempt for their premodern tribal countrymen. Hence, destroying tribalism was featured as an important concern for each of these modernite elites. To illustrate this, one has merely to look at the writings of key Southern African leaders, for example, South Africa's Govan Mbeki (Mbeki, 1964, p. 145); Zimbabwe's Ndabaningi Sithole (Sithole, 1959, pp. 69-70); and Mozambique's Eduardo Mondlane (Mondlane, 1969, p. 164).

11. Formal township houses (often called "ANC areas") near hostel sites and squatter areas have been burned down during raids from hostels and squatter settlements. Likewise hostels (called "IFP areas") have been torn down during raids launched by formal township dwellers.

12. "The minority" means white people. The term is clearly pejorative.

13. If the ANC developed a color-blind modernization program it could probably hegemonically incorporate most nonblack moderns. But presently, the ANC's (a) black nationalism, (b) advocacy of black affirmative action (wherein "black" excludes coloreds and Indians), and (c) adherence to "majoritarianism" ("majority" = "black") has generated a nonblack antipathy toward the ANC. Thus most colored, Indian, and white moderns now support the NP.

14. An unpredictable factor will be the response of white moderns to any repression of pre- and postmodern opposition. There is a strong correlation between being a white modern and being a lower-middle-class bureaucrat or member of the security services (because lower-middle-class status limited access to postfordist technology and significations). If the ANC ruling elite played its cards right, white modernites would probably be prepared to assist the new modernizing elite implement their plan. In March and April 1994 they certainly helped the ANC-dominated Transitional Executive Authority subdue the premodern power bases in Bophuthatswana and Kwa-Zulu.

15. If the ANC fails to deliver on the land issue it will likely face a backlash from land hungry premodernites who voted for the ANC. But redistributing white farms will disrupt the commercial farming industry. Because agriculture is a large component of the modern economic sector, this will, in turn, destabilize the wider modernization program. Further land redistribution holds the danger of generating a white right-wing backlash.

16. Estimates of South Africa's post-1993 net loss (emigration over immigration) of mainly professional people are 32,790 people (McNeill, 1996, p. 48). And from 1996 the "brain drain" began accelerating (McNeill, 1996, p. 48). So serious is the problem that Deputy President Mbeki has directed the Department of Arts, Culture, Science and Technology to investigate skills loss due to emigration and to create a database of experts

who have emigrated so they can be hired back as consultants for specific projects (Edmunds, 1996).

17. No teleology is implied in the modernity-to-postmodernity shift, just as no teleological "progress" is assumed in the premodernity-to-modernity shift. These three cultural discourses are simply seen as "different." None is inherently superior, although it is valid for someone to "prefer" one of these discourses over another because she or he feels more comfortable operating within it.

REFERENCES

African National Congress. (1990). *Joining the ANC.* Johannesburg: Author.

African National Congress. (1993). Resolutions adopted at the ANC DIP National Media Seminar. In P. E. Louw (Ed.), *South African media policy: Debates of the 1990s* (pp. 329-340). Bellville: Anthropos.

African National Congress. (1994, February 17). *Reconstruction and development program* [African National Congress internal discussion document].

Anonymous. (1996a, May 1). Can Telkom actually deliver? *Weekly Mail* [from the Internet].

Anonymous. (1996b, August 30). Technology versus development. *Financial Mail* [from the Internet].

Anonymous. (1996c, February 9). Telkoms gargantuan task. *Weekly Mail* [from the Internet].

Anonymous. (1996d, April 4). Zwelithini, Inkatha and the ANC: Royal miscalculation. *Financial Mail* [from the Internet].

Benyon, J. (1980). *Proconsul and paramouncy in South Africa.* Pietermaritzburg: University of Natal Press.

Campschreur, W., & Davendal, J. (1989). *Culture in another South Africa.* London: Zed.

Dalton, R. J., & Kuechler, M. (Eds.). (1990). *Challenging the political order: New social and political movements in Western democracies.* Cambridge, MA: Polity.

Davenport, T. R. H. (1977). *South Africa: A modern history.* New York: Macmillan.

Edmunds, M. (1996, September 13). The government examines its losses too late. *Weekly Mail* [from the Internet].

Fanon, F. (1963). *The wretched of the earth.* New York: Grove Press.

Hammond-Tooke, W. D. (1975). *Command or consensus: The development of Transkei local government.* Cape Town: David Philip.

Harvey, D. (1989). *The condition of postmodernity.* Oxford, UK: Basil Blackwell.

Janicke, M. (1990). *State failure.* Cambridge, MA: Polity.

Lash, S. (1990). *Sociology of postmodernism.* Boston: Routledge & Kegan Paul.

Lipton, M. (1985). *Capitalism and apartheid.* Aldershot: Wildwood House.

Louw, P. E. (1994). Shifting patterns of political discourse in the new South Africa. *Critical Studies in Mass Communication, 11*(1), 22-53.

Makhanya, M. (1996a, July 12). Constitution will undermine African customs, Contralesa tells court. *The Star* [from the Internet].

Makhanya, M. (1996b, May 13). Contralesa's Holomisa likely to leave parliament soon. *The Star* [from the Internet].

Malala, J. (1996, May 22). Government aims to build new bourgeoisie. *The Star* [from the Internet].

Masekela, B. (1989). Keynote address on behalf of the Department of Arts and Culture of the ANC. In W. Campschreur & J. Divendal (Eds.), *Culture in another South Africa* (pp. 250-256). London: Zed.

Masmoudi, M. (1979). The New World information order. *Journal of Communication, 29*(2).

Mbeki, G. (1964). *South Africa: The peasant's revolt.* New York: Penguin.

Mboweni, T. (1992). Growth through redistribution. In G. Howe & P. Le Roux (Eds.), *Transforming the economy: Policy options for South Africa* (pp. 201-210). Durban: Indicator SA.

McMenamin, V. (1992). Shifts in ANC economic policy. In G. Howe & P. Le Roux (Eds.), *Transforming the economy: Policy options for South Africa* (pp. 245-254). Durban: Indicator SA.

McNeill, R. (1996, August). Emigration. *Natal Style* [from the Internet].

Mondlane, E. (1969). *The struggle for Mozambique.* New York: Penguin.

Naidoo, P. (1996, July 10). Constitutional court rules on the payment of Zulu King and chiefs. *Saturday Star* [from the Internet]

Schlemmer, L. (1977). Theories of plural societies and change in South Africa. *Social Dynamics, 3*(1), 3-16.

Sithole, N. (1959). *African nationalism.* Oxford, UK: Oxford University Press.

Stadler, A. (1987). *The political economy of modern South Africa.* Cape Town: David Philip.

Streek, B. (1996, July 5). Warning of conflict if ANC acts on Holomisa. *Cape Times* [from the Internet].

Tomaselli, R., Tomaselli, K. G., & Muller, J. (1987). *Currents of power: State broadcasting in South Africa.* Bellville: Anthropos.

Van den Berghe, P. (1967). *Race and racism.* New York: John Wiley.

Wa Thiong'o, N. (1981). *Education for a national culture.* Harare: Zimbabwe Publishing House.

Wilson, F., & Ramphele, M. (1989). *Uprooting poverty: The South African challenge.* Cape Town: David Philip.

Worsley, P. (1984). *The three worlds: Culture and world development.* London: Weidenfeld & Nicolson.

Wright, H. M. (1977). *The burden of the present.* Cape Town: David Philip.

FURTHER READING

Louw, E., & Tomaselli, K. (1991). Semiotics of apartheid: The struggle for the sign. *European Journal for Semiotic Studies, 3*(1-2), 99-110.

Lyotard, J. F. (1984). *The postmodern condition: A report on knowledge.* Manchester: Manchester University Press.

III

FORUM: IDENTIFYING NATION-STATES THROUGH CHANGE

9

Distinguishing Cultural Systems

Change as a Variable Explaining and Predicting Cross-Cultural Communication

JAMES W. CHESEBRO • *Indiana State University,*
Terre Haute

Comparative research has been identified as the "communication field's 'extended and extendable frontier,' " a part of the shift toward an "advancing globalization," part of the fact that "researchers' international contacts" continue to "multiply," and part of the growing recognition that "scholars from different countries naturally think of working together on common problems" (Blumler, McLeod, & Rosengren, 1992, p. 3). The motives for these shifts and transformations were aptly articulated in the first volume of the *International and Intercultural Communication Annual* when this annual's first editor Fred L. Casmir (1974) maintained that "our search" is "for commonalities, for common experiences, for common perceptions to make our human interaction possible, meaningful, happy, more satisfying" (p. iii).

At the same time, these shifts and transformations have generated a self-reflexivity and explicit consciousness of the meaning of comparative research. Indeed, the quest to compare and contrast communication systems is as old as the discipline of communication itself. The classical impulse is an exemplar. Distinguishing genres, in terms of context, time, content, and purpose, Aristotle (1932, pp. 16-20) sought to classify all discourses as *deliberative, forensic,* and *epideictic.* Black (1965) has reported that one of the "primary and identifying ideas of neo-Aristotelianism" was its "classification of rhetorical discourses into forensic, deliberative, and epideictic" (p. 31). Nevertheless, Black has also argued that the quest for a more universal formulation of these neo-Aristotelian genres was hampered or "restricted" (p. 39) by the neo-Aristotelian emphasis on a speaker's immediate "results with a specific

AUTHOR'S NOTE: An earlier draft of this chapter was presented as the "Keynote Address" at the annual meeting of the Speech Communication Association of Puerto Rico, San Juan, Puerto Rico, December 8, 1995.

audience on a specific occasion" (p. 31) and by appraisals of "discourse in terms of its effects on a relatively immediate audience" (p. 39).

As a discipline, comparative research's quest has now manifested itself in international, intercultural, and cross-cultural studies. In this analysis, the nature of cross-cultural communication research is examined. It goes without saying that a host of different approaches to cross-cultural communication have been employed. In some cases, personal experiences have been used to generate hypotheses regarding how cultural systems can differ (see, e.g., Fayer, 1993). In other cases, a single measurement has been employed, suggesting that cultural systems can differ in degree, if not in kind (see, e.g., McCroskey, Fayer, & Richmond, 1985). Others have suggested that single cultures must be compared to other cultural systems along multiple dimensions. In this regard, maintaining that this method is more precise and "more accurate" than other techniques, Scollon and Scollon (1995) have observed, "One strategy which has been used, of course, is to use multiple dimensions to contrast cultures" (p. 162). For example, the dominant symbol-using system[1] of the United States might be compared to Japan's, in terms of its reliance on individualism or collectivism, context using, authority references, and achievement or nurturance. Even though a systematic and universal system is used, as cultures are compared and contrasted on an increasing number of continua, we gain an increasing appreciation and understanding of the distinct and discrete nature of each of the cultures being compared. In this sense, as cultures are compared and contrasted to each other on an increasing number of dimensions, the unique identity of each cultural system begins to emerge.

In this chapter, the nature of cross-cultural communication research is examined by considering the range of multiple dimensions used to compare and contrast cultures. Toward this end, I initially look at an excellent example of what I take to be provocative cross-cultural communication research, then examine some problems with this kind of research, move on and offer a minisurvey of how cultures have been distinguished and, finally, consider an additional way of distinguishing cultures. Thus, this analysis is guided by four objectives. First, the nature of cross-cultural communication research is illustrated. Second, some of the conceptual and definitional issues involved in cross-cultural communication research are isolated. Third, a summary of some of the major concepts used to distinguish the unique cultures of different nation-states is provided. Finally, another system or method for distinguishing nation-state cultural systems is outlined. This method emphasizes change as a means of explaining and predicting cross-cultural communication.

ILLUSTRATING THE NATURE OF
CROSS-CULTURE COMMUNICATION RESEARCH

A rich variety of diverse cross-cultural communication studies now exists. These studies differ in objectives, philosophical approaches to research, methods, and the kinds of understandings that are reported. A study that intrigues and provides one understanding of cross-cultural communication research was reported by Tamar Liebes.[2]

Liebes (1989) was interested in how peoples from different cultures perceive the same event, yet tell different stories about it. She decided to ask people from different cultures to watch the same episode of the television series *Dallas*. Liebes asked 54 groups to watch the episode of *Dallas*. Each group was composed of five to six people. The 54 groups were selected from Israel and United States, and Liebes attempted to select groups from "widely different subcultures" (p. 278) in each of these two nation-states. In Israel, the subcultures represented in her study included Arabs, Moroccan Jews, new immigrants from Russia, and second-generation Israelis living on a kibbutz. In the United States, second-generation Americans living in Los Angeles were used as participants. In all, five different cultures were represented in this study. As cultures, each of these five groups differed dramatically, especially in "mother tongue, media literacy, socio-historical experience, and location in the social structure" (Liebes, 1988, p. 278).

Although different in cultural background, with respect to other demographic variables, the members of these groups were roughly the same. In all cases, Liebes (1988) reported that, "Age, education, and regular viewing of the program were essentially homogeneous for all participants." Given her other participant-recruiting techniques, Liebes could additionally report that, whereas "we cannot make a claim on formal randomness or representativeness," nonetheless "we have no reason to suspect any systematic bias" and have reason to believe that the participants were "demographically alike for reasons of relatedness and propinquity" (Liebes, 1988, p. 278).

After each group viewed the episode of *Dallas*, Liebes asked each of the different cultural groups, "How would you retell the episode you just saw to somebody who had not seen it?" Using focus group techniques and recording responses, Liebes characterized how each of the five cultural groups retold the story they had just viewed on the episode of *Dallas*.

The results suggested, Liebes (1988) concluded, that "different cultures interpret American television texts" differently and, specifically, that "the group retellings reveal correlations between ethnicity and choice of narrative form" (p. 277). Particularly, the Arabs and Moroccans were shocked at what they saw, especially the roles that women played in the program. In Liebes's words, the Arabs and Moroccans were "more traditional," telling their story in a linear form, in which events were characterized as having an inevitable and sequential progression within the context of the extended family. In contrast, the Americans and kibbutzniks adopted a more ironic, tongue-in-cheek attitude about the program. The Americans and kibbutzniks told their story in a segmented form, emphasizing the intrapersonal and interpersonal emotional problems of the characters. Finally, employing yet a different conception, the Russians were political in their retelling of the program. The Russians ignored the story and characters in the episode, and they prided themselves on exposing an overall principle in the episode that—in their view—fostered a "false picture of reality" about the material well-being of Americans, and they ultimately highlighted "the potential persuasive power of the program" (p. 289).

The Liebes report suggests three major interim conclusions. First, cross-cultural communication differences exist. Second, communication systems—at least—reflect cultural differences. Third, communication systems may actually constitute cultural differences. The "data" used to establish the existence of cross-cultural communication are ultimately symbol based, with meanings used to justify the existence of cross-cultural differences. The immediate evidence suggests, then, that cross-cultural differences are grounded in communication differences. Ultimately, cross-cultural differences should be apprehended and understood as a function of communication differences. With this kind of study as a guide, it is appropriate to isolate some of the definitional issues involved in this type of cross-cultural communication research.

CONCEPTUAL AND DEFINITIONAL ISSUES IN CROSS-CULTURAL COMMUNICATION RESEARCH

A host of conceptual and definitional issues obviously confound cross-cultural communication research. It is appropriate to recognize these problems at the outset, isolating potential problems explicitly and directly.

Of the host of issues that might be examined here, not the least of these is the meaning of the word *culture*. Some 45 years ago, Kroeber and Kluckhohn (1952) identified 164 definitions of culture. They concluded that "each individual selects from and to a greater or lesser degree systematizes what he experiences of the total culture in the course of his formal and informal education throughout life" (p. 157). And since 1952, the number of definitions has increased geometrically. Particularly when making cross-cultural comparisons, a lack of agreement on what is meant by culture could be disastrous.

At the same time, it is possible to distill some important characteristics of a culture that are particularly relevant to cross-cultural communication research. Three of these characteristics are important to underscore. Ultimately, these characteristics will provide an operational definition of the object of study in cross-cultural communication research.

First, a culture is a system-center or transcendent concept. A culture does not exist phenomenally; a culture does not exist as a physical entity. A culture is a social construction; it is a composite term that refers to a socially perceived pattern, or integration, of diverse elements within a societal system. Accordingly, when studying culture, researchers must necessarily examine self-report information regarding what the members of a culture identify as their standards and criteria for assessing and evaluating. Lustig and Koester (1993) reflect this orientation when they define "culture" as "a learned set of shared perceptions about beliefs, values, and norms" (p. 41).

Second, a culture is constituted with and transmitted through symbols. Consistently, as Kroeber and Kluckhohn (1952) found in the 164 conceptions of culture, researchers have concluded that cultural patterns are acquired through and transmitted by symbol-using activity. Reflecting this norm, Lindesmith and Strauss (1956) have aptly reported, "The term 'culture' is generally used to refer to behavior patterns, including beliefs, values, and ideas, which are the shared possession of groups and which are symbolically transmitted" (p. 38). They have argued that "language is both an integral part of culture and the indispensable vehicle for its transmission" (p. 6). Reasoning that "man is a symbol manipulator—the only symbol-manipulating animal," Lindesmith and Strauss (1956) have maintained that

> Man's immersion in a cultural environment depends on the existence of language behavior, or the creation and manipulation of high-order signs (symbols). Society means communication. Language is both the vehicle by means of which culture is transmitted from generation to generation and also an integral part of all aspects of culture. (p. 6)

From a functional and pragmatic perspective, then, certain language choices and patterns can be studied as a reflection and integrating force of a cultural system.

Third, a culture refers to societal understandings that are transferred from one generation to the next. A key questions emerges at this juncture: When is symbol-using "cultural," when is it not? Granted, there is one sense in which all symbols are inherently and necessarily always cultural, for they are an outcome and product of a commonly shared value system. Nevertheless, not every symbol is understood to represent a collective's shared standards for evaluating. In this regard, some symbols are used, and only function, in "private" and "personal" domains. Although serving a host of other functions, certain symbol systems do seem to function culturally, and these symbol systems are understood to be cultural, because they convey understandings from one generation to the next. In this regard, Scollon and Scollon (1995, p. 205) have maintained that a generational affiliation is similar to a membership in an "involuntary discourse system" that determines, in part, the personal ideology and identity. Because these generational ideologies and identities are learned "early life experiences," Scollon and Scollon maintain that this generational identification constitutes one of "the strongest influences" in a person's life.

Beyond using a common definition of *culture* when studying cross-cultural communication, researchers must also determine if a nation-state can be said to be constrained by one cultural system (see, e.g., Scollon & Scollon, pp. 154-163). In terms of the practical, we need to study nation-state cultures. In an ideal world, we might examine cultures regardless of nation-state boundaries. But data and understandings are now linked to and collected by nation-states, not by cultural systems. Accordingly, we need to explore how meaningful it is to equate nation-states and cultural systems. In dealing with this issue, Triandis and his colleagues have concluded that it is often necessary to generate "stereo-types as hypotheses of national character." Triandis, Vassilious, Vassilious, Tanaka, and Shanmugam (1972) have maintained that,

> Our view is that we can employ the stereotypes of different culture groups as *estimates* of the probable differences in the mean value of their traits.
>
> We can then ask if the trait differences are consistent with historical and ecological analyses of the experiences of subjects in different cultures. (p. 304)

As Triandis and his colleagues develop their research methods, using semantic differential scales and interviews, they ultimately survey both self-conceptions and conceptions of others with a wide variety of participants in different kinds of relationships or societal stratifications, from each of the nation-state cultures involved in the cross-cultural communicative exchange (also see Hui & Triandis, 1986; Triandis, Bontempo, Villarcal, Asai, & Lucca, 1988).

Besides the issues involved in equating nation-states and cultural systems, researchers must also recognize that nation-state cultures are frequently more similar than different in several ways. Cross-cultural communication research tends to focus on the differences between nation-state cultures, as if only the differences explained human communication. Yet Edelstein (1983) has suggested that it may be possible to search for universals across cultural systems, as well as cultural differences. He has recommended that one pursue "commonalities until" one encounters "culturally derived differences." Thus, one might seek to "enjoy the best of both worlds—universality across and differences within cultures" (p. 304).

In all, there is no denying that conceptual and definitional issues exist in cross-cultural communication research. Yet once a researcher is sensitive to these issues, design methods seem to exist to bypass many of the concerns. Accordingly, it is possible to consider some of the ways in which cultural systems have been distinguished. The question we now need to address is, "How are cultural systems distinguished in cross-cultural communication research today?" This aptly brings us to a third consideration, a summary of some of the major schemes currently used to distinguish the unique cultures of different nation-states.

SCHEMES FOR DISTINGUISHING
NATION-STATES AS CULTURAL SYSTEMS

For some three decades, efforts have been under way to distinguish nation-state cultural systems in systematic and researchable ways. Essentially, all of these efforts seek to determine the nature of the "subjective" understanding people within nation-state cultures have of themselves, others, and their environment. In this regard, several "dimensions of subjective culture" have been posited, and it is maintained that any single nation-state culture can be placed—probably quantitatively—along these different dimensions.

If a single nation-state culture is placed along several of these dimensions, several benefits might be derived. First, a more profound understanding of each culture would be rendered. Second, the dimensions would establish a common foundation for comparing cultures systematically. And third, pragmatically, a research foundation would exist for describing and predicting the meanings of different communicative acts in specific cross-cultural communication situations. Accordingly, let me consider four schemes or ways in which cultures are distinguished today.

The Individual-Collectivist Dimension

For some researchers, cultures can be distinguished along a continuum with "extremely individual" at one end and "extremely collectivist" at the other end (see, e.g., Triandis et al., 1972). The basis for classifying a nation-state culture along this continuum is whether or not the articulated or communicated standards, values, and beliefs of a community emphasize the significance of individual action or the importance of collectivist action. In summarizing the research generated in terms of this dimension, Singelis and Brown (1995) have concluded,

> It is true that cultures are not exclusively individualist or collectivist. As complex and many-faceted, cultures no doubt encourage the development of both types of self-construal to some extent. Nevertheless, using aggregate data, several large-scale analyses have found cultures fall on a single continuum with individualism and collectivism at the extremes. (p. 358)

In particular, Miller (1984) found that India was predominantly collectivist, whereas the United States was predominantly individualist. Specifically, she reported that 40% of Hindu adult Indian references were collectivist, whereas only 18% of the responses from adults in the United States were collectivist. A second dimension is now appropriately considered.

The Context Dimension

In 1972, writing in *Beyond Culture,* Edward T. Hall maintained that any transaction is affected by the cultural context in which it occurs. Hall specifically noted,

> Any transaction can be characterized as high-, low-, or middle-context. HC transactions feature preprogrammed information that is in the receiver and in the setting, with only minimal information in the transmitted message. LC transactions are the reverse. Most of the information must be in the transmitted message in order to make up for what is missing in the context (both internal and external).
>
> In general, HC communication, in contrast to LC, is economical, fast, efficient, and satisfying; however, time must be devoted to programming. If this programming does not take place, the communication is incomplete.

> HC communications are frequently used as art forms. They act as a unifying, cohesive force, are long-lived, and are slow to change. LC communications do not unify; however, they can be changed easily and rapidly. (p. 101)

In Hall's view, on the basis of the predominant communication pattern within a culture, any single nation-state can be classified along this context continuum from high, to middle, to low context.

In particular, high-context countries included Japan, Korea, and China, as well as many Latin and African cultures. In contrast, low-context countries included the United States, Australia, and most Northern European cultures.[3] A third dimension is now appropriately considered.

The Power Distance Dimension

Nation-state cultural systems also have been distinguished by their "relation to authority" (Hofstede, 1980, p. 47) and particularly how they perceive authority, how much they fear authority, and the type of authority that is preferred in a culture. The power distance dimension reflects a universal recognition that (a) power inequalities exist in all cultures (Hofstede, 1980, p. 94), (b) a dynamic equilibrium exists in power relationships in which "the more powerful seek to maintain or increase the power distance to the less powerful" whereas less powerful "individuals will strive to reduce the power distance between themselves and more powerful persons" (Hofstede, 1980, p. 98), and (c) cultures maintain "consistently different power distances in hierarchies" (Hofstede, 1980, p. 99).

When the power distance dimension is cast as a continuum, at one pole, the "monolithic," cultures are characterized by power held by a few people. At this end of the continuum, language choices and patterns reflect a strong sense of hierarchy, and there are apparently few ways of transcending hierarchical levels. Linguistic and nonverbal communication across these hierarchical levels are restricted. At the other pole, the "pluralistic," "competition between groups and leaders is encouraged, control by leaders is limited since members can join several organizations, democratic politics are fostered and information sources are independent of a single organization" (p. 99). At this end of the continuum, hierarchies are not as relevant, and there are ways of transcending the hierarchical levels that exist. Linguistic and nonverbal communication across hierarchical levels are accepted, if not appreciated (see, e.g., Hofstede, 1980, p. 99).

In Hofstede's formulation, of the 40 countries under investigation, the five "most afraid" countries were the Philippines, Mexico, Venezuela, India, and Yugoslavia. The five least afraid countries were Austria, Israel, Denmark, New Zealand, and Ireland.[4]

A fourth dimension is now appropriately considered.

The Masculinity-Femininity Dimension

The masculinity-femininity dimension is cast as a traditional, if not sexist, metaphor. It explores the degree to which cultures pride themselves on their preference for achievement and assertiveness, at one end of the continuum, or for nurturance and social support, at the other end of the continuum. Accordingly, as Lustig and Koester (1993) have noted, "an alternative label is achievement-nurturance" (p. 147).

Hofstede (1980) has developed a "masculinity index" or MAS to determine the place of a particular culture along the achievement-nurturance dimension. High-MAS cultures emphasize achievement and ambition, judge people on the basis of performance, and encourage material displays of these achievements. Low-MAS cultures emphasize life choices that improve intrinsic aspects of the quality of life, service to others, gender equality, and less prescriptive role behaviors.

On the basis of employees' self-reported relationships to their managers in 40 different countries, Hofstede (1980) reported that the five most "achievement"-oriented or "masculine" countries were Japan, Austria, Venezuela, Italy, and Switzerland. The five most "nurturant" or "feminine" countries were Sweden, Norway, the Netherlands, Denmark, and Finland.

In all, these four schemes for distinguishing nation-states as cultural systems, although intriguing, do not exhaust all of the ways in which cultural differences can be understood. Cultures would also appear to differ in how they respond to change.

CHANGE AS A VARIABLE EXPLAINING AND PREDICTING CROSS-CULTURAL COMMUNICATION

With respect to face or content validity, it is certainly easy to imagine that nation-state cultural systems differ in how positively or negatively they respond to change.[5] In some nation-states, if a religious, moral, or ideological discourse dominates, members of a cultural system seldom advocate basic changes in the structure and processes of their society. For example, certain religious sects will not only avoid change, but they will prevent their members from making contact with those elements of the larger society that are associated with change. In other nation-states, a drive to implement scientific advancements and technological developments may reflect a receptivity, commitment, and perhaps even an eagerness, to change the nature of society. The discourses promoting and rationalizing the Industrial Revolution would seem to have possessed such a commitment to change.

The response to change could, of course, be motivated by a host of such factors as the nature of a situation, the behaviors of adjacent societies, access to technological developments, and types of governing bureaucracies and decision-making systems, as well as antecedent or historical constraints. Yet a cultural orientation can also overpower each of these factors. Hence, if members of a cultural system decide, they can promote or avoid change by redefining situations, negotiating treaties with adjacent societies, changing the ways in which technologies are used, bypassing or adjusting government systems, or reconceiving historical precedents. The decision to change or not to change can be a powerful, if not primary and controlling, motivating force unto itself.

When change is cast as a dimension for distinguishing nation-state cultural systems, it is useful to view one continuum marked by four different focal points or clusters along the continuum. At one end of the continuum, revolutionary change can be posited. But revolutionary change can gradually evolve and blend into another form of change. Revolutionary change can be displaced by a discourse advocating evolutionary change. And evolutionary change itself can give way to rhetoric that emphasizes stability. Finally, the discourse of stability can give way, at the other end of the continuum, to a form of involutionary change. Hence, the response-to-change dimension suggested here would highlight four clusters of change: revolution, evolution, stability, and involution.

Each of these four types of change requires more detailed consideration. In describing these four forms of change, at this point, the conceptual definitions provided by Service (1971) are particularly instructive.[6]

Of the first form of cultural change, identified as *revolution,* Service (1971) has maintained, "Revolution is a radical, relatively abrupt change of the fundamental characteristics of a system" that also "implies that the change involves some kind of struggle *against* something or somebody" that is "characterized by visible disruption" (p. 13). Thus, the political discourse of the radical revolutionary of the 1960s and early 1970s functioned as a form of revolution. In other nation-state cultures, this call for political revolution manifests itself in dramatic, sometimes brutal, changes in the form of government, as in Mao's China and Lenin's and Stalin's Soviet Union.

Service (1971, pp. 11, 12) has argued that cultural *evolution,* a second and distinct form of change, is characterized by a form of discourse in which change is described as occurring at a "reasonable" rate, developments are cast as "progressive" and "unfolding," activities are described as proceeding in a common "direction" or "along some kind of linear scale," and when programs are interpreted as "very significant solutions to important local problems." In this regard, Watkins (1964) has argued that the United States was able to shift to a form of representative democracy, because the "traditional class distinctions" that had plagued the emergence of the democracies of Europe were absent in 18th-century America. As Watkins maintained, "legal and customary restrictions on social mobility were comparatively mild, which meant that the break with Great Britain could be accomplished without any very drastic changes in the established social order" (pp. 20-21).

Of the third form of cultural change, *stability,* Service (1971) has reported,

> Stability, after all, is merely indicative of the success of the adaptive process: When the culture is successfully adapted, it tends to reject subsequent changes. This can render explicable what might seem paradoxical: that a culture "high" in one stage might fail to advance to further heights in the next, simply because of its earlier success. Of course, the more specialized and complicated its form of adaptation, the more deeply entrenched and committed to its extant environment it becomes. (p. 11)

In many respects, it can be argued that the foundation for a period of cultural stability now exists in the United States. In this regard, two factors are outstanding.

First, the complexity and interrelationships of the United States economy and technology may not be suited to change. The United States economic-scientific-technology establishment can become so complex that it cannot be comprehensively or systematically changed. As Service (1971) has argued, "With all other factors equal, the more backward a nation's technology and economy in terms of today's equipment, the greater the potentiality for the basically different Second Industrialization" (p. 59).

Second, insofar as American education affects cultural change, the American educational system has increasing evolved into a set of discrete enclaves of specialized information as reflected, for example, in the departmental structures of the contemporary university in the

United States. The United States is now appropriately understood as adapting through specialization.

In all, the United States now satisfies the definitional requirements as a stable culture.[7] Its rhetoric is one of specialized adaptation. Within this context, historian H. Stuart Hughes (1949) has maintained that the United States now emphasizes, as a definition of its civilization, its efficiency and specialization, which means, in Hughes's words, that "the U.S.A. is now stabilized and coming to occupy a conservative position in the world" (p. 36).

In contrast, Service (1971) has defined cultural *involution* as an attempt "to preserve an extant structure, solving its new problems by 'fixing it up' " (p. 12). Rhetoric designed to control dissenters and analyses that ultimately hinder the diffusion of innovations are explicit signs of involution. In these schemes, advocates maintain that existing systems can be adjusted to and/or possess ready remedies for all emerging problems.

CONCLUSION

Overall, then, cultures appear to differ in how they respond to change. Cultural change appears to generate an interrelated set of options, spanning a continuum, ranging from revolution to evolution to stability to involution. Only a brief outline of this scheme has been explored and sketched here. The utility of this dimension requires that systematic cross-cultural communication research be undertaken. Moreover, the relationships that might exist between these four forms of cultural change need to be compared to the description of the rhetorical characteristics of the radical, liberal, conservative, and reactionary political positions that Brock (1965) has provided. Nonetheless, a potentially exciting area of research is revealed here, an area that could provoke, intrigue, excite, and stimulate others to act. Such undertakings should be heuristically valuable and theoretically generative for cross-cultural communication as a research area.

NOTES

1. The expression "dominant symbol-using system" should not be equated with, or assumed to be equivalent to, the identification and selection of the communication system of a single or more powerful group from a cultural system. Rather a "dominant symbol-using system" of a cultural system is determined by a systematic (perhaps random or cluster) sampling technique and comprehensive content analysis system of all of the

diverse sociocultural groupings within a single nation-state cultural system. In this regard, a researcher might hypothesize that the "dominant symbol-using system" of the United States should be identified as "multiculturalism." Furthermore, various standards and tests exist for determining whether or not the sampling and content analysis systems used are appropriate (see, e.g., Rubenstein, 1995). In terms of validity, Lustig and Koester (1996, pp. 93-99) have maintained that a description of the dominant symbol-using system of a culture should reflect the beliefs, values, and norms of that culture. In a similar vein, Scollon and Scollon (1995, pp. 127-128) have maintained that a description of the dominant symbol-using system of a culture should reflect the ideologies, socialization processes, forms of discourse, and face systems of a culture.

2. Liebes published this study in a variety of publications, each with a different emphasis and, in some cases, with different groups of participants included in the analyses (see Katz & Liebes, 1986; Liebes, 1988; Liebes & Katz, 1986). For my purposes, I am using the summary of this study provided by Liebes in the December 1988 issue of *Critical Studies in Mass Communication.*

3. It should also be noted that high-context countries also tend to be collectivist (e.g., Japan, Korea, China, India, and Latin and African countries), whereas low-context countries tend to be individualistic (e.g., United States, Australia, and most Northern European countries) (see Gudykunst & Ting-Toomey, 1988; Singelis & Brown, 1995, p. 361).

4. In Hofstede's (1980, p. 101) formulation, the power distance dimension can also be conceived as a "willingness to disagree with supervisors" as well as a "fear of disagreement" measure. As Hofstede (1980, p. 76) has observed in this formulation, the "central question measuring 'Power Distance' " was, "How frequently are employees afraid to express disagreement with their managers?"

5. This dimension explores "reactions to change" or "stated beliefs and values about change," which has functioned as a traditional orientation and domain of the discipline of communication. This dimension *does not* explore or seek to measure any type or form of societal change itself.

6. It should be noted that Service's definitions are not entirely satisfactory for our purposes, because he believes that he has described forms of societal change rather than symbolic conceptions of change, responses to change, and beliefs and values about change.

7. For some, it is extremely difficult to perceive the United States as entering a period of cultural stability, because of the apparent upheavals and changes initiated by a host of "minorities" and "marginalized" groups within the United States, of which women, African Americans, gay males and lesbians, and Latins constitute only a modest indication of the scope of cultural change in the United States. It should be noted, however, that cultural change itself is not being denied here. Rather the effort undertaken here is to identify the kind or type of cultural change that is occurring, and specifically the effort is to identify the nature of the rhetoric of cultural change that is emerging in the United States. In this regard, the multiple voices of diverse minority and marginalized groups are viewed here as completely consistent with the claim that the United States is increasingly advocating adaptation through specialization. Indeed, each of the vocal minority and marginalized groups in the United States has insisted that the unique historical and lifestyle cultures of each group constitute a dominant symbol system in the United States. Of course, it is impossible for any one of the symbol systems of these diverse groups to dominate. Yet in this sense, each of these competing voices constitutes a demand for adaptation to its specialized voice. From a larger perspective, the United States has reacted in powerful ways to these different demands for specialized adaptation, and as

long as this form of cultural change persists, the United States can do little to move past the demands for specialized adaptations required of each of these groups and find themes and modes that are common to all of these groups.

REFERENCES

Aristotle. (1932). *Rhetoric* (L. Cooper, Trans.). New York: Appleton-Century-Crofts.

Black, E. (1965). *Rhetorical criticism: A study in method.* New York: Macmillan.

Blumler, J. G., McLeod, J. M., & Rosengren, K. E. (1992). Introduction to comparative communication research. In J. G. Blumler, J. M. McLeod, & K. E. Rosengren (Eds.), *Comparatively speaking: Communication and culture across space and time* (pp. 3-18). Newbury Park, CA: Sage.

Brock, B. L. (1965). *A definition of four political positions and a description of their rhetorical characteristics.* Unpublished doctoral dissertation, Northwestern University, Evanston, IL.

Casmir, F. L. (1974). Editor's notes. *International and Intercultural Communication Annual, 1,* iii-iv.

Edelstein, A. S. (1983). Communication and culture: The value of comparative studies. *Journal of Communication, 33,* 302-310.

Fayer, J. (Ed.). (1993). *Puerto Rican communication studies.* San Juan, PR: Fundacion Arqueologica, Anthropologica, e Historica de Puerto Rico.

Gudykunst, W. B., & Ting-Toomey, S. (1988). *Culture and interpersonal communication.* Newbury Park, CA: Sage.

Hall, E. T. (1976). *Beyond culture.* New York: Anchor.

Hofstede, G. (1980). *Culture's consequences: International differences in work-related values.* Beverly Hills, CA: Sage.

Hughes, H. S. (1949). *An essay for our times.* New York: Knopf.

Hui, C. H., & Triandis, H. C. (1986). Individualism-collectivism: A study of cross-cultural researchers. *Journal of Cross-Cultural Psychology, 17,* 225-248.

Katz, E., & Liebes, T. (1986). Decoding *Dallas*: Notes from a cross-cultural study. In G. Gumpert & R. Cathcart (Eds.), *Inter/Media: Interpersonal communication in a media world* (3rd ed.). New York: Oxford University Press.

Kroeber, A. L., & Kluckhohn, C. (1952). *Culture: A critical review of concepts and definitions* (Papers of the Peabody Museum of American Archaeology and Ethnology, Vol. 47, No. 1). Cambridge, MA: Harvard University Press.

Liebes, T. (1988, December). Cultural differences in the retelling of television fiction. *Critical Studies in Mass Communication, 5,* 277-292.

Liebes, T., & Katz, E. (1986, June). Patterns of involvement in television fiction: A comparative analysis. *European Journal of Communication, 1,* 151-171.

Lindesmith, A. R., & Strauss, A. L. (1956). *Social psychology* (Rev. ed.). New York: Holt, Rinehart & Winston.

Lustig, M. W., & Koester, J. (1993). *Intercultural competence: Interpersonal communication across cultures.* New York: HarperCollins.

Lustig, M. W., & Koester, J. (1996). *Intercultural competence: Interpersonal communication across cultures* (2nd ed.). New York: HarperCollins.

McCroskey, J. C., Fayer, J. M., & Richmond, V. P. (1985, Summer). Don't speak to me in English: Communication apprehension in Puerto Rico. *Communication Quarterly, 33,* 185-192.

Miller, J. (1984). Culture and the development of everyday social explanation. *Journal of Personality and Social Psychology, 46,* 961-978.

Rubenstein, S. M. (1995). *Surveying public opinion.* Belmont, CA: Wadsworth.

Scollon, R., & Scollon, S. W. (Eds.). (1995). *Intercultural communication: A discourse approach.* Oxford, UK: Basil Blackwell.

Service, E. R. (1971). *Cultural evolutionism: Theory in practice.* New York: Holt, Rinehart & Winston.

Singelis, T. M., & Brown, W. J. (1995, March). Culture, self, and collectivist communication: Linking culture to individual behavior. *Human Communication Research, 21,* 354-389.

Triandis, H. C., Bontempo, R., Villarcal, M. J., Asai, M., & Lucca, N. (1988). Individualism-collectivism: Cross-cultural perspectives on self-group relationships. *Journal of Personality and Social Psychology, 54,* 323-338.

Triandis, H. C., Vassilious, V., Vassilious, G., Tanaka, Y., & Shanmugam, A. V. (1972). *The analysis of subjective culture.* New York: John Wiley.

Watkins, F. M. (1964). *The age of ideology—Political thought, 1750 to the present.* Englewood Cliffs, NJ: Prentice Hall.

10

Problematizing "Nation" in Intercultural Communication Research

KENT A. ONO • *University of California, Davis*

> We must again, as in the 1970s, seriously consider whose interests are served by continuing to construct "culture" primarily in terms of national boundaries and by maintaining the current focus on the development of "intercultural cookbooks" for interaction.
>
> —Dreama Moon (1996)

Given recent attention in the U.S. academy to issues of transnationalism brought on by government, corporate economic trends toward globalization (e.g., NAFTA), and the dissolution of the "Soviet Union" into multifariously governed entities, it is with some trepidation that I read James Chesebro's (this volume) chapter, "Distinguishing Cultural Systems: Change as a Variable Explaining and Predicting Cross-Cultural Communication," which resurrects what I was hoping would ultimately be a casualty of the Cold War: the nation-state. "Distinguishing Cultural Systems" (hereafter, DCS) argues for a cross-cultural model for understanding communication among national cultures. In equating culture with *national* culture, Chesebro unwittingly reproduces many of the nationalist assumptions in intercultural research that scholars doing intercultural research have recently attempted to correct.[1] Although his chapter improves contemporary intercultural communication research, it also draws on problematic assumptions of intercultural communication research for some of its own primary assumptions; and whereas it then adds the concept of cultural change, which by itself holds fruitful possibilities, it nonetheless also rearticulates and enforces a nationalist, U.S.-*centric* model of cultural exchange and interaction. My goal in this chapter will be to problematize "nation." By abandoning the nationalist focus of prior research reproduced by DCS, a more radical cultural studies approach to cross-cultural communication, one that addresses experiences of people in everyday life, may be possible.

AUTHOR'S NOTE: The author would like to thank Carole Blair, Rona Halualani, and Wen Shu Lee for their helpful comments on this chapter.

DCS articulates a model for comparing and contrasting national cultures to determine "commonalities" and "differences." It assumes that culture is a socially constructed phenomenon "transmitted" through symbols and "transferred" from one generation to the next. To understand the uniqueness of national cultures and their similarities to others, DCS suggests that they be compared and contrasted with as many different variables as possible. Chesebro writes, "single cultures must be compared to other cultural systems in terms of and along multiple dimensions." Through a process of finding similarities between and among national cultural groups and then through a coordinated process of differentiation, unique statements about cultural identity and process can be made.

DCS assumes two principal tenets with regard to cross-cultural studies of national cultures. First, it assumes that national cultures are legitimate units of analysis. Chesebro writes, "In an ideal world, we might examine cultures regardless of nation-state boundaries. But, data and understandings are now linked to and collected by nation-states, not by cultural systems." From this perspective, Chesebro finds that "nation-state cultures are frequently more similar than different in several ways."

Second, DCS assumes that a national culture's predilection toward change, stability, or both be taken as one factor among other traditional intercultural communication variables as a measure of national character. Chesebro discusses factors already used regularly in mainstream intercultural communication research to understand national character and cultural groups, namely, whether or not different national cultures tend to be (a) individualist or collectivist, (b) low context or high context, (c) authoritative or obedient, and (d) masculine or feminine. To this, DCS adds a focus on national change, arguably the most significant contribution his specific chapter offers to communication and cultural studies. As Chesebro writes, "The decision to change or not to change can be a powerful, if not primary and controlling, motivating force unto itself."

There is much to admire in DCS's model for distinguishing cultural systems. First, DCS's comparative approach to the study of communication helps move beyond a U.S.-centric focus on understanding international communication and world cultures. It encourages us to understand cultures different from those researchers might typically identify. It further asks that researchers not assess culture on the basis of internally produced methods of comparison. Subtly, DCS pushes researchers to think beyond cultural blinders. Second, this chapter moves to contextualize similarities and differences by increasing the number of possible points of comparison, hence complexifying and, therefore, not simply relying on past intercultural models of analysis. Third, DCS encourages better communication and the sharing of information, ideas, and values. Its approach recognizes the significance of cultural difference and acknowledges the importance of communicating uniqueness for purposes of cooperation. Finally, the chapter encourages us to account for a nation's position on social change. With this perspective, DCS is able to provide an apt and laudable critique of U.S. politics and its relatively "conservative position" within the realm of international politics and cultures.

Whereas there are many fine aspects to his chapter, many ideas may need further research and theorization. DCS's primary limitations stem from problems in the literature used as the basis for the study. For example, DCS relies heavily on Tamar Liebes's (1988) article "Cultural Differences in the Retelling of Television Fiction," which studies five international cultural audiences and their responses to watching one episode of the U.S. television program *Dallas*. In the process, "Cultural Differences" (hereafter, CD), like DCS, relies heavily on decontextualized concepts of culture. I will provide an extended analysis of CD, because DCS focuses so much attention on it, and so that I might demonstrate the problematic conception of "nation" in CD and the reproduction of that problematic conception in DCS.

CD focuses on four Israeli subcultural audiences and one U.S. audience. After watching the episode, all groups answered specific questions, and viewers gave their own versions of what they saw. Through analysis of viewers' responses, CD extracts general cultural principles. In the process, the article assumes a psychological intent behind the answers given. CD suggests that the Russian participants, in particular, are "suspicious" of the researchers and of *Dallas* and that they are not willing to talk about the narrative as it unfolds but would rather read *Dallas* as an ideological commodity produced within a capitalist society. CD suggests that Russians "perceive the story as being a false picture of reality" (Liebes, 1988, p. 289), implying that they see television programs as embodiments of capitalist ideology and, therefore, see television as *false consciousness.* This analysis is not only limiting but also objectifying; it assumes that, because the Soviet Union was a socialist society, participants within that society necessarily read television through a socialist lens. Moreover, it implies that no other subjective aspect (e.g., personal quirks; other ideological configurations, such as ethnicity, sexuality, or gender; trauma; or, more generally, diasporic experiences) are relevant to the reading process. In short, CD implies that Russian subjects do not read with as much human complexity as do U.S. and Israeli participants. Furthermore, CD implicitly employs the same ideological analysis of all five groups' discourse that the article critiques the Russian participants for using when they discuss the producers, characters, and narrative of *Dallas*; CD reduces them to the ideological position to which it assumes they subscribe and, in the process, diverts attention away from Liebes's own ideological position as critic.

Rather than research Russian culture, for example, by asking for self-reports, or even having a conversation with the participants about their questions and answers to determine their own perceptions of why they answered the way they did,[2] CD arguably draws on negative Western stereotypes of Russian people (i.e., common or "typical" representations of cultural groups in Western media) to explain microlevel differences in audience reactions to the show.[3] In one rather tautological statement, Liebes (1988) writes, "This suspiciousness on the part of the Russians seems overdetermined; it is almost too easy to explain" (p. 289). To prove this, CD uses "personal communication" from Dmitri Segal, presumably drawing from this *evidence* to assess the Russian subjects. Liebes writes, "Russians, especially Russian Jews, learn early to scan their environment for signs of where true power is hidden: they learn to read between the lines" (p. 289).

Not surprisingly, given the stereotyping perspective of CD's assessment of Russian immigrants in Israel, the study concludes with positive representations of the second-generation U.S. and Israeli participants. CD argues that, as opposed to the Russians, U.S. and Israeli viewers are complex readers of narrative texts, not simply readers who ignore the text in order to make ideological pronouncements with "flaunted superiority" (pp. 289-290). Liebes (1988) writes that U.S. and Israeli participants' "retellings are 'open,' future oriented, and take account of the never-ending genre of the soap opera" (p. 290). Liebes concludes an otherwise academically impersonal article with this assessment of her U.S. and Israeli participants: "Their definition of both the viewing and the retelling as liminal permits a playful subjunctivity in their negotiations with the program, with fellow viewers, and with the discussion leaders" (p. 290). Ultimately, that the Russian participants viewed *Dallas* skeptically and U.S. and Israeli participants viewed it as part of a genre of soap operas renders the Russian participants' critiques malfeasant. Indirectly, CD affirms television production and texts, rather than centering the cultural context in which viewing takes place. That CD privileges a pro-U.S., pro-Israeli perspective is not surprising, given the focus of the article on the complex "pleasures" of viewing a U.S. media object, especially one with so much nationalist capital as *Dallas*.

Overall, CD makes surface assumptions about the psychology and intent of subjects and renders an ideologically laden analysis that implies that U.S. citizens and Israelis have common viewing practices and give complex readings of television narratives, whereas Russians are unfriendly and uncommunicative and make ideological pronouncements about the show without taking into account its more complex narrative design. Without asking for self-reports by participants, or simply by problematizing the ideological focus of the study itself, this article ends up implying that the most important thing about people is the nation and the general ideology practiced within that nation, as understood by the "nonpartisan" Western researcher. For the Russian participant, national culture *determines* his or her readings; for U.S. and Israeli participants, national culture *frees* them to provide their own individual and creative readings.

DCS's focus on contextualizing the practice of comparative research is in many ways a nice corrective to CD's decontextualizing approach. Yet, in promoting CD's approach, and in borrowing so much from it, many of the same critiques of CD's work I have made so far also apply to DCS. Moreover, DCS relies heavily on other problematic research besides CD. The well-established intercultural communication model on which DCS relies—(a) individual versus collective action, (b) low versus high context cultures, (c) conceptions of authority and obedience, and (d) masculinity versus femininity as exhibited in different national cultures—is, for the most part, specious (González & Peterson, 1993; Moon, 1996; Xi, 1994). It is surprising, given the range and breadth of intercultural communication, that the field of research has relied for so long on this ethnocentric and limiting research paradigm that tends more toward stereotypes of marginalized cultures than toward collaboration with them. The attempt to make broad, general claims about nations, and then to extrapolate those speculations to apply to the people who live in the geographical spaces those nations circumscribe, especially given the multiracial and multicultural world in which we live, is fraught with problems these foci may serve to make worse rather than better. As Moon (1996) suggests about much contemporary intercultural research,

"Culture," at this level, is most often defined as nationality, and the constructedness of this position and its intersection with other positions such as gender and social class is not considered. The outcome is that diverse groups are treated as homogeneous, differences within national boundaries, ethnic groups, genders, and races are obscured, and hegemonic notions of "culture" are presented as "shared" by all cultural members. (p. 76)

The very attempt to force a generalizing principle out of every study is a practice handed down to us throughout Western intellectual history, a history that dominant U.S. and European national cultures have strongly participated in shaping, simultaneously denying the specific nature of that process—a process I problematize here. That is, the legacy of at least enlightenment thinking, especially perhaps in this country, is one fraught with the logical notion that eliminating all falsity will produce a positivity. Moreover, the academic approach that searches for a generalizing principle, especially as that principal is then affixed to people, demonstrates the degree to which objectivity can serve as a kind of antiseptic scientism, relentlessly in pursuit of a unifying principle and willing to sacrifice any variable or subject that fails to bear out its claim on knowledge.

Basically, these generalizing claims, no matter how far reduced they may be, are, as DCS asserts, "stereotypes" of people, premised on a U.S.-centric model of cultural relations, with a narrow understanding of nation, race, class, gender, and sexuality. They are stereotypes; they do not portray people as they see themselves. Rather, they portray people in ways that are advantageous for those who study them, categorize them, and then use those categories for self-serving purposes. For instance, blanket stereotypes of a society (as if there is ever one society) as a collective, high context, authoritative, and masculine people, which is the typical construction in intercultural communication research, is a move toward controlling the people in that country. These stereotypes differentiate the culture (as if there is or could be such a thing as "a culture" given the contradictory, overlapping, hybrid, multifaceted, diverse, and geopolitical tapestry of all cultures) from (yet another misnomer) U.S. culture. The differentiation usually is for the purposes of arguing U.S. superiority, for providing inexperienced U.S. students (arguably not the ones being studied) with tools for survival in the increasingly competitive world of business, and for providing quick fix solutions for students in introductory intercultural communication courses who envision, perhaps one day, communicating and interacting with the people under study. Not only do these stereotypes not hold up, they offend and objectify. They assume that a people and a culture are homogeneous entities; that they function in a systemic, logically consistent fashion; that people act predictably over time; and that the most important part about communication is reading moments of idiosyncratic behavior rather than, for instance, deconstructing one's own ideological education and position and interacting in an informed and reformed way that recognizes self-consciousness about similarity and difference, generally, in daily life. Furthermore, stereotypes assume that a self-produced model, without the benefit of models for, by, and of its participants, is a sufficient beginning for cultural research. Whereas DCS does add to, and thus alters, an intercultural model built on stereotyping logics, by insisting that we build on (rather than replace) this model, DCS necessarily perpetuates many of the stereotypes and research problems it critiques.

Part of the problem, here, may be that the conception of nation-centered research is insufficiently theorized in the research that DCS cites and, more important, is then also undertheorized in DCS. Although it is beyond the scope of this chapter to provide a full, detailed sketch of the research being done in this area, I would point out that much recent scholarship has been dedicated to theorizing "nation" and its typical collaborator "colonialism." Benedict Anderson's (1983) ground-breaking book, *Imagined Communities,* argues that nations are a fairly new idea, actually a post-Gutenberg press invention. That is, the very idea of a nation was not conceived until the possibility for reading a single text by people across a wide expanse of geographical (newly typographical) space became theoretically possible and practically accomplished. From there, people could imagine extending empires and gaining collective responses from disparate peoples within the empire in an efficient enough fashion to conceive of nation-building and its administration. Certainly, production and distribution of the Bible served to unify broad publics who read the book and who were aware that other people far away from their local experiences were reading it, too. Nevertheless, even today, not all people understand themselves as part of a nation; nor is the concept of a nation likely to be similar across great geographical distances. In brief, even today a nation never fully or adequately reflects the lives of the diverse people living in the nation that the nation pretends and sometimes appears to represent. The very focus on a nation, then, as a *given* unit of understanding in communication or other research, is problematic. For a person to understand herself or himself as part of a nation requires years and years of socialization and a civilization in which that is a taken-for-granted assumption. That is, a nation only makes sense when *nation becomes a taken-for-granted, hence naturalized, part of one's daily experiences.* For those without that kind of socialization, a nation is not an understandable or representative symbol of unity, identity, or existence. And even for those of us who live in a culture with highly technological means for communicating, our *sense* of nation and national identity can vary enormously, given Anderson's (1983) argument that nations exist only in socially imagined spaces—in a fictional world ontologically distinct from the world in which we live our lives.

In addition, DCS does not address the spate of research on cultural studies, some of which follows and builds on Anderson's (1983) research and could inform a cross-cultural communication model. Given the international interest in cultural studies, the number of associations, departments, conventions, journals, books, articles (both academic and newsworthy), and general conversations about cultural studies within the past 20 to 30 years (let alone, as Bruce Gronbeck suggested on a discussion panel at the Speech Communication Association in 1994, since the early 20th century), and given communication scholars' role in producing this deluge of discourse, a student of cross-cultural communication could expect DCS to provide at least a chance reference to the potential collaborative opportunities possible between cross-cultural communication research and cultural studies. Nevertheless, I would point out that overlooking cultural studies is itself not a problem specific to DCS. The insularity of communication research generally, despite all of the recent arguments that our field borrows far too many theories from other fields, is becoming more and more frequent.[4] Nevertheless, especially with regard to the issue of cross-cultural communication, at least a little bit of communication outside of our own backyard might be advisable. The critique I make of CD for not being willing to talk and learn from participants applies here: If we are to take cross-cultural communication research seriously, and I think we certainly should, then (a) we will have to practice communicating with people likely to have something to say about the matter without prejudices about who they are and where they are from, and (b) we will have to make sure that various voices, positions, and perspectives are heard on the matter, for the benefits of self-reports may be the first lesson we learn from doing such research. As Alberto González (1990) writes, "Communication studies interpreting the discourse of a particular co-culture may be enhanced when attention is given to the discovery of the historical symbolism to which the co-culture responds" (p. 289).

Many of my criticisms so far are directed at the research DCS cites and not at DCS itself. For instance, DCS itself recommends that self-reports be used in cross-cultural research. In addition, because DCS regards culture as socially constructed, its definition of "nation" implicitly must also be so, though the chapter does not make this point specifically. Moreover, DCS's theory of cultural change has real possibilities with regard to cross-cultural communication research. Although I think a lot more discussion about this focus needs to take place, the notion of comparing and contrasting cultural conceptions and enactments of change is quite intriguing. A model of cultural change could help account for various levels of conservative and revolutionary policies and could help avoid fast-starting despotic rulerships—something many cultural, social, and political groups throughout the world, I might add, think happens every 4 to 8 years in the United States on the first Tuesday in November. A focus on change would encourage continued change and help to make communication scholarship more socially effective. Although a theory of culture that addresses the issue of cultural change would be helpful, a model that makes universal claims or rests on universal assumptions about how people act would not. My purpose here is to break away more fully from traditional models, in part by looking outside of the insularity of a nationalist paradigm, and then to enact, really and realistically, what DCS only touches on as a vague possibility and what it tries to incorporate into the current structure of communication research. This approach, I hope, can alter rather than expand that current structure. Moreover, the definition of change and how change can be examined would have to be well-formed, yet it could not rest on rigid conceptions of nations. It could not conclude, as Chesebro (citing Triandis and his collaborators) argues, that, "it is often necessary to 'generate stereotypes as hypotheses of national character.' " Finally, a better justification for a model of change could be made.

Whereas a focus on cultural change could lead to more egalitarian and theoretically useful communication research, a retreat to field-specific models, which themselves represent much of what cultural studies research has worked so hard to change, would not be advisable. Moreover, a cross-cultural paradigm that engages cultures and recognizes the legitimacy of unique cultural perspectives, and especially a paradigm willing to be transformed by a multiplicity of peoples and conversations with peoples, would not only be helpful but purposeful and praiseworthy. DCS allows us to move in either direction. I hope we do not retreat back to models that rest on making broad generalizations about massive numbers of diverse peoples with complex cultural organizations, performances, identities, and experiences. By broadening the possibilities rather than narrowing them, a study of cultural change would, I hope, eliminate the need to study "national" culture at all.

NOTES

1. For critiques of U.S.-centric models of intercultural communication, see, for instance, González (1990), González and Peterson (1993), Moon (1996), Shome (1996), and Xi (1994).

2. For example, one question that might have been helpful is, "What do you think has led you to see television in this way, that is, as an embodiment of U.S. cultural values and ideology?"

3. A stereotype conveys information efficiently. It is a representative anecdote, or a metaphor that stands in for complex cultural phenomena, and as such it reduces people to the most generalizable features available at the moment, one that makes sense within the context of the conversation. Hence, a stereotype serves a limiting function, by reducing the conversation to the feature most people privy to the conversation, could agree to, often at the expense of the perspective of those the stereotype is meant to represent. Stereotypes tend to be like sound bites: Once spoken, they recruit their participants to recognize consciously the feature about themselves to which the hailer of the participant refers. In addition, stereotypes attempt to contain meaning: that is, to limit understandings of complex cultural realities to the most easily graspable element of a person's or people's overall humanity.

4. Key here is the insularity and protectiveness within the communication discipline, as if all questions can be answered within the discipline, as if "home-grown" is best, and as if communication principles are sufficient to answer all questions. The focus becomes, "Communication is never not relevant."

REFERENCES

Anderson, B. (1983). *Imagined communities: Reflections on the origin and spread of nationalism.* London: Verso.

González, A. (1990). Mexican "otherness" in the rhetoric of Mexican Americans. *Southern Communication Journal, 55,* 276-291.

González, A., & Peterson, T. R. (1993). Enlarging conceptual boundaries: A critique of research in intercultural communication. In S. P. Bowen & N. Wyatt (Eds.), *Transforming visions: Feminist critiques in communication studies* (pp. 249-278). Cresskill, NJ: Hampton.

Gronbeck, B. E. (1994, November). *Rhetoric and cultural studies: A new constellation.* Symposium conducted at the meeting of the Speech Communication Association, New Orleans, LA.

Liebes, T. (1988). Cultural differences in the retelling of television fiction. *Critical Studies in Mass Communication, 5,* 277-292.

Moon, D. G. (1996). Concepts of "culture": Implications for intercultural communication research. *Communication Quarterly, 44,* 70-84.

Shome, R. (1996). Postcolonial interventions in the rhetorical canon: An "other" view. *Communication Theory, 6,* 40-59.

Xi, C. (1994). Individualism and collectivism in American and Chinese societies. In A. González, M. Houston, & V. Chen (Eds.), *Our voices: Essays in culture, ethnicity, and communication* (pp. 152-158). Los Angeles, CA: Roxbury.

11

Response to Chesebro's Change Variable to Explain Cross-Cultural Communication

CARLEY DODD • *Abilene Christian University*

Timely essays that advance a category system of research concerning international and intercultural communication contribute a significant dimension to the human communication discipline. Even more specific, any attempt to clarify an understanding of "culture" further enables researchers to explain cultural variability and its association with human communication. In that regard, Casmir (1995) affirms Shuter's (1990) earlier concern that much of the research in intercultural communication "is conducted to refine existing communication theories: Culture serves principally as a research laboratory for testing the validity of communication paradigms" (Shuter, 1990, p. 238). Casmir underscores a concern defining culture and its communication concomitants when he emphasizes how culture has not been as powerful a driving force in intercultural communication research as much as in psychology and in research to support other communication models (Casmir, 1995, p 34). Casmir's entire volume is dedicated to examining the role of common national experiences and their influence on communication between nations as well as viewing national cultures as a way of understanding intracultural communication.

Chesebro's chapter in this current volume enters into the arena that calls for more precision in defining culture and its role in shaping inter- and intracultural communication research. His concern and discussion of "culture" coordinates with frequent critiques in papers, articles, and books, which by the dozens, and at almost every convention program, often present a common concern over the meaning of "culture." Chesebro's chapter underscores selected foundations in cross-cultural communication, highlights communication systems as a reflection of culture, and then specifically develops "cultural change" as an additional cultural dimension.

This review of Chesebro's (this volume) work first offers a critical analysis of his position. Then, by extending Chesebro's base into a matrix and then adding categories in a matrix for cultural research, I believe researchers will have a more expanded repertoire of categories around which to improve intercultural and cross-cultural research.

CROSS-CULTURAL RESEARCH

Chesebro (this volume) first presents a case "to compare and to contrast communication systems" that, he argues, is a process inherent in the communication discipline's tradition. The discussion, after acknowledging how comparative research has been expressed as "international, intercultural, and cross-cultural studies," then isolates "the nature of cross-cultural communication research." He illustrates with an analysis of Liebes's (1988) work, comparing the responses of Arabs, Moroccans, Israelis, Russians, and Americans on how they each would retell an episode of *Dallas* that they had just viewed. These five cultures each responded differently in their communication response to the story. Beyond comparisons, this variability is then advanced as the second point—that is, how cultures reflect dominant symbols in their communication systems.

In other words, the chapter next highlights how cross-cultural communication research is a matter of comparing cultures as dominant symbol-using systems. That is, a way to differentiate between cultures is to contrast and compare them along an increasing number of continua. One of those, bolstered by citing Liebes's (1988) research, appears to be dominant symbol usage as part of a culture's communication system that lies at the core of understanding cultural differences. Or as Chesebro cited, "communication systems—at least—reflect cultural differences . . . or may actually constitute cultural differences," since meanings are "used to justify the existence of cross-cultural differences."

To consider the chapter's position here is to thoughtfully reflect on several key points. First, scholars traditionally have advanced a clear appreciation of cross-cultural comparisons. The earliest days of cultural and social anthropology emerged in the 1920s and 1930s, as a discipline to study cultures, in contrast to traditional categories of archeology. Such names as Ruth Benedict, Edward Hall, Bronislaw Malinowski, and Margaret Mead, along with the next generation of such cultural anthropologists as Robin Fox (1971), Marvin Harris (1968), and Serena Nanda (1980), pioneered the study of comparing living cultures. Their quest was not so much for an understanding of communication or communication systems, except for Hall, as for an understanding of how cultures are similar or different. Their debates centered on systems of analysis to compare cultures. The resulting taxonomies became the tools to develop comparative ethnographies that could ascertain answers to cultural categories. The system was believed to ensure adequate "scientific" comparisons and replications of these observer-based techniques. Their debates sounded like those of communication scholars today because they borrowed the terms *emic* and *etic* from linguist Kenneth Pike. One group argued for etic taxonomies to conduct massive comparison studies that now appear in many libraries as "The Human Relations Area File" or can be found under "Ethnographic Studies." A second group, with such authors as Ward Goodenough (1956), argued that such approaches are missing the internal or emic view of a culture, as he articulated the case for "cognitive anthropology" whereby researchers were to "get inside the mind" of the culture.

Chesebro's call to isolate cross-cultural contrast and comparison research pertaining to communication is appreciated. We must be reminded that scholarly efforts to advance "newly developed" cultural dimensions must stand the test of earlier and current debates from intercultural communication and anthropology. In this sense, we can put any effort to expand cultural dimensions as enlarging our view of any taxonomy of comparison research for the purposes of (a) providing profiles to examine culture A and culture B differences and (b) providing insight into intracultural communication.

It is also very important to differentiate cross-cultural communication from inter- and intracultural communication research. Perhaps Chesebro (this volume) would agree that cross-cultural comparisons can never quite tell us what is inside the individual, or whether or not the individual is actually influenced and guided by cultural values, worldview, beliefs, customs, and norms in interactional encounters between people.

The chapter further suggests that symbol using is the common experience, and we must agree that language, codes, and symbols are part of the commonalities that make a culture (Lustig & Koester, 1996, p. 33; Smith, 1966). But there are several pitfalls to avoid in using this argument. One is that symbol usage and "meaning" are basically outsider perspectives (etic) applied to culture A, culture B, and so on. In that sense, Johnson and Tuttle (1989) observe that symbols are "static communication, ritually oriented communication . . . with scripts operative to a greater extent than our own." In other words, "they have a time frame that is much longer than our own, so that intercultural encounters that U.S. cultural members consider failures . . . may be proceeding quite nicely in the view of cultural members who have a different temporal frame of reference" (pp. 466-467). Another pitfall in arguing that symbol usage is a reflection of cultural differences, and then drawing cross-cultural comparisons and contrasts, is the recognition that these profiles are often unidimensional, simplistic, and based on convenience samples, points illustrated in Casmir's (1995) critique of Hofstede's sampling from within the Hermes organization in 40 countries. The influence of individual differences and corporate culture do not seem to matter in these profiles of national cultures.

A final caution and limitation to cross-cultural research is that by its nature it lacks the interactive qualities of intercultural communication. Cross-cultural comparisons seem static, bounded by averages and modalities of themes that can be predictive but that lack the qualities of what *actually* happens in the interpersonal intercultural "encounter" that characterizes much of current intercultural research. Thus, our applause goes to Chesebro for highlighting the importance of cross-cultural research, as we also recognize its long-standing tradition in all cross-cultural comparisons efforts. Yet caution must be exerted against overgeneralization that cultural differences, ascertained by comparisons, can be predictive without additional dynamics of communication style differences, relationship history, attribution, cultural competency, worldview, values, and numerous other intercultural factors influencing the communication encounter (Dodd, 1995, pp. 4-13). It is a stronger case to point out that to isolate *only* the "cross-cultural" aspects of this field is to rob researchers of potentially rich diversity, interactional options, adaptation strategy, competency skills, cultural attitudes, value themes, and worldview perspectives influencing the communication process (Brislin, 1993; Dodd, 1995; Elashmawi & Harris, 1993; Klopf, 1995; Lustig & Koester, 1996). In essence, cross-cultural, and for that matter international, communication studies apply an etic perspective to an *etic-emic* process and thus limit the study of the moment of actual encounter. Numerous researchers have noted the intercultural relationship, the encounter itself, as the defining moment of intercultural communication often identified with metaphors such as communication with "strangers" (Barnlund, 1989; Gudykunst & Kim, 1984), "attachment," "intimacy," "partnership," "disclosure," "affiliation," (Barnlund, 1989), and "interaction with cultural differences" (Dodd, 1995).

THE RELATION OF CULTURE AND SYMBOLS

The Chesebro chapter (this volume) articulates the problem of confounding issues and conceptual problems in defining "culture." The chapter prefers the Lustig and Koester (1993, p. 41) definition of culture as "a learned set of shared perceptions about beliefs, values, and norms." From that point, the chapter maintains that language and culture are inseparable, a point that has been made traditionally and contemporarily. The work continues to underscore throughout the chapter how symbols lie at the core of culture. Evidence from Scollon and Scollon (1995) is cited to note that, because symbols are cultural, and because symbols convey understandings from one generation to the next, generational affiliation correlates with a culture's discourse system, connected through ideology and identity.

This sequence of logic is intriguing. Certainly, as Chesebro states, language and culture are inseparable, and language choices and patterns can be studied "as a reflection and integrating force of a cultural system." There is no question that rhetorical and linguistic factors reify certain elements of culture. Nevertheless, these are not the fundamental questions about culture as much as the question of ultimate cause of individual behavior in culture, *including* language. There is something inside of individuals influenced by their culture that belies language. If he is saying that, to study symbols is to study culture, then the chapter's emphasis implies that to examine discourse or symbols offers an etic approach as if examining rhetoric, symbols, and language itself would be the ultimate "keyhole" through which scholars could see culture more fully. Without in any way denying the power of language, we must entertain the notion that thought, value, worldview, spirituality, ecology, economics, literacy, urbanization, cultural catastrophe, and crisis are but a few of an individual's cultural experiences that also lead to symbol usage selected from within the pool of possible symbols. Consideration must be given to how individuals modify and recalibrate symbol usage on the basis of features happening inside the individuals and factors with the high context and privately understood aspects of a culture, a theme supporting Chesebro's point. Nevertheless, we would argue that symbols offer a look in part but that an etic-emic perspective flourishes within culture's vast array of elements, institutions, and cognitive systems to offer a still more holistic view.

CULTURE AS NATION-STATE AND VARIABLES UNDERLYING CULTURAL SYSTEMS

The chapter exits the concept of culture and language to embrace the notion of nation-state as a cultural system. The support for this position has been posited in the chapter and by Casmir (1995) and Shuter (1990). An exciting note is Chesebro's search for meaningful categories in

TABLE 11.1 Values Compared by Nations

What Japanese Say These Cultures Value			
Americans	Chinese	Arabs	Japanese
Personal life	Bicycles	Religion	Information
Wealth	History	Allah	Harmony
Fairness	Health	Koran	Honesty
One answer	Obeying power	Status	Options
Family	Family	History	Loyalty
Liberty	Money	Family	Social status
Materials	Age	Nationality	Tradition
Education	Civilization	Islam	Respect
Time	Gold	Moustache	Company
Frontier spirit	Relationships	Gold	Status
Success	Respect		Job
Dreams	Group		Cooperation
Freedom	Food		Society
Directness			Hard work
Money			Politeness
Reasons			Family
Religion			Modesty
Power			Uniformity
			Adjustment

SOURCE: Adapted from Elashmawi and Harris (1993).

using the nation-state as a unit of analysis, particularly his citation of Edelstein's insistence that one should pursue commonalities until cultural differences are encountered. This laudable goal should invite more exacting probes into cultural universals, it is suggested.

Two observations could be added, one to advance this point and one to limit it. Elashmawi and Harris's (1993) analysis of extensive value differences between national cultures underscores thematic and value differences, both real and perceived. For instance, Table 11.1 illustrates what Japanese value in relation to what they say Americans, Chinese, and Arabs value. Other lists and comparisons abound in the intercultural literature (Brislin, 1993; Harris & Moran, 1995; Klopf, 1995). The point is that national cultures can be distinguished, a point supporting Chesebro's chapter. The chapter can be extended, however, when we recognize that many national cultural comparisons are profiles of value-oriented differences. These, in turn, promise potential prediction of perceptual and attributional influence on relationships and communication. But the forecast is a profile. The question then raised is how such profiles, values, and categories give insight into interpersonal intracultural encounters, as well as interpersonal intercultural encounters. What is the link to actual communication?

A second point, and a cautionary note, is to question the validity limits of national culture. We would hope that the colonial traditions and the melting pot theme from the United States have not led to an assumption that national culture and cultural systems necessarily overlap. The Islamic cultures, bounded by political entities in the Middle East and Asia, illustrate high consistency of national culture and actual or internal cultural systems within those national borders. The former Soviet Union, however, illustrates a nation-state with multicultural diversity bounded by economic and geopolitical forces but lacking correlation with the diverse cultural systems contained in its borders. Furthermore, some global regions of the world are significantly more tribal and familial in nature than "national." Tribal systems in Africa can cut across national boundaries that, by all standards of measure, are realities of geopolitical factors and not necessarily shared perception. Such tribal groups as the Ashanti, Ga, Fanta, Ewe, Ibo, and Hausa can be found concentrated in such national boundaries as Ghana and Nigeria, but they are clearly not limited to such boundaries. The hundreds of tribal groups on the New Guinea island fall into two politically determined halves of the island, Irian Jaya, belonging to Indonesia, and the independent half, Papua New Guinea.

CHANGE AS A VARIABLE EXPLAINING CROSS-CULTURAL COMMUNICATION

Following the discussion of the nation-state as a significant cultural system unit of analysis for research, Chesebro moves toward the significant contribution in the chapter. He reviews the Triandis and Hofstede notions of the individual-collectivist dimension of culture, along with Hofstede's "Power Distance Dimension," Hofstede's "Masculine Feminine Dimension" (inappropriately named, and appreciatively indicated in Chesebro's analysis by Lustig and Koester, 1993, who prefer the term "achievement-nurturance"), and Hall's "Context Culture." Curiously, Chesebro does not mention Hofstede's fourth factor, "Uncertainty Reduction." The omission is especially intriguing in light of the intercultural research employing variations of this dimension. These categories have generated a breakthrough in intercultural and cross- cultural research, initiating numerous articles and papers that began appearing from approximately the early to mid-1980s until the present time. It is these important underlying dimensions of culture and their research roots from Hofstede and Hall, in comparisons of national cultures, which sets the stage for Chesebro's additional underlying dimension: change.

Chesebro adds the construct of "change" as a significant cultural variable, pointing to potential variability of cultural systems responding positively or negatively to change. Nation-states that advocate a dominant ideology, and where such discourse dominates, we presume are cultures predicted to react negatively to change. Chesebro envisions certain religious sects that insulate cultural members from contact with the larger society and thus impede structural and process change. By contrast, other cultures respond positively to change, explained by multiple causes for consequent change. The chapter informs its readers of a developmental type model that was developed by Service (1971), and although Chesebro is not entirely content with Service's definition (and, we presume, the model), it nevertheless is presented as an example of stages explaining culture. A culture experiences revolutionary change (radical, abrupt), evolutionary change (reasonable rate, unfolding), stability (when successfully adapted, the culture rejects subsequent changes), and involution (preservation, control of anything new by the already possessed remedy from the existing system). Each stage, moreover, is marked by forms of discourse or rhetoric, which are designed to fit the outcomes associated with each stage.

The benefits of reminding us of "change" as an added category to cross-cultural research are intriguing and should be underscored for future researchers to consider. Some researchers might object to the developmental stages presented in the model (we resist here such a critique that might involve assumptions of uniformity, homogeneity, and linearity of any developmental models). The emphasis on rhetoric, symbol usage, and discourse as seemingly the primary communication aspect associated with the model might reasonably be argued as a limitation in contrast to exploring a variety of additional communication themes and behaviors we noted earlier. Although some fine tuning or major overhaul might be posited, this category convincingly invites many researchers to use it as a new category for research. Particularly, the linking of stages of change in culture to rhetorical outcroppings associated with those stages could prove helpful (if researchers accept the assumptions of the stage or developmental model presented). The opportunity to further advance this category is irresistible at this point.

The intercultural communication field has not overlooked the "change" variable, if we consider a number of other communication perspectives. To outline aspects or dimensions of change could be useful, as we further the purpose of this review to be more inclusive and build on the chapter's direction concerning change.

Young Kim has discussed the application of change in numerous papers, articles, and books. Her notion of "adaptive change" or "adaptation" is well documented and modeled (Kim, 1989). In the context of strangers adapting to new cultures, Kim asserts adaptation as the "internal transformation of an individual challenged by a new cultural environment in the direction of increasing fitness and compatibility in that environment" (Kim, 1988, p. 9). She also concludes that "adaptation to the environment is the main causative agent of a human system's evolution" (p. 45). Whereas Chesebro is dealing with macrocultural change and stages of receptivity, the models provided by Kim, and the measures indicated in much of her research, suggest additional ways to unfold the change metaphor. Particularly, Kim's development of the "Stress-Growth-Adaptation Dynamic" could prove a useful model for refinement and application to Chesebro's notion of nation-state change potential.

The model presented in Chesebro's work not only lacks the individual's role in coping with adaptation and change, but it does not penetrate the depths of interpersonal networking and relationship roles influencing the change process. From an interpersonal network perspective, Roger's (1995) prolific work in innovation decision and cultural change (diffusion and adoption of change) has illuminated this set of causes to change. He focuses on many information roles people play to exert influence and advance information within a system.

Harris and Moran (1995) and Elashmawi and Harris (1993) indicate the convergence of culture and organization in the change process. Their models are based on the nature of organizations working in global environments and the emphasis that must be placed on "cultural synergy" to adapt to changing conditions. Their goal is not one of domination but of a blending of the best of two or more cultures when such a blend serves a functional purpose.

Another system change perspective can be drawn from family studies and family therapy literature. The work of Olson (1976) and other associates presents a model of two axes of family systems: cohesion and change. Each axis has four categories on a continuum, resulting in 16 combinations. His axis of change (developed widely in this literature tradition) offers rich metaphors regarding autonomy, intimacy, power, and enmeshment. Whereas the application of this model to family communication has been developed (Galvin & Brommel, 1996), attempts to adapt this model to the cross-cultural or intercultural literature have not surfaced but appear promising.

TABLE 11.2 A Matrix of Cultural Dimensions by Nation-State by Dominant
Symbols or Discourse Applied from Chesebro's Categories

	Nation-State Culture		
Dimensions	*Culture A*	*Culture B*	*Culture C*
Individual-Collectivist			
Power-Distance			
Masculine-Feminine			
Context Culture			
Change			

The dependent or outcome variable is Dominant Symbols or Discourse Systems to be completed in the blank areas.

TOWARD AN EXPANDED CATEGORY SYSTEM FOR INTERCULTURAL AND CROSS-CULTURAL COMMUNICATION RESEARCH

The Chesebro chapter illuminates the important question of major categories and adds the component of change and associated rhetorical consequence within each change stage. The work can be analyzed into a matrix of (a) national cultures by (b) individual-collectivist, power-distance, masculine-feminine, context dimensions by (c) a discourse system or content analysis of dominant symbols. An example is presented in Table 11.2. The blanks to be analyzed are the kinds of dominant symbols or a representation of a discourse system. This system organizes the complex issues presented in Chesebro's chapter by presenting a form for us to begin, in some way, to analyze systematically and maintain comparability for other researchers.

I think the system is valuable. Nevertheless, I can add to the category system additional elements that I believe serve to enrich the research process. An expanded model in Table 11.3 is a matrix of cultural systems, with a broader list of cultural factors by communication interactions encountered. These illustrate research models and guides for ultimately refining the most significant and potentially powerful predictive variables possible in explaining intercultural communication.

Ultimately, the questions of culture as a unit of analysis, the benefits of etic versus emic analyses, the viability of nation-state as predictive of cultural communication, the benefits of discourse symbols as a meaningful outcome variable, and the most meaningful set of categories appropriate for intercultural communication research must continue to

TABLE 11.3 An Expanded Matrix of Cultural Factors by National Culture by
Intercultural Relationship Outcome

	National Culture		
Cultural Factor	*Culture A*	*Culture B*	*Culture C*
Individual-Collectivist			
Power–Distance			
Masculine–Feminine			
Uncertainty Reduction			
Change Potential			
Worldview (Hi-Lo Control)			
Time Orientation			
Spatial Orientation			
Spiritual Quest Potential			
Adaptation Motivation			
Logic & Thought–Linear/Sequential			
Face Saving Motivation			
Doing–Being Continuum			
Task–People Continuum			

The dependent or outcome variable is the positive or negative relationship outcome resulting from intercultural encounters.

be sorted out. This chapter builds on Chesebro's advancement and seeks to refine and further advance theoretical constructs for research.

REFERENCES

Barnlund, D. C. (1989). *Communicative styles of Japanese and Americans: Images and realities.* Belmont, CA: Wadsworth.

Brislin, R. (1993). *Understanding culture's influence on behavior.* Orlando, FL: Harcourt Brace.

Casmir, F. L. (1995). *Communication in eastern Europe: The role of history, culture, and media in contemporary conflicts.* Hillsdale, NJ: Lawrence Erlbaum.

Dodd, C. H. (1995). *Dynamics of intercultural communication* (4th ed.). Madison, WI: Brown & Benchmark.

Elashmawi, F., & Harris, P. R. (1993). *Multicultural management: New skills for global success.* Houston, TX: Gulf.

Fox, R. (1971). *Kinship and marriage.* New York: Penguin.

Galvin, K. M., & Brommel, B. J. (1996). *Family communication: Cohesion and change* (4th ed.). New York: HarperCollins.

Goodenough, W. (1956). Componential analysis and the study of meaning. *Language, 35,* 195-216.

Gudykunst, W. B., & Kim, Y. Y. (1984). *Communicating with strangers.* New York: Random House.

Harris, M. (1968). *The rise of anthropological theory*. New York: Thomas Y. Crowell.

Harris, P., & Moran, R. (1995). *Managing cultural differences* (4th ed.). Houston, TX: Gulf.

Johnson, J. D., & Tuttle, F. (1989). Problems in intercultural research. In M. Asante & W. Gudykunst (Eds.), *Handbook of international and intercultural communication* (pp. 461-483). Newbury Park, CA: Sage.

Kim, Y. Y. (1988). *Communication and cross-cultural adaptation: An integrative theory*. Avon, UK: Multilingual Matters.

Kim, Y. Y. (1989). Intercultural adaptation. In M. Asante & W. Gudykunst (Eds.), *Handbook of international and intercultural communication* (pp. 275-294). Newbury Park, CA: Sage.

Klopf, D. W. (1995). *Intercultural encounters: The fundamentals of intercultural communication* (3rd ed.). Englewood, CO: Morton.

Liebes, T. (1988). Cultural differences in the retelling of television fiction. *Critical Studies in Mass Communication, 5*, 277-292.

Lustig, M. W., & Koester, J. (1993). *Intercultural competence: Interpersonal communication across cultures*. New York: HarperCollins.

Lustig, M. W., & Koester, J. (1996). *Intercultural competence: Interpersonal communication across cultures* (2nd ed.). New York: HarperCollins.

Nanda, S. (1980). *Cultural anthropology*. New York: Van Nostrand Reinhold.

Olson, D. H. (1976). *Treating relationships*. Lake Mills, IA: Graphic.

Roger, E. M. (1995). *Diffusion of innovations* (4th ed.). New York: Free Press.

Scollon, R., & Scollon, S. W. (1995). Generational discourse. In R. Scollon & S. W. Scollon, *Intercultural communication: A discourse approach* (pp. 205-228). Oxford, UK: Basil Blackwell.

Service, E. R. (1971). *Cultural evolutionism: Theory in practice*. New York: Holt, Rinehart & Winston.

Shuter, R. (1990). The centrality of culture. *Southern Communication Journal, 55*, 237-249.

Smith, A. F. (1966). *Communication and culture*. New York: Holt, Rinehart & Winston.

12

Change, Nation-States, and the Centrality of a Communication Perspective

JAMES W. CHESEBRO • *Indiana State University,*
Terre Haute

Dialogue is an essential dimension of the scholarly process, but a dialogue can incorporate a tremendous range of perspectives. Goaded by political and ideological objectives, Kent A. Ono (this volume) is specifically concerned about basic intercultural research techniques that could, he fears, promote unwarranted generalizations and harmful stereotypes. From quite a different perspective, questioning central assumptions of all cross-cultural communication research, Carley Dodd (this volume) maintains that, "There is something inside of individuals influenced by their culture that belies language." In this regard, Dodd suggests that individuals "modify and recalibrate symbol usage" on the basis of such factors as spirituality, ecology, economics, literacy, urbanization, cultural catastrophe, and crisis. Accordingly, admitting that "Chesebro is dealing with macrocultural change and stages of receptivity," Dodd believes that several notions of change also exist that emphasize individual and interpersonal cultural experiences. Going far beyond my argument for the inclusion of change, Dodd concludes by proposing that several new and additional factors be considered in cross-cultural communication research.

THE ORIGINAL POSITION REMAINS

Given these responses, I must initially note that neither critic actually deals with the central principle of my chapter. I have maintained that the sense of change and the response to change within a cultural system dramatically affect what transformations and actions mean and how a nation-state will act on these meanings. If a nation-state values change, it is more likely to foster revolutionary and evolutionary changes in all of its customs, mores, and institutions. If a nation-state denigrates change, stability and involution are more likely to determine future actions. Accordingly, I maintained that the four existing schemes for characterizing cultures—the individual-collectivist dimension, the context dimension, the power distance dimension, and the masculinity-femininity dimension—will become more useful, meaningful, and predictive when a nation-state's approach to change is also considered. An example illustrates my point. In the early 1970s, a researcher might have provided a detailed description of these four dimensions in Iran. Logically and conceptually, a reasonable extension of these descriptions would have suggested that Iran would become increasingly Westernized. Nevertheless, such an analysis would have generated an extremely misleading view of the future of Iran, for the analysis ignores the understandings of change that permeated the Iranian culture. In the case of Iran, the power of tradition was overwhelming and fostered a commitment to involution. In this case, if change had been recognized as a cultural dimension, and if change had been recognized as a factor affecting transformation, a researcher would be encouraged to consider those elements of change that produced the return of the Islamic republic in 1979, the emergence of fundamentalist Muslim codes, and the suppression of Western influences.

In "Distinguishing Cultural Systems," I am attempting to emphasize the role that change can produce, as a construct in cultural analyses. In my view, the sense or understanding of change that dominates a nation-state is an essential dimension that profoundly qualifies what the analyses of the individual-collective, context, power distance, and masculinity-femininity dimensions reveal about cultural transformation and developments in a nation-state. As I see it, an analysis of change can exert an overwhelmingly powerful difference in how a culture is understood.

But the respondents, here, predominantly bypass the essence of this perspective and analysis. I deal, then, with the respondents as they state their cases, which focuses our attention on the value of the nation-state as a construct and the power of a communication perspective.

"IF ONLY THE WORLD WOULD DISSOLVE ITS NATION-STATE BOUNDARIES"

Kent A. Ono uses my chapter on cultural change as an opportunity to promote his specific political and ideological agenda. Although Mr. Ono is worried that my chapter will "unwittingly" promote an ideological position he dislikes, he does little to underscore the ideological position he himself argues for, nor does he offer the kind of reasons and evidence for his position that one might expect in an academic exchange. As I see it, Mr. Ono virtually assumes that his ideological posture is unquestionable. Accordingly, he maintains that he was "hoping" that the "nation-state" would become a "casualty of the Cold War." Of course, the "end of the Cold War" has increased, not decreased, the importance of the *nation-state* as a concept and the number of nation-states. For example, when the Union of Soviet Socialist Republics dissolved on December 25, 1991, some 12 new nation-states immediately replaced it, each fiercely and profoundly nationalistic. As other nation-states achieved independence throughout the late 1980s and into the 1990s, citizenship and nation-state identification has become an even more important way of identifying and characterizing one's cultural orientation. Peoples of different nation-states—be they from Iraq, Ireland, Mexico, Argentina, or even the more recently formed Estonia, Georgia, and Armenia—are increasingly defining themselves as struggling for a nation-state cultural identity, nation-state self-determination, and as cultural agents seeking independence and sovereignty for their respective nation-states.

As I mentioned, Mr. Ono is also worried that my chapter will "unwittingly" reproduce "nationalist assumptions in intercultural research" and that it "rearticulates and enforces a nationalist, U.S.-*centric* model of cultural exchange and interaction." The exploration of nationalistic tendencies in intercultural communication research is more likely to be the product of the actions and changes of world governments rather than the analysis I offer in my chapter. But I do hope that my chapter will draw attention to, and begin to unravel, some of the power politics, nationalistic struggles, and nation-state cultural factors that increasingly control cross-cultural communication.

Regarding his belief that the world should dissolve its nation-state boundaries, Mr. Ono would "eliminate the need to study 'national' culture at all." At this juncture, he is simply presumptuous. He implies that researchers should determine what can and should be studied. In contrast, I would hope that researchers will study the communication systems that exist and record how various cultural groupings identify and describe themselves. If they use their nation-state—its unique customs, its special mores, and its particular institutions—as self-descriptive of their cultural orientation, I would hope researchers recognize such self-definitions as central to the study of cross-cultural communication. The participants in communicative processes, rather than the researchers studying the processes, should determine the frame of reference governing participants' communication systems.

ELIMINATING THE "U.S.-CENTRIC MODEL" AND THE "PRO-U.S., PRO-ISRAELI PERSPECTIVE"

In "Distinguishing Cultural Systems," I used Tamar Liebes's (1988) cross-cultural examination of *Dallas* to "illustrate" the "nature of cross-cultural communication research." Mr. Ono believes "Distinguishing Cultural Systems . . . relies heavily on Liebes's article." Point of fact, my analysis of culture does not rely, at all, on Tamar Liebes's article. My decision to introduce change as a cultural variable does not rely on Liebes's survey of literature, Liebes's concepts of culture, nor on the specific methods used by Liebes. Given the audience I was initially addressing when this chapter was originally presented, it was important to illustrate the nature of cross-cultural communication research. I used Liebes's article to "illustrate the nature of cross-cultural communication research," because it has been one of the most widely distributed examples of cross-cultural research, with various forms of the essay published in *Intermedia* (1984), the *European Journal of Communication* (1986), the third edition of Gumpert and Cathcart's *Inter/Media: Interpersonal Communication in a Media World,* and in *Critical Studies in Mass Communication.* Accordingly, when addressing an audience new to cross-cultural communication research, I did not need to defend all dimensions of a study to maintain that it "illustrates," "intrigues" and "provides one understanding of cross-cultural communication research." Likewise, I believe Mr. Ono is simply wrong when he asserts my chapter "relies heavily on Liebes's article" and when he asserts—without proof to establish the analogy—that the "problematic conception of nation" in Liebes's article is a "reproduction" of the "problematic conception" in my chapter.

At the same time, I believe that Mr. Ono's reading of the Liebes article distorts her analysis, as well as the nature of cross-cultural communication research. Mr. Ono maintains that the Liebes article "decontextualizes concepts of culture, . . . assumes a psychological intent behind the answers given [by participants]," ignores such variables as "personal quirks," "ethnicity, sexuality, or gender; trauma; or more generally diasporic experiences," and ultimately reflects only "Liebes's own ideological position as critic" and "draws on negative Western stereotypes" to characterize one group.

To avoid these problems, Mr. Ono would "ask for self-reports, or even have a conversation with the participants about their questions and answers to determine their own perceptions of why they answered the way they did." Yet Liebes has reported that she used just the kind of self-report data recommended by Mr. Ono, that she had conversations with the participants in her study, and that she sought to determine why the participants in her study answered the way they did. Particularly, Liebes used an "open-ended question" (e.g., "How would you retell the episode [of *Dallas*] you just saw to somebody who had not seen it?"). Indeed, to illustrate her methods, Liebes provided extensive direct quotations from the participants in her study. In addition, Liebes sought to equivocate demographic differences across the five different cultural groupings involved. And she explicitly reported that "age, education, and regular viewing of the program were essentially homogeneous for all participants" across all cultural groupings. She concluded, "We cannot make a claim on formal randomness or representativeness," but she reported that "we have no reason to suspect any systematic bias" and reason to believe that the subjects were "demographically alike for reasons of relatedness and propinquity." Certainly, Mr. Ono might disagree with these claims, but if he does, he needs to identify explicitly the problems he finds with Liebes's procedures, methods for selecting participants, and for claiming that the participants' reported statements reflected their own cultural orientation.

Nevertheless, Mr. Ono's claims are disturbing on another level. He implies that a researcher can somehow avoid having a cultural bias ("Pro-U.S., Pro-Israeli," or otherwise). Granted, a researcher may have a perspective and bias different from the participants. But a researcher always has some sort of ideological bias and cultural orientation that affect descriptions, interpretations, and evaluations. Every research method and procedure—social scientific, ethnographic, critical, and applied—necessarily reflects the political orientation of the researcher. Every researcher has a sense of what is significant and relevant that affects and shapes the design of the researcher's efforts, descriptions, interpretations, and evaluations. Perfect objectivity cannot be achieved. The alternative to a goal of perfect objectivity is to describe one's methods and procedures as clearly and as precisely as possible, so that the reader might discern the meanings the researcher has imposed on the data identified and why it was characterized as it was. In my view, then, Mr. Ono is unnecessarily harsh with Liebes, proposing a standard of objectivity that no researcher can achieve.

STEREOTYPING AND GENERALIZATIONS

Mr. Ono is particularly concerned that researchers avoid stereotyping when conducting cross-cultural communication research. He would avoid "general claims about nations" that "extrapolate" to "the people who live in the geographical spaces those nations circumscribe," the attempt to "force a generalizing principle out of every study," using a "U.S.-centric model of cultural relations," "blanket stereotypes of a society," and stereotypes that "offend and objectify." Mr. Ono concludes this analysis by quoting me, when I report that "it is often necessary to generate 'stereotypes as hypotheses of national character.'"

In response, a degree of "research reality" is required. First, culture is a *socially* constructed *concept* that seeks to characterize the *shared* meanings about perceptions, beliefs, values, and means *by and among unique individuals* who are distinct in a tremendous number of ways. Whenever communication interactions are characterized, the patterns described will always reflect both the unity and division inherent in every communicative exchange. Second, every social unit—from a dyad, to a small group of five, to a composite intergroup unit—possesses variance and differences in terms of individual statements about perceptions, beliefs, values, and means. For example, when discussing the concept of *culture* unifying entire racial groups (such as Latinos, African Americans, Native Americans, and European Americans), variance and differences about perceptions, beliefs, values, and means will necessarily exist. Third, every cultural grouping will contain a host of subcultures. For example, every racial culture contains a great deal of diversity and subcultures who can disagree with one another on significant issues. Accordingly, it is impossible to make any claim about a culture without— to some degree—stereotyping or generalizing. Fourth, stereotyping is an inherent feature of all language use by researchers. Whenever language is used, descriptions and interpretations will provide only an incomplete reflection of what participants report at the time of interviews. Language simply cannot capture the dynamic lived experiences, historical and future processes, and the internal reactions involved when individuals participate and reflect their cultures. In this sense, whenever researchers use language as their mode for reporting findings, they stereotype. Nevertheless, as Williams and Giles (1996, p. 221) have noted, the issue is not whether or not stereotyping is used (for any degree of variance should be reported whenever possible) but whether the stereotyping leads to "negative evaluations, misunderstandings, and even conflict." Fifth and finally, not all communicative acts will be treated by a researcher as cultural. As Mr. Ono has put it, some communicative acts are best viewed by a researcher as "personal quirks," "ethnicity, sexuality, or gender; trauma; or, more generally, diasporic experiences" rather than reflective of a particular culture. Whereas Mr. Ono is silent on how a researcher should make these distinctions, cross-cultural communication researchers must possess a set of explicit procedures for identifying certain communicative acts as reflective of a culture and for distinguishing these cultural communication acts from alternative forms of communication.

Part of the motive for any generalization about the culture of a group stems from the fact that the communication system of the groups involved is used as the database for the generalization. Allen, Hecht, and Martin (1996) have argued that "the identity of a cultural group becomes established on the basis of the communication pattern of that group" (p. 69). In their view, the "use of 'culture' here emphasizes speech in language communities," with the "defining element [of a culture being] whether the quality of interaction by the collective of persons create a 'lens' for the grouping and understanding of the environment" (pp. 69-70).

Given this view of culture, it is appropriate to ask if any particular communication act is or is not cultural. To address this question, a researcher must have a procedure for identifying what should be viewed as "cultural" and what should not. In the Liebes study, for example, she independently and separately interviewed several different groups she felt reflected the same culture. Certainly, individual members in each group differed dramatically in several ways. Nevertheless, what are treated as reflective of a cultural orientation are the same kinds of content statements about perceptions, beliefs, values, and norms that are repeatedly expressed by all of these groups, independently, under different circumstances. In this regard, Allen et al. (1996, p. 70) have maintained that "the basis of the culture" stems "from the common construction of symbols to form the lens by which the members illuminate their symbolic world." In their view, the "key is the *consistency* of response to the items by the person" (p. 71). Consistency involves a question of degree and involves a judgment call about when the degree of consistency should be viewed as important. Accordingly, the degree of agreement among participants determines the degree to which participants share a common cultural orientation. For those seeking formal social scientific methods for making these determinations, Allen et al. (1996, pp. 70-74) identify techniques and measures that a researcher can use to determine when communication commonalities and differences should be treated as significant cultural markers.

CREATIVE ALTERNATIVES

The analysis provided by Carley Dodd (this volume) departs sharply from the perspective outlined by Mr. Ono. Mr. Dodd's analysis can be viewed in several ways. I do not think his analysis is directed specifically at what I have suggested. As I understand his statement, it challenges all cross-cultural communication researchers. It offers intriguing, exciting prospects that each of us must profitably consider. Rather than argue with Mr. Dodd, I have found it more useful to isolate some of the compelling—in many cases, troublesome, but in all cases, interesting—questions that he raises about how cross-cultural communication research has been and should be executed. To isolate, underscore, and highlight these questions, I have found it useful to identify and cast these ideas as five propositions.

1. *Cross-cultural communication research should provide both an external or researcher's view as well as an internal or participant's perspective of cultures.* Certainly, a cultural analysis should capture and reflect the frame of reference of the participants within a cultural system. At the same time, cultures are affected by the symbol systems of those external to a cultural system. Cross-cultural communication research may ultimately require that a researcher master ethnographic, social scientific, critical, applied, and performance studies methods. At the same time, if a researcher is truly an "outside," "foreign," or "objective" observer of a culture—even if the researcher seeks to be as sensitive, caring, responsible, and open-minded as possible to the views of others—it may be extremely difficult for the researcher to serve as a participant observer, conscious of all dimensions of another's culture, and to capture the frame of reference of a culture as it is experienced by those within the culture system. In this sense, despite their best efforts, researchers will always possess their own perspective, ideology, and political view when they examine cultures other than their own.

2. *Symbol-using may be a consequent, rather than generative, factor in cross-cultural interactions.* Perhaps one of the most challenging claims for the entire discipline of communication, symbolic analysis, Mr. Dodd notes, can be viewed as static and ritualistic as well as unidimensional, simplistic, and convenient. In a larger sense, Mr. Dodd maintains that symbol systems may inherently provide an incomplete view of the multiple, multilayered, and diverse activities and processes involved in actual cross-cultural interactions. In this sense, language inherently stereotypes. Language isolates and focuses on only part of the interactive process, and it presumes that this part is reflective of the entire process. In this sense, a language statement is inherently a highly selective and incomplete claim about a process that precedes the language statement and continues after the language statement is made. In all, Mr. Dodd questions and challenges a basic set of assumptions about

using symbols that has dominated most cross-cultural communication research.

At the same time, I think it is fair to note that Mr. Dodd's conception of using symbols is but one—and not the only one—view about the roles and functions of using symbols in the construction of cultural systems. Symbols may, as he presumes, serve as a passive consequent of other prior factors. Or in contrast to Mr. Dodd's view, using symbols has also been cast and understood as an active determinant of cultural systems in which using symbols is the process by which people attribute significance and meaning to the other factors in a cultural system. To mention but one example, the foundation for this more activist view of symbols was forcefully articulated by Kenneth Burke (1952a, 1952b, 1953a, 1953b), when he held that the development and use of the negative allowed human beings to symbolically construct the existence of motivations and propositions (such as goals, ideals, standards, and ethics) that go beyond what physical entities warrant. In this sense, it is possible to hold that, even though using symbols may not be the only or initial variable affecting cultural systems, it may be an essential human act that imposes critical and essential meanings on these other factors affecting cultural systems.

Or a third possibility may also exist. Regardless of which view of using symbols is "correct," we may need to adopt a more interdisciplinary perspective when conducting cultural analyses. In this view, a large set of factors—of which using symbols is but one of these variables—may each actively interact to determine a cultural system. In this sense, cultures may be a product of multiple factors, and cultural analysis may require the integration of the contributions of all of the diverse disciplines that represent the full power of each of these factors. Nevertheless, mastering the understandings required to effectively manipulate all of these factors within a single analysis may make this option less viable and practical than we would hope.

In any event, the power of Mr. Dodd's analysis is that he requires that the basic assumptions, regarding the roles and functions attributed to using symbols, be reconsidered when cross-cultural communication research is executed. In my view, this call for a reconsideration is long overdue.

3. *Cultures can be examined, studied, and characterized as intrapersonal, interpersonal, group, intergroup, organizational and institutional, mass, and international events.* It may be essential to pay attention to all of these "levels" of the communication process, for these perspectives reveal both internal and external understandings of a culture. Certainly, we need to be aware of both the internal meanings governing

a cultural system and the responses this cultural system solicits from those external to the culture. Both sets of understandings determine the meaning of a cultural system.

4. *A culture is far more than the use of symbols.* Offering a logical extension of his view that using symbols may be a consequent rather than generative factor in cross-cultural communication, Mr. Dodd maintains that "we must entertain the notion that thought, value, world-view, spirituality, ecology, economics, literacy, urbanization, cultural catastrophe, and crisis are but a few of an individual's cultural experiences that also lead to symbol usage selected from within the pool of possible symbols." This more "holistic view" stems, in part, from Mr. Dodd's belief that, "There is something inside of individuals influenced by their culture that belies language."

5. *Cultural analysis should be tremendously expanded beyond the constructs currently contained in cross-cultural communication research.* Mr. Dodd aptly implies that I am too shy, because I propose only one new scheme for understanding, comparing, and contrasting cultural systems. In Table 11.3, Mr. Dodd outlines an entire series of new and additional factors that should be considered. As I see it, Table 11.3 is one of the most comprehensive and creative recommendations for future cross-cultural communication research we currently have. Mr. Dodd's recommendations—as reflected in Table 11.3—should initially be viewed positively, as new and exciting options for the development of cross-cultural communication research designs. Accordingly, I would not qualify Mr. Dodd's recommendations. At the same time, I do think we will need to work through each of the factors included within Mr. Dodd's "matrix of cultural factors" in Table 11.3, and we will need to ask how each of these factors can affect and is affected by the other factors. At a minimum, for example, we will need to identify the various ways and scope of ways in which "uncertainty reduction" occurs in diverse cultural systems. At the least, researchers should be able to anticipate the range, kinds, and types of "uncertainty reduction" that can be used in diverse cultures. Equally important, we need to know the relative significance of "uncertainty reduction" in the complex of other cultural factors. Accordingly, whereas I fully support the directions proposed by Mr. Dodd, I would also note that his "expanded matrix" cannot be immediately achieved. I suspect the kind of analysis I have suggested for including change within the analysis of cultural systems must be done for all 11 of the new and additional factors Mr. Dodd has proposed.

In all, this dialogue has been successful. As I see it, beyond responding to my chapter, Mr. Ono and Mr. Dodd provide challenges that all cross-cultural communication researchers can appreciate and benefit from when the meanings embedded in cross-cultural communication processes are explored.

REFERENCES

Special Note: References listed in Chesebro's "Distinguishing Cultural Systems" are not repeated here.

Allen, M., Hecht, M., & Martin, J. (1996). Examining the impact of culture social scientifically: Some suggestions from examining Martin, Hecht, and Larkey. *World Communication, 25*, 69-78.

Burke, K. (1952a, October). A dramatistic view of the origins of language: Part one. *Quarterly Journal of Speech, 38*, 251-264.

Burke, K. (1952b, December). A dramatistic view of the origins of language: Part two. *Quarterly Journal of Speech, 38*, 446-460.

Burke, K. (1953a, February). A dramatistic view of the origins of language: Part III. *Quarterly Journal of Speech, 39*, 79-92.

Burke, K. (1953b, April). Postscripts on the negative. *Quarterly Journal of Speech, 39*, 209-216.

Katz, E., & Liebes, T. (1984). Once upon a time, in Dallas. *Intermedia, 12*, 28-32.

Liebes, T., & Katz, E. (1986). Patterns of involvement in television fiction: A comparative analysis. *European Journal of Communication, 1*, 151-171.

Williams, A., & Giles, H. (1996). Intergenerational conversations: Young adult's retrospective accounts. *Human Communication Research, 23*, 220-250.

Index

Abrahams, R., 65
Achebe, C., 27
Act-sequence structure of razzing ritual, 69-70
Adaptation, cultural, 35-36, 47, 89
Affirmative action programs, 156-157
Africa and validity limits of national culture, 209
African National Congress (ANC), 150, 164
  See also South Africa
Agonistic terms, 100-103
  See also Self and society opposition
Agriculture in South Africa, 149
Alcoff, L., 40
Allen, M., 221
Alliances, intercultural relationships as interpersonal, 142
Allport, G. W., 133
Ambivalence, globalization and experiential, 35
American Indians:
  ascription/avowal processes, 137, 138
  blood quantum and Indianness, 64, 85-86, 91, 95
  Bureau of Indian Affairs, 59, 85, 86
  children separated from their families, 85, 92-93
  contact Indians, 58
  cultural competence, determining, 57
  Five Civilized Tribes, 83
  Indianness, problematic and consequential nature of, 62-65
  qualitative-ethnographic methods for studying, 59-62
  Trail of Tears, 83
  See also Cherokee family, one Oklahoma; Razzing ritual (American Indians)

Analytical frames, asking respondents to share their, 142-143
ANC. See African National Congress
Anderson, B., 199, 200
Anderson, J. A., 138
Anthropological approaches, essentialism in, 140
Anzaldúa, G., 3, 35, 36
Apartheid, 148, 150-151
  See also South Africa
Arabs and cross-cultural communication research, 179, 180
Argumentation and identity, link between, 23
Aristotle, 177
Asai, M., 183
Ascription of identity, 133, 137-138
Ashanti people and validity limits of national culture, 209
Ashcroft, B., 128
Asian Indian women in America:
  adaptation, cultural, 35-36
  displacement and identity, 37-39
  interethnic and intraethnic contexts, 42-50
  multiple hierarchies of race/class/gender, 50-51
  past and present, merging of the, 34-35
  standpoint of Asian Indian women, 39-42
Assimilation:
  American Indians, 81, 93-94
  Asian Indian women in America, 39, 44
Assumptions, power of invisible, 143
Attneave, C., 85
Australia and context dimension, 185
Austria:
  femininity-masculinity dimension, 186

power distance dimension, 186
Authenticity:
    Asian Indian women in America, 48-50
    myth of, 141
Authorial self-reflexivity, 5, 28-29
Avowal of identity, 132-133, 137-139
Axes, cultural identity framed by two,
    38, 42-43, 47-48

Bammer, A., 35
Banks, A., 4
Banks, J. A., 128
Banks, S. P., 4
Bantu education programs (South
    Africa), 151
Bantustans (South Africa), 149-150
Barnlund, D. C., 206
Basso, K., 65
Bateson, G., 23, 24
Bateson, M. C., 23, 24
Baxter, L., 101
Benedict, R., 204
Benevolent discourse and rhetorical
    presents/voids, 17-21
Berkhofer, R., Jr., 85, 86, 91
Berthold, C., 101
Beyond Culture (Hall), 184
Bhabha, H., 35, 140
Bhattacharjee, A., 48
Bhavani, K., 37
Bible, the, 117-118
Billig, M., 81, 82
Binarism of settler or colonized, 128
Binary opposition, problem of, 23
Black speakers and sounding, 65
Blair, C., 193
Blending in, process of, 44
Blind review procedures, 144
Blood quantum and Indianness, 64,
    85-86, 91, 95
Blumler, J. G., 177
Bochner, S., 81
Bogden, R., 59
Bolt, C., 83, 89-91, 94
Bontempo, R., 183
Book of Changes, 23
Borderlands, 35
Bornman, E., 132, 136-139
Boudinot, E., 95

Boundaries, desire to dissolve
    nation-state, 216-217
Bowker, J., 133, 136
Boyle, A., 87, 88
Brah, A., 39
Brinton, H., 117
Brislin, R., 94, 206, 208
Brock, B. L., 189
Brommel, B. J., 211
Brown, P., 131
Brown, W. J., 184
Bureau of Indian Affairs (BIA), 59, 85,
    86
Burke, K., 81, 101, 223
Buthelezi (Chief), 150, 161
Butler, J., 23-25
Byrd, J., 95

Cai, B., vii
Campschreur, W., 161
Candidate Indians, 72-73
Canning, K., 26
Carbaugh, D., 100-102, 104, 115, 116,
    123, 131
Casmir, F. L., 177, 203, 206, 207
Certificate of degree of Indian blood
    (CDIB), 85-86, 91, 95
Chang, M., 14
Change explaining/predicting
    cross-cultural communication
    research, 186-189, 194, 209-211,
    215-216
Chatterjee, P., 48
Chaudhuri, N., 27
Chen, D., 12, 20
Chen, V., 4, 37, 127
Cherokee family, one Oklahoma, 80
    assimilation to dominant culture,
        93-94
    changing language/dress/
        religion, 92
    Civil War, 90-91
    grandmother keeping the old ways,
        92-93
    history of Indians in Oklahoma,
        83-88
    Irish immigrants, 92
    rediscovery, cultural, 94-96
    separation from other Cherokees, 91

theoretical foundations and methods
   for studying, 81-83
westward migration, 89-90
Cherwitz, R., 81
Chesebro, J. W., 1, 6
Chiang Kai-Shek, 28
Chickasaw tribe, 83
Childrearing and Asian Indian women,
   49-50
China and context dimension, 185
   See also Footbinding in China
Chinese Americans and
   ascription/avowal processes,
   137-138
Choctaw tribe, 83
Choice, self-identity as, 5
Chomsky, N., 61
Chow, R., 27
Chung, J., 23, 24, 28
CIT. *See* Cultural identity theory
Civil War, 90-91
Clark, A. K., 19
Class as a political and oversimplified
   category, 127-128
   See also Multiple hierarchies of
   race/class/gender
Classification of rhetorical discourses,
   177
Clifford, J., 129
Coding and interpretive procedures in
   CIT research, 138
Cognitive anthropology, 205
Collectivist-individual dimension,
   184
Collier, M. J., 1, 6, 38, 57, 130-134,
   136-140, 142
Colonial/imperial influences on identity
   formation, 139
Commonalities and differences,
   determining, 194
Communication process, levels of the,
   223-224
Communication studies, 200
   See also Cross-cultural
   communication research
Comparative research, 177-178, 197
   See also Cross-cultural
   communication research;
   Distinguishing cultural systems
   (critique of)

Competence based on implicit privilege,
   142
Conditioning processes and oppression,
   14
Condon, S., 81, 82
Conquergood, D., 38, 129, 132, 137,
   142
Constructionist view of communication,
   135
Contact Indians, 58
Context dimension, 184-185
Contextualization, rhetorical, 16-21
Contralesa organization (South Africa),
   163, 166-167
Cook-Gumperz, J., 4
Cope-Robinson, L., 117
Creek tribe, 83, 91
Crenshaw, K., 37
Critical Studies in Mass Communication,
   218
Critical theory, viewing interpretation in
   context of, 142
Cronen, V., 135
Cross-cultural communication research:
   change as a variable explaining and
   predicting, 186-189
   conceptual and definitional issues,
   180-183
   conclusions, 189
   different approaches to, 178
   illustrating the nature of, 179-180
   propositions for the future,
   222-225
   shifts and transformations, 177
   See also Distinguishing cultural
   systems (critique of); Nation-state
   cultures
Cuban Americans and ascription/avowal
   processes, 137
Cultural competence, determining,
   56-57, 67-68
Cultural differences. *See* Distinguishing
   cultural systems (critique of)
Cultural genocide, 85
Cultural identity theory (CIT), 130
   epistemological assumptions,
   134-138
   ontological assumptions, 131-134
   reconciliation and the need for
   continued dialogue, 139

respondent and researcher, relationship between, 143-144

Dallas (TV show) and cross-cultural communication research, 179-180, 195-196, 218
Dalton, R. J., 160
Daly, M., 25
Dasein, concept of self as, 3-4
Davendal, J., 161
Davenport, T. R. H., 150
Davies, A., 103
Davis, K. E., 37
Dawes Commission, 88, 90, 92, 94
Decolonization of the mind, 126
De Klerk, F. W., 152
de Lauretis, T., 39
Delgado, F. P., 124, 126
Deloria, V., Jr., 66, 84, 86, 89, 91, 94
Denmark and femininity-masculinity dimension, 186
Denzin, N., 135
Deprivation, cultural. *See* Cherokee family, one Oklahoma
Dialogical intersubjectivity based on hermeneutics, 135
Diaspora experience and identity, 38
Difference and rupture, axis of, 38, 42-43
Differentiation and identification, simultaneous processes of, 24
Discernment as a Quaker term, 110, 116
Displacement and identity, 37-39
Distinguishing cultural systems (critique of), 203
  boundaries, desire to dissolve nation-state, 216-217
  change, focus on national, 194, 209-211
  commonalities and differences, determining, 194
  contextualizing the practice of comparative research, 197
  cross-cultural communication research, 204-206
  cultural change, focus on, 200-201
  culture with national culture, equating, 193

  expanded category system for inter/cross-cultural communication research, 212-213
  ignoring spate of research on cultural studies, 200
  limitations, primary, 195-197
  nation-centered research insufficiently theorized, 199
  nation-states and variables underlying cultural systems, 207-209
  stereotyping and generalizations, 197-199, 219-221
  symbols, relation of culture and, 206-207
  U.S.-centric model, 218-219
Diversity *vs.* national unity. *See* South Africa
Dodd, C., 1, 6, 206, 215
Domestic issues for Asian Indian women, 48-50
Domination, structures and functions of, 126, 127
Donahue (TV show) and self and society opposition, 100, 115-117, 123
Donald, J., 35, 39
Double-description, process of, 23, 28
Drucker, A. R., 19

Eco, U., 81
Edelstein, A. S., 183
Edwards, D., 81, 82
Elashmawi, F., 206, 208, 211
Englishwoman's Review, 19
Epistemological assumptions toward the goal of inquiry, 124-125, 127-128, 134-138
Essentialism in anthropological approaches, 140
Etatist worldview, modernist, 156, 160
Ethnic and national identities, dialectic tensions between, 140
Ethnicity as a political and oversimplified category, 127-128
  See also Interethnic/intraethnic contexts and identity negotiation; Multiple hierarchies of race/class/gender
Ethnographic traditions, postcolonial critique of, 129-130

European Americans in cultural identity
  theory, 140
European Journal of Communication,
  218
Evolution, cultural, 188
Evolution, identity as an, 5
Ewe people and validity limits of
  national culture, 209
Excess, notion of, 24, 28

Faith and Practice, 104, 110, 116, 119
Family systems, model of two axes of,
  211
Fanon, F., 158-160
Fayer, J., 178
Federal policies and cultural deprivation
  of American Indians, 85-86
Femininity-masculinity dimension, 186
Feminist theory:
  footbinding in China, 5, 22-28
  multiple hierarchies of
    race/class/gender, 127-128
  participatory research, 141
  sexuality and gender, insistence on
    separation of, 126
Filler, L., 83
Finland and femininity-masculinity
  dimension, 186
Fisher, M. P., 40
Fiske, J., 135
Fite, R., 95
Five Civilized Tribes, 83
Flemming, L. S., 27
Fluid nature of identity, 38
Folb, E., 84
Folk theories of communication,
  100
Fontana, A., 138
Footbinding in China:
  authorial self-reflexivity, 28-29
  history of, 12-16
  paradox for Chinese women with
    bound feet, 11
  patriotic breeders or colonized
    converts after, 21-22
  postcolonial feminist approach to
    identity and, 22-28
  rhetorical presents and voids of
    discourse on, 17-21

Fordist modernization program in South
  Africa, 157-161
Foss, S. K., 126
Foucault, M., 124
Fox, R., 204
Franz, C. E., 41
Frey, L., 138

Galvin, K. M., 211
Game, M., 81, 82
Ga people and validity limits of national
  culture, 209
Garfinkel, H., 76
Garner, T., 65
Gender:
  race as separate from, attempts to
    study, 36
  sexuality separated from, feminist
    theory and, 126
  See also Footbinding in China;
    Multiple hierarchies of
    race/class/gender
General Allotment Act of 1887, 88, 90,
  92, 94
Generalizations and stereotypes, 43-44,
  197-199, 219-221
Genocide, cultural, 85
Gergen, K. J., 37, 38, 50
Gestalt vs. linear process, 113
Giles, H., 4, 220
Glenn, L. D., 84-87
Globalization, relocation/experiential
  ambivalence and, 35
God and self as oppositional terms,
  101-102
  See also Self and society opposition
Goffman, E., 133
González, A., 1, 127, 197
Goodenough, W., 205
Government policies and cultural
  deprivation of American Indians,
  85-86
Gregg, N., 39, 40
Griffiths, G., 128, 141
Griping in Israeli discourse, 69
Gronbeck, B., 200
Gudykunst, W. B., 206
Gumperz, J. J., 3
Guttman, A., 83

Hall, E. T., 184, 204
Hall, S., 35, 36, 38, 42, 126, 128
Halualani, R., 193
Hammond-Tooke, W. D., 149
Han people and footbinding in China, 18-20, 22
Harding, S., 41
Hare, A. P., 110
Harris, M., 204
Harris, P. R., 206, 208, 211
Harvey, D., 153, 162, 167
Hausa people and validity limits of national culture, 209
Hecht, M. L., 37, 57, 130, 131, 136, 221
Hegde, R. S., 1, 2, 5, 42
Hegemonic notions of culture, 197
Heidegger, M., 3-4
Hermeneutic inquiry, science and, 4, 135
Hertel, E., 23, 24, 28
Hikins, J., 81
Hill, L., 71
History and social construction of group identities, 140, 141
Hofstede, G., 185, 186
Hollway, W., 39
Holomisa, P., 163
Home environment and Asian Indian women, 48-50
Homelands in South Africa, 149-150
Hooks, B., 26, 43, 126, 127, 144
Houston, M., 37, 127
Hubbard, G., 117
Hughes, H. S., 189
Hui, C. H., 183
Humor, ritualized. *See* Razzing ritual (American Indians)
Hunter, J., 27
Hybrid zone, ambiguity of the, 35
Hymes, D., 60, 61, 66

Ibo people and validity limits of national culture, 209
Identification and differentiation, simultaneous processes of, 24
Identities played off one another, Quaker, 118-119
Ideology and social construction of group identities, 140
Imagined Communities (Anderson), 199

Imperialism, international, 27
Imperialist *vs.* the colonized, 128
India and collectivist-individual dimension, 184
  See also Asian Indian women in America
Indianness, problematic and consequential nature of, 62-65, 81, 87
  See also American Indians; Cherokee family, one Oklahoma
Indian Self-Determination Act of 1975, 86, 91, 95
Indian Territory (Oklahoma), 83
Individual-collectivist dimension, 184
Individualist approach to the study of immigrants, 36
Indonesia and validity limits of national culture, 209
Industrial realism, 151-152
Information age media technology, 152-153
In-group cultural identities, 132-134, 136, 138
Inkatha Freedom Party (IFP), 150, 161, 164, 166
  See also South Africa
Inn, A., 81
Insults, ritualized. *See* Razzing ritual (American Indians)
Interaction and Identity (Mokros), 56
Interethnic friendships, 141
Interethnic/intraethnic contexts and identity negotiation:
  authenticity and modernity, representations of, 48-50
  difference and rupture, axis of, 42-43
  misidentification and continuity, axis of, 47-48
  other, isolation of the, 46-47
  racist encounters, 44-45
  stereotypical representations, 43-44
Interlocutor identity, 131
Intermedia: Interpersonal Communication in a Media World, 218
International and Intercultural Annual, 177
Interpretive approaches to researching cultural identity, 122, 130

See also Cultural identity theory (CIT)
Interrelationships among gender/race/class. *See* Multiple hierarchies of race/class/gender
Intuitive *vs.* logical process, 112
Invisible assumptions, 143
Involution, cultural, 189
Iranian Americans and ascription/avowal processes, 137-138
Ireland and power distance dimension, 186
Irish immigrants, 89, 92
Islamic cultures, high consistency within, 209
Israel:
    cross-cultural communication research, 179, 180, 195-196
    griping in Israeli discourse, 69
    power distance dimension, 186
Italy and femininity-masculinity dimension, 186
Iziphakanyiswa Amendment Bill of 1995 (South Africa), 163

Jacobs, S. M., 27
Jane, L., 88-95
Janicke, M., 156
Japan:
    context dimension, 185
    footbinding in China, 18-19, 22
Johnson, J. D., 205
Jordon, P., 168

Kahn, M., 169
Katriel, T., 69, 100
Kauffman, B., 41
Kennan, W., 71
Kennedy, oppositional terms and John F., 101
Kim, Y. Y., 35, 36, 87, 88, 130, 206, 211
Kiowa tribe, 71
Klopf, D. W., 208
Kluckhohn, C., 180, 181
Kochman, T., 65
Koester, J., 181, 186, 205, 206, 209
Korea and context dimension, 185
Kramarae, C., 37

Krejci, C., vii
Kroeber, A. L., 180, 181
Kuechler, M., 160
Kwan, K. M., 47
Kwa Zulu-Natal Amakosi Amendment Bill of 1995 (South Africa), 163

Labov, W., 65
Land and American Indians, 84
Lang, P., 135
Langsdorf, L., 140
Language as integral part of culture:
    Cherokee tribe, 92, 93
    cross-cultural communication research, 181
    distinguishing cultural systems (critique of), 207
    self-identity, 4
    South Africa, 155
Lash, S., 148, 150, 158, 167, 168
Leading as a Quaker term, 109-110, 114, 119
Lee, W. S., 1, 2, 5, 23, 24, 28, 193
Levinson, S., 131
Levy, H., 11, 14, 18, 19, 21, 25
Li, Y., 20
Liebes, T., 179, 195, 196, 204, 218-219
Lin, Y., 20
Lindesmith, A. R., 181
Linear *vs.* gestalt process, 113
Location, politics of, 42
Logical *vs.* intuitive process, 112
Louw, E., 6
Lucca, N., 183
Lugones, M., 39
Lujan, P., 84-88
Lustig, M. W., 181, 186, 205, 206, 209
Lytle, C., 86, 91, 94

Mackie, D. M., 4
Makhanya, M., 164
Malala, J., 158
Malhotra, V. A., 3
Malinda (Cherokee), 92-93
Malinowski, B., 204
Manchus people and footbinding in China, 18, 20, 22
Mandela, N., 163

Mani, L., 40, 48
Mankiller, W., 86, 88, 95
Marcus, G. E., 129
Marriage, arranged, 39-40
Martin, J., 26, 133, 221
Marxism, 24, 156
Masculinity-femininity dimension, 186
Masekela, B., 161
Masmoudi, M., 160
Mboweni, T., 151, 152, 160
McCall, G., 59
McClintock, A., 22, 27, 125-127, 139
McCroskey, J. C., 178
McGoldrick, M., 127, 139
McKerrow, R., 82
McLeod, J. M., 177
McLoughlin, W., 88, 89, 95
McMenamin, V., 152, 160
McNickle, D., 84
Mead, M., 204
Mexico and power distance dimension, 186
Middleton, D., 81, 82
Migrant sensibility, 35
    See also Asian Indian women in
        America
Miller, J., 184
Mind, Self and Society (Mead), 3
Ming dynasty and footbinding in China,
    12
Minh-ha, T. T., 125
Minority rights, 86
Mirande, A., 136
Misidentification and continuity, axis of,
    47-48
Modernity and Asian Indian women in
    America, 48-50
Modernization process in South Africa,
    148-152, 157-161
Mohanty, C. T., 37
Mokros, H. B., 56
Moleketi, J., 158
Monolithic cultures, 185
Monolithic representations of Third
    World women, 37
Moon, D., 193, 197
Moraga, C., 36
Moran, R., 208, 211
Morgan, R., 138, 143
Moroccan Jews and cross-cultural
    communication research, 179, 180

Morris, R., 4
Moss Island Friends. *See* Self and
    society opposition
Motivations for identifying as an Indian,
    63
Muller, J., 149
Multiple dimensions to contrast cultures,
    178
Multiple hierarchies of race/class/gender:
    Asian Indian women in America, 37,
        50-51
    cultural identity theory, 134
    feminist theory, 127-128
    postcolonial perspective, 125-126
Murray, J. H., 19

Naidoo, P., 163
Nanda, S., 204
Nandi, P., 40
National and ethnic identities, dialectic
    tensions between, 140
National Party (South Africa), 148
    See also South Africa
Nation building, state-directed, 156-158,
    160, 165-167
Nation-state cultures:
    boundaries, desire to dissolve
        nation-state, 216-217
    change as a dimension for
        distinguishing, 186-189
    context dimension, 184-185
    cultural identity theory, 131-132
    footbinding in China, 20-22, 27-28
    individual-collectivist dimension, 184
    masculinity-femininity dimension,
        186
    power distance dimension, 185-186
    reasons for studying, 182-183
    See also Distinguishing cultural
        systems (critique of)
Native Americans. *See* American Indians
Neo-Aristotelianism, 177-178
Neosocialist etatist development, ANC's,
    156
Netherlands and femininity-masculinity
    dimension, 186
New Guinea Island and validity limits of
    national culture, 209
New world information order, 160

New Zealand and power distance
   dimension, 186
Ngugi, T., 27
Nonverbal cues and assessing cultural
   identity, 55-56
Norway and femininity-masculinity
   dimension, 186

Oklahoma Territory, 83
   See also Cherokee family, one
   Oklahoma
Olson, D. H., 211
Ono, K. A., 2, 6, 19, 20, 215, 216-217
Ontological assumptions toward the goal
   of inquiry, 124-127, 131-134
Oppositional terms, identifying, 100-103
   See also Self and society opposition
Oppression:
   conditioning processes, 14
   dialogue between
      oppressors/oppressed, 126, 127
Other, seeing oneself represented as the,
   34, 42, 46-47, 50-51
Out-group members, 132-134, 136, 138
Overlapping nature of identities, 131

Papua New Guinea Island and validity
   limits of national culture, 209
Parmar, P., 42
Parry, B., 128
Participatory research, 141
Past and present, merging of the, 34-35
Patriarchy, globalized, 26
Pearce, W. B., 135
Performance-based ethnography, 142
Phallocratic morality, universal sameness
   of, 25
Philippines and power distance
   dimension, 186
Philipsen, G., 100, 102, 115, 116
Physical characteristics as criterion of
   Indianness, 64
Plethoraphobia, 17
Pluralistic competition between groups
   and leaders, 185
Polyphonic voices of respondents, 141
Population statistics on American
   Indians, 86-87, 90

Postcolonial perspective on cultural
   identity:
   defining postcolonialism, 123-124
   epistemological claims, 127-128
   ethnographic traditions, critique of,
      129-130
   feminist theory and footbinding in
      China, 22-28
   ontological claims, 125-127
Postmodernites, South African, 152-154,
   167-169
Postmodern skepticism, 123
   See also Postcolonial perspective on
   cultural identity
Potter, J., 81
Power:
   distance dimension, 185-186
   and identity, 126, 133-134, 140, 141
   sociocultural, 143
   sociopolitical, 133-134
Power/Knowledge: The Politics of Social
   Science (Cameron, Frazer, Harvey,
   Rampton & Richardson), 123
Pratt, S. B., 2, 5, 57, 58, 62, 64, 81, 87,
   129, 131, 134, 135, 141
Premoderns, South African, 148-150,
   161-165
Privilege and identity, 126, 133-134,
   140, 143
Process (spiritual) vs. product (secular)
   oriented, 114
Processual epistemology, 23, 24

Qing dynasty and footbinding in China,
   18, 20
Quakers. See Self and society opposition
Qualitative-ethnographic methodology,
   59-62

Race:
   cultural identity theory, 139
   and gender as separate, attempts to
      study, 36
   political and oversimplified category,
      127-128
   racist encounters, 44-45, 87-88
   See also Interethnic/intraethnic
      contexts and identity negotiation

Rader, B., 86, 87, 94
Radio in South Africa, 149-150
Radley, A., 81, 82
Ramphele, M., 149
Rattansi, A., 35, 39
Razzing ritual (American Indians), 65
  act-sequence structure, 69-70
  contextual and reflexive nature of, 69
  an exemplar of, 74-77
  humor, distinctively Indian, 73-74
  participants, 72-73
  purpose of, 67-68
  settings, 70-71
  songs, 71-72
  topics, 66-67
Rediscovery, cultural, 5, 94-96
Religious boarding schools and
    American Indians, 85
Religious Society of Friends (Quakers).
    See Self and society opposition
Relocation in context of contemporary
    globalization, 35
Renaissance view of divinity, 119
Representation, crises of, 141
Researching cultural identity:
  American Indians, 59-62, 81-83
  comparative research, 177-178. *See
    also* Cross-cultural
    communication research
  feminist theory and participatory
    studies, 141
  interpretive perspective, 122, 130.
    See also Cultural Identity theory
    (CIT)
  philosophical problematics, 124-125
  postmodern skepticism, 123. *See also*
    Postcolonial perspective on
    cultural identity
  respondent and researcher,
    relationship between, 143-144,
    222
Resource allocation threat in South
    Africa, 169
Respondent and researcher, relationship
    between, 143-144, 222
Revolution, 187
Rhetorical contextualization, 16-21
Ribeau, S., 38, 130, 131, 136
Richmond, V. P., 178
Robert's Rules of Order, 115

Roger, E. M., 211
Romanticism's self over society, 102
Ropp, P. S., 20
Rosengren, K. E., 177
Rosenthal, P., 101
Rosselli, F., 4
Rueckert, W., 101
Rushdie, S., 34, 35
Russians and cross-cultural
    communication research, 180,
    195-196
Rutherford, J., 35

Sachs, H., 130, 131
Sado-Ritual Syndrome, 25
Said, E., 11, 23, 27, 29, 35, 51
Saldivar, R., 4
Saran, P., 40, 47
*Saturated Self: Dilemmas of Identity in
    Contemporary Life* (Gergen), 4
Schlemmer, L., 154
Scollon, R., 178, 182, 207
Scollon, S. W., 178, 182, 207
Self and society opposition:
  conclusions, 119-120
  identities played off one another,
    two, 118
  method for studying, 102-104
  oppositional terms, 100
  origins of, 101-102
  personal control given up to God's
    will, 115-117
  spiritual and secular process, 104-111
  truth, two-step process for finding,
    117
  vocabulary, special, 118-119
Self as socially constructed, view of the,
    37
Self-consciousness, 3
Self-determination by tribal
    governments, 86, 95
Self-doubt, 5051
Self-face, 133
Self-objectification, 3
Self-reflexivity, 122
  authorial, 5, 28-29
  comparative research, 177
  cultural identity theory, 144
Seminole tribe, 83

Sense-making processes, respondents sharing, 142-143
Service, E. R., 187, 188, 210, 211
Sexuality:
  Asian Indian women, 49
  gender and, insistence on separation of, 126
Shanmugam, A. V., 182, 184
Shaver, L. D., 2, 5, 82, 93
Shaver, P., 82, 87, 88
Shibutani, T., 47
Shome, R., 4, 27, 29
Shotter, J., 38
Shuter, R., 203, 207
Shutiva, C., 66
Similarity and continuity, axis of, 38
Simmons, J., 59
Singelis, T. M., 184
Smith, A. F., 205
Socialization and razzing ritual (American Indians), 68
Society:
  God's guidance, collectively seeking, 117
  self-identity and, interdependence of, 3
  societal understandings, transferring, 182
  See also Self and society opposition
Sociocultural power, 143
Sociopolitical power, 133-134
Songs and razzing ritual (American Indians), 71-72
Sounding (verbal dueling), 65
South Africa:
  cultural identity theory, 132, 133, 139
  fordist modernization program, 157-161
  future of, 170-171
  nation building, 165-167
  postmodernization, resistance to, 167-169
  premodern/modern/postmodern culture, conflicts between, 148-154
  premoderns, conservative, 161-165
  rethinking the struggle in, 154-157
Soviet Union, nation-state concept and former, 217
Speech codes, 100

Speech Communication Association in 1994, 200
Spelman, E., 16, 17, 24, 26, 36, 51
Spiritual and secular agon. *See* Self and society opposition
Spivak, G. C., 14, 24, 128
Stability, cultural, 188
Stadler, A., 154
State-directed nation building, 156-158, 160, 165-167
Stedmon, R., 85
Stereotypes and generalizations, 43-44, 197-199, 219-221
Stewart, A. J., 41
Stoler, A. L., 27
Strauss, A. L., 181
Streek, B., 164
Stress-growth-adaptation dynamic, 211
Strickland, R., 83, 85, 86
Strobel, M., 27
Structural factors and postmodern ethnographers, 135
Sung dynasty and footbinding in China, 12, 20
Sweden and femininity-masculinity dimension, 186
Switzerland and femininity-masculinity dimension, 186
Symbols:
  cross-cultural communication research, 181-182, 222-224
  distinguishing cultural systems (critique of), 206-207
  Quakerism, 5-6, 111-115
  self-consciousness, development of, 3
System-center concept, culture as a, 181
Szalay, L., 81

Taiwan and footbinding in China, 18-19
Tajfel, H., 132
Tanaka, Y., 182, 184
Tanno, D. V., 3, 80, 136, 140
Taylor, S., 59
Third World modernization, 156
Thomas, M., 57, 130
Thomas, R., 84, 87
Thomas-Rogers Oklahoma Indian Welfare Act of 1936, 86

Thompson, J., 132, 140
Tiffin, H., 128
Ting-Toomey, S., 131, 133
Tintern Abbey (Wordsworth), 101
Tomaselli, K. G., 149
Tomaselli, R., 149
Trail of Tears, 83
Transcendent concept, culture as a, 181
Transparency, power of, 143
Traveling between worlds, 39
Triandis, H. C., 182-184
Tribalism, role of Indianness with regard
    to, 63
Trinh, T. M., 23, 36, 39
Truth:
    regimes of, 127
    two-step process for finding, 117
Tuttle, F., 205

Understanding Indian Tribal
    Governments, 86
United States:
    collectivist-individual dimension,
      184
    context dimension, 185
    cross-cultural communication
      research, 179, 180, 195-196
    stability, cultural, 188-189
    U.S.-centric model of cultural
      exchange and interaction, 193,
      218-219
Unity and Quakerism, 110, 116

van Dijk, T., 127, 133
Vassilious, G., 182, 184
Vassilious, V., 182, 184
Veblen, T., 20
Venezuela:
    femininity-masculinity dimension,
      186
    power distance dimension, 186
Verbal dueling games, 65
    See also Razzing ritual (American
      Indians)
Villarcal, M. J., 183
Viswesaran, K., 41
Vocabulary and Quakerism, 115,
    118-119

Wahrhaftig, A., 84, 87
Waite, B., 95
Waley, A., 25
Wander, P., 16, 23, 24
Wang, J., 23, 24, 28
Wardell, M., 85, 87, 91, 94
Washburn, W., 84
Wa Thiong'o, N., 161
Watkins, F. M., 188
Weber, D., 132
Western imperial powers and footbinding
    in China, 19-20
Western industrial modernity and
    race/class categories, 127
Wetherell, M., 81
White bourgeois view of feminism, 26
Whiteman, American Indians ridiculing
    behaviors of, 65
White scholars researching people of
    color, 138
Wick, N., 3, 5
Wieder, D. L., 56, 57, 60, 64, 131,
    141
Williams, A., 4, 220
Willis, J., vii
Wilson, F., 149
Wittgenstein, L., 132, 135
Wolf, D. L., 135, 141
Woodward, G. S., 84, 88, 90
Working class, policing the, 127
Worsley, P., 150
Wright, A., 83
Wright, R., 83-86, 90, 93

Xhosa people (South Africa), 163
    See also South Africa
Xi, C., 197

Yamada, M., 14, 42
Yugoslavia and power distance
    dimension, 186
Yung, J., 19

Zhuo, Y., 18
Zulu people, 161
    See also South Africa
Zwelethini (King), 163

About the Contributors

JAMES W. CHESEBRO (PhD, University of Minnesota, 1972) is Professor in the Department of Communication at Indiana State University. He has specialized in the study of culture and media as symbolic systems, maintaining a sustained focus on dramatistic theory, methods, and criticism. He has written several books and has published in *Quarterly Journal of Speech, Critical Studies in Communication,* and *Communication Monographs* as well as in journals outside the discipline.

MARY JANE COLLIER (PhD, University of Southern California, 1982) is Associate Professor in the Department of Human Communication Studies at the University of Denver. Her research focuses on cultural identity and intercultural relationships. In addition to being a coauthor of *African American Communication,* her work appears in *Communications Monographs, International Journal of Intercultural Relations, Communications Quarterly,* and *Howard Journal of Communications.*

CARLEY DODD (PhD, University of Oklahoma, 1974) is Professor of Communication and Dean of the Graduate School at Abilene Christian University. He has served in a variety of professional organizations and has spoken, traveled, and consulted widely. He has presented extensively in intercultural communication and is known for his textbook, *Dynamics of Intercultural Communication,* which is going into its 5th edition.

ALBERTO GONZÁLEZ (PhD, Ohio State University, 1986) is Associate Professor in the Department of Interpersonal Communication at Bowling Green State University. His research interests combine intercultural communication, rhetorical criticism, and new technologies and culture.

RADHA S. HEGDE (PhD, Ohio State University, 1991) is Assistant Professor in the Department of Communication at Rutgers University. Her teaching and research interests center around issues of race and gender, with specific emphasis on questions of identity pertaining to South Asian immigrant and Third-World women. Her work has appeared in *Communication Quarterly* and *Women's Studies in Communication.*

ERIC LOUW teaches in the School of Social Sciences and Liberal Studies, Charles Sturt University, Bathurst, Australia. He previously taught at the Rand Afrikaans University and the University of Natal in South Africa. He has a PhD in Media and Cultural Studies from the University of Natal, Durban. He has published widely on the South African media.

WEN SHU LEE (PhD, University of Southern California, 1989) is Associate Professor of Communication Studies at San Jose State University. Her research interests include humor, idiom, paradox, and discursive differences among women of different cultures. She has been published in *Journal of Applied Communication Research, Howard Journal of Communications, Western Journal of Communication,* and *Journal of Communication.*

KENT A. ONO (PhD, University of Iowa, 1992) is Assistant Professor of American Studies and Asian American Studies at the University of California, Davis. His research and teaching focuses on rhetorical, cultural, film, and media studies, especially as they relate to issues of cultural marginalization. He has contributed essays to *Communication Monographs, Philosophy and Rhetoric, Western Journal of Communication, Women's Studies in Communication,* and various anthologies. He is coeditor of *Enterprise Zones: Critical Positions on* Star Trek and is currently completing a cowritten book on rhetoric and poststructuralism.

STEVEN B. PRATT (PhD, University of Oklahoma, 1985) is Professor in the Department of Communication at the University of Central Oklahoma. His research interests focus on cultural identification, as well as language and social interaction, with an emphasis on identifying American Indian communicative behaviors. He serves as a traditional and ceremonial leader of the Osage Nation and developed the Osage National Language.

LYNDA DIXON SHAVER (PhD, University of Oklahoma, 1990) is Associate Professor in the Department of Interpersonal Communication at Bowling Green State University. She is an Oklahoma Cherokee whose research interests include multicultural and gender issues in health, education, and business contexts. She has published in *Intercultural Communication Studies* and has written several book chapters.

DOLORES V. TANNO (PhD, University of Southern California, 1990) is Associate Professor in the Department of Communication Studies at California State University, San Bernardino. Her research interests combine intercultural communication, rhetorical criticism, and ethics of communication.

NANCY WICK (PhD, University of Washington, 1997). Her research interests are in the ethnography of communication applied to a variety of settings.